THE SOUTH SEAS DREAM

An Adventure in Paradise

D1567981

John Dyson

THE SOUTH SEAS DREAM

An Adventure in Paradise

LITTLE, BROWN AND COMPANY
BOSTON–TORONTO

LIBRARY OF CONGRESS CATALOG CARD NO. 82–9929

FIRST AMERICAN EDITION

ISBN: 0–316–20024–7

Library of Congress Cataloging in Publication Data

Dyson, John, 1943–
    The south Seas dream.

    Includes index.
    1. Islands of the Pacific—Description and
travel. 2. Dyson, John, 1943– . I. Title.
DU23.5.D96 1982   990   82–9929
ISBN 0–316–20024–7   AACR2

PRINTED IN GREAT BRITAIN

To
my Mother, who set me dreaming,
my Father, who kept my feet on the ground,
and especially Kate and
my children, who let me go,
this South Seas tale is offered
with all my love and thanks

Time is brilliantly blinded: there is nothing to see. This is the reason so many people are apologetic about taking planes. They say, "What I'd really like to do is forget these plastic jumbos and get a three-masted schooner and just stand there on the poop deck with the wind in my hair."

Paul Theroux
The Old Patagonian Express

Happy he who, like Ulysses, has made an adventurous voyage.

Joseph Conrad
The Mirror of the Sea

Many a green isle needs must be
In the deep wide sea of misery,
Or the mariner, worn and wan,
Never thus could voyage on.

Percy Bysshe Shelley
Lines Written Amongst the Euganean Hills

The thought came to me in Tahiti:
"I shall sail away like the white man,
I shall paddle to some distant country,
I shall hunt in some amorous land."

Mako Manuwiri (A Wander's Chant)
Quoted by Robert Dean Frisbie
The Book of Puka-puka

CONTENTS

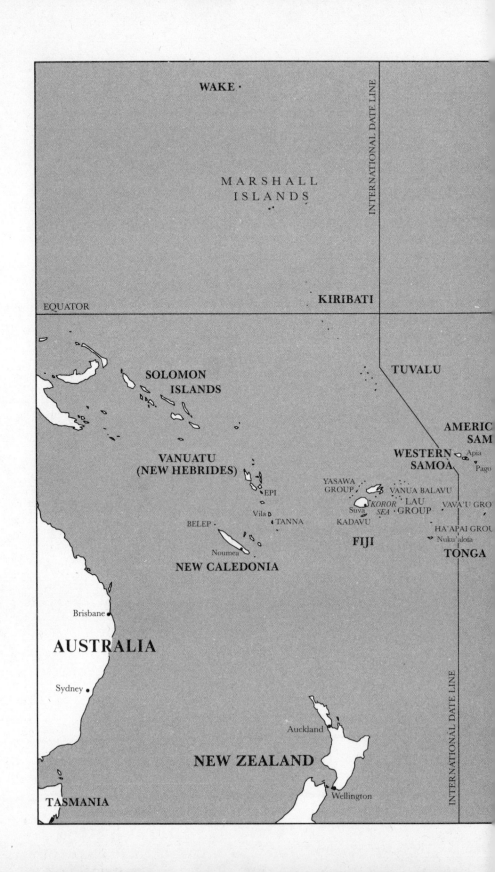

Honolulu

HAWAII

EQUATOR

MARQUESAS
ISLANDS

PUKAPUKA
NASSAU

SUVAROV

T U A M O T U
A R C H I P E L A G O

BORA BORA HUAHINE
MOOREA Papeete
TAHITI

PALMERSTON

FRENCH
POLYNESIA MURUROA

RAROTONGA

COOK
ISLANDS

AUSTRAL
ISLANDS

GAMBIER
ISLANDS

PITCAIRN

S O U T H   P A C I F I C   O C E A N

Miles
0   100 200 300 400 500

0   400   800
Kilometres

AUTHOR'S NOTE

In these times of fluctuating rates of exchange it is difficult to be precise when talking of costs. Throughout this book the dollar sign refers to a median value, for the American, Australian and various Pacific Island dollars are all approximately equal to within about ten per cent.

My pictures were taken with a Minolta XD7 through-the-lens reflex camera fitted with 24–50mm f4 and 50–135mm f3.5 zoom lenses. This equipment performed perfectly, was light to carry, excellent in use, and survived even a brief dip in the surf at Lubalea.

Along the way I was helped by many individuals and organisations, in addition to those mentioned in the book. To one and all I extend my warmest appreciation. In particular, I would like to thank Air Pacific, the Fiji airline, for help with travel within the Pacific Islands, and P & O Cruises.

Tourist officers in every country provided a great deal of practical help and good advice. I would like to extend my appreciation to the Intercontinental Island Inn of Port Vila, Vanuata; the Tradewinds Hotel, Blue Lagoon Cruises and Beachcomber Island, of Fiji; Gerard Gilloteaux of Papeete and the Captain Cook Hotel of Moorea.

No project of this kind would have made a landfall without the keenest support and enthusiasm of my publishers. My warmest thanks to those who helped to push out my boat – Roland Gant and Nigel Hollis in London, England, and Mary Tondorf-Dick in Boston, Massachusetts.

DEAR DOROTHY

A CARGO
OF DREAMS

Heavily laden with building bricks, cement, timber and drums of fuel, the old ketch rolled to her rails with a quick snatchy rhythm. Veils of clammy spray shot through with rainbows drifted over the deck with each shouldering thrust of the lee bow. Under a tempest of blue sky, the spray-fall turning to a salty dust on my skin, I was basking face-down on the tarpaulin hatch cover when a hot, moist, slithery thing oozed along my back. Startled, I jerked upright and the black mongrel puppy licking the salt from my skin danced away, barking joyfully, the brass bell round its neck tinkling like a wind-chime.

The lounging Kanaks travelling as deck passengers laughed. A piratical bunch they looked, with tattered track suits, ankle charms, and rolled cigarettes stuck behind the ear. One had a towel tied in a band round his head, so his hair stuck out like a fuzzy ginger thistle. Two children regarded me solemnly with big eyes and snotty noses; when I clapped my hands at the puppy they hid in their mother's brilliant purple skirt.

Sticky and sweaty and sunburned, and on the rebound after a flight halfway round the world, I got to my feet and stretched, staggering as the little ship lurched awkwardly over a wave. The sunshine was so brilliant and thick that it seemed to pour over me like a hot, sweet fluid. Squinting over *Hawk's* starboard rail I saw the jagged peaks of Grand Terre. All day we had been voyaging along the coast of this large main island of New Caledonia. Owner and skipper of a South Seas trading ketch, Jacques had set the jib and mainsail to boost the efforts of the rumbling diesel so we motor-sailed, bound for the Belep Islands.

His black eyes as expressionless as sunglasses, Hake (*Har-Kay*) the Solomon Islander crewman was on the fo'c'sle hauling buckets of frothing water out of the ocean and filling the open barrel used to dip water for flushing the lavatory, washing dishes and boiling rice. When I tapped my chest he grinned and shot me full in the face. The water dried off stickily in seconds. I clambered on the bowsprit and lay face down, watching the tiny flying fish winging to safety from the black bow cutting through the water. Suddenly there was a shriek, as if the ship were being ambushed. Everyone on deck rushed aft, where Jacques and Hake wrestled with a bar-taut rope trailing in the wake. The line jumped in their hands as, far astern, a silver shaft thrashed above the surface like a piece of cartwheeling shrapnel. Then a second line trailing over the taffrail quivered and sprang. The puppy ran between everybody's legs, barking and clanging its bell. A pair of Spanish mackerel or *wahoo* hit the deck in a thunder of panic and the bell could be heard tinkling hesitantly at a safe distance amidships.

Conning from the ratlines halfway up the mainmast, Jacques turned the ship towards the reef. Big swells uncoiled from the ocean, tripped headlong on the underwater cliff rising almost vertically from great depths, and roared in seething avalanches over the ledge of coral. With anxious glances at Hake, now ludicrously wearing a policeman's cap, the young skipper shaded his eyes against the sun's glare to distinguish the darker blues and greens that indicated deep water, and brought his ketch into the placid lagoon. Then he returned to the wheelhouse and watched for a time, checking that Hake had the new course fixed in his mind.

I was on the bowsprit again, watching the fringe of coconut palms along the shore and the high arid slopes beyond, and gazing down from time to time at the shifting shades of azure blue and turquoise sliding beneath the keel, when Jacques caught my eye. The old ship was eighty feet long and we were at opposite ends of her, but I could see the satisfaction in his quick happy grin.

You wanted to sail in a South Seas trader, Jacques was telling me, and this is what it *can* be like. Then he dipped his thumb into his mouth and hitched it towards the galley. Good, George had put the kettle on.

This adventure in paradise had started long ago with a banana. I was a schoolboy in New Zealand, doing the weekend errands, when the greengrocer piled potatoes on the scales until the pointer quivered at five pounds. As he tumbled them into my basket he said he had a love letter for me. From the South Seas, he added, licking the stub of a pencil hanging from his neck on a string and jotting the cost of the spuds on a paper bag.

That a letter of any kind should be addressed to me care of the fruit and veg. man at the end of our road was mystifying. That it should be a love letter, and from the South Seas, was lunatic. Then Jan, a grave Dutchman not usually given to practical jokes, handed me a banana and urged me to read it.

The sneer died in my throat as I realised the banana did indeed bear a message. In rough cuts of a broad thumbnail, which would have been invisible when the banana was hard and green and packed in its crate but now were clearly legible in brown on mottled yellow, the banana proclaimed:

DEAR JOHN I LOVE YOU SEXY DOROTHY

New Zealand, where I was raised on adventure stories imported from England and bananas imported from Samoa, regarded itself as a South Pacific nation but its outlook was that of an English county adrift somewhere off Cornwall. I had never seen a coral reef, never paddled an outrigger, neither picked a banana nor tasted a fresh coconut. But my imagination had been fired by tales of reef and palm. The gin-sodden schooner skippers with hoary fists and hairy language in Jack London. The dissolute beachcombers and traders bewitched by beautiful island maidens in Robert Louis Stevenson. The saga of *Mutiny on the Bounty* which, besides being an exciting sea-story with tones of lust, had also the thrill of men deliberately escaping civilised authority to try their luck with Nature in her most appetising image. But these stirring adventures did not seem to me to take place among islands that were our nearest neighbours: I regarded the South Seas as an Englishman would, as mysterious isles of desire on the furthest, least accessible, backside of the planet.

After all, it was inconceivable that my sexy Dorothy could be a fat and giggling nymph in a gym slip and sandshoes, like the Samoan girl called Alamein in my class. She had been christened after the name of the desert battle in which her father was engaged on the day she was born. When she ran into a skipping rope clacking in lazy revolutions her beautiful black hair streamed like a banner and her bosom wobbled like a chocolate marshmallow, a characteristic of some curiosity in one aged eleven. But her right hand could strike like a snake and flick an unwary young gent's fly buttons wide open, and her cackle of victory would be heard clear across the playground. This was no tender sultry nymph tempting sailors (or schoolboys, for that matter) with such delights of Venus that they would risk flogging, hanging, or worse. Could such a girl be the inspiration of Stevenson's

THE SOUTH SEAS DREAM

description of Samoan people as "God's best, at least God's sweetest work"? Or the seductress to knock the poet Rupert Brooke head over heels and cause him to write of Samoa:

"... I know an island
where Beauty and Courtesy, as flowers, blow."

It was the banana that set me wondering, because it held some faint promise that the stories were no fiction and the islands were by no means far away.

To raise cash for an overseas trip, my first job was labouring in a wool warehouse where most of the other workers were young islanders from the several South Pacific groups that had fallen under New Zealand's bureaucratic wing. Straight out of the academic hot-house, I was priggish about the shiftlessness of these handsome and happy-go-lucky contemporaries, and appalled at their chain-smoking, the way they guzzled junk food, their angry consumption of beer that swept them willy-nilly into vandalism and casual crime; it was many years before I recognised culture shock when I saw it. But those lads never stopped laughing and ragging and there was not a mean streak in any of them. Carefreeness was their religion. The only thing they worried about was which sheila they would get down the gully after the flicks. With a jab of a cargo hook any of them could twist a 400-pound wool bale as lightly as I might have managed had it been hay. They teased me non-stop and made a tally man of me, not because I could count but because I was earnest. My nickname was Biggles.

Sprawling in mountains of greasy wool at tea break swilling Coke and stuffing meat pies and Minties down my throat with the best of them, I heard blood-tingling yarns. Of community fish-driving in dazzling lagoons, of turtle-hunting trips by sailing canoe to an uninhabited *motu* across the atoll, of sexual sports engaged in as uninhibitedly as playground tag, of the massive blue and purple land crabs that climbed palm trees to clip coconuts with pincers that could take your hand off.

For these boys the gates of paradise had opened. They had real jobs and lots of money. They could drive cars and drink milkshakes and go to the pictures. Life, they reckoned, was okay. Meanwhile, I nourished a dream of my own. I hid in the lavatory as long as I dared to gaze at the brochure, dog-eared and sticky with lanoline, showing plans and pictures of the passenger liner on which I had booked for England.

Oh for a life of sensations rather than thoughts, John Keats had sighed. He would have been content enough on the sundeck of the giant liner on that brilliant, glossy morning as it slid into the lagoon and was engulfed by the maelstrom of violent, passionate colour, noise and dust that was Tahiti on a Ship Day. I was sixteen years old, travelling in a cabin with twenty-six berths, and it was my first foreign country. Schooners and cruising yachts were moored to the quay beneath scarlet flamboyants of breathless beauty. Green over-growth seemed about to overwhelm the trim white wooden buildings with their shady, creeper-festooned verandahs. A sea of brown faces jostled and waved noisily on the dusty wharf, as if this was the first vessel to arrive for months. The dome of hot blue sky burned like fire, while the vault of shot-silk blues and greens beneath the ship held a promise of chill refreshing rejuvenation. Hordes of small boys gambolled on the mooring warps and dived for coins into the window-clear water; not a shoal of square white jellyfish drifting listlessly down there, I realised with a jolt, but ship's toilet tissues.

The eager tourist, I swam in the lagoon, swigged from a freshly cut green coconut, walked beneath the wind-rattled palms, watched the mighty rollers of the Pacific beating the reef, sat on a bag of copra – the strong-smelling dried coconut meat that is the main crop of the South Seas – and watched a trading schooner battening down before it let go, hoisted sail, and turned out into the boisterous white horses of the blue ocean beyond the reef. In the soft, sweet-smelling evening I watched the sunset over Moorea. Then to Quinn's, a waterfront shack with a tin roof and woven cane, one of the most famous dives in the Pacific. Amplified guitars and hollow-log drums beat out a *tamure*, the fast-pulsing traditional dance that fills the air with a thunder of kisses. In every booth, girls with flowers behind their ears and bright dresses sprawled languidly upon sailors and tourists. As I walked past a stand of bamboo, on my way back to the ship, there came a piercing shriek. Was it a night bird or somebody being murdered? The street was deserted and I had no idea what to do. Then it came again, blood-chilling to begin with, but fading into a throaty chuckle and a strange plucking noise. With a gulp and a blush I realised it was the music of passionate kissing. The bushes were alive with copulating couples. Shaken, Biggles retired to his bunk.

In these meagre experiences and curiosities the seeds of my own love affair with visions of sunlit islands of the South Seas were sown. Images of colour, dazzle, sensuality, carefreeness, closeness to a Nature at her most benign and beautiful, warmth of heart and high adventure haunted my thoughts. Now I was a newspaper reporter hunting stolen babies among the chimney pots of Manchester, and I began to long for the far-away islands that had once been so close to home.

It started as the Blue Water Dream. I fell in love with sailing, devoured books on the subject, studied for a certificate at navigation school, and sailed in the English Channel to prepare myself for the great adventure. I would roam those parts of the world where the air was sweetest and freshest, where the only hand on the tiller of life is your own, where your anchor splashes down into depths of your own choosing. I pictured myself, bearded and in shorts, sailing a yacht adorned with baggy-wrinkle and faded flags into some dazzling lagoon where the ocean's stern grace would be exchanged for an interval of leafy calm. I would beat the typewriter for the few dollars I would need to survive until the heat of the morning grew too demanding and I would peel over the side for a languid swim to the palm-shaded beach where a tender, lithesome, admiring Dorothy would have brought a mango for my breakfast. And it was by no means an impossible dream for every year more people were living it. For every 100 dreamers I calculated, one actually took a step towards it by attending navigation school or buying a boat. For every 100 who took such a step, one actually set a course for the west horizon. What happened to me? I got married.

Now a different reel flickered on the picture screen of my mind. Up to my neck in sawdust, wallpaper paste and mortgage, the simplicities of an island lifestyle seemed a tempting option. Willingly enough – I thought – I would trade bricks and mortar in London for a thatched hut by a sunny lagoon stocked with fish. Strap-hanging to and from the office by train, I would see my spear skewering a parrot fish in the shallows, feel the sting of the fat on my bare skin as I turned the spit over the fire, sense the cool touch of the sunset-flamed water as I rinsed the grease off my fingers and looked round for a papaya. It was hard, sometimes, to remember to get off at my station.

Then, as our children multiplied and grew bigger, and the suburban rut threatened to become all-engulfing, my thoughts began to dwell on other values of the South Seas Dream. It struck me after all these years that obese and dim though she was, there had never been a moment when Alamein, the Samoan girl in class, was not smiling. I remembered the boys in the wool-store and realised it had been the conflict of our own materialistic society with their own lend-and-borrow, community-oriented culture, that had led them into what our courts termed crime but which they – by their own reckoning – saw simply as a practical way of life: theft was a concept which did not exist in their minds.

In the islands of the South Seas there were no mortgages, no insurance, no serious untreatable diseases, no starvation, no old folk dying in need, no orphanages, no welfare to undermine the spirit, not taxes to speak of, no clock-watching, no nuclear targets, no pollution, no drugs problem, no urban decay, no advertising hoardings, no electric pylons to mar the view, no traffic lights, no danger of cataclysmic event beyond the odd cyclone or tidal wave, no organised crime ... The islands might have been held back by dim-witted administrations but had never been victimised nor exploited because they had nothing worth taking except a bit of sandalwood and pearl-shell so there was no residue of aggression. The islands had nothing to sell but their beauty when the weather was nice, yet political development was occurring with its own steady momentum in an atmosphere of dignity and tranquillity, and without a gun in sight. Surely this, too, was a dream?

The South Seas Dream takes many forms, even if it is not a concept specifically of waving palms, thundering surf, and a semi-naked lifestyle in the sunshine. It is ironic that in this affluent and comfortable high-tech age which Westerners enjoy we do not stop at questioning the quality of the air we breathe, the food we eat, and the reason we should fear to walk the streets in the dark. We have leisure to question – and worry about – the direction of life itself. With all our wealth and technical ability, with all our comforts, education and entertainment, we are basically a discontented lot. So we dream.

We dream of an existence somewhere fresher and calmer. We imagine the satisfactions of being more creative with our own hands, of growing and farming our own food, of thatching our own roof, of being self-sufficient. We supplement with expensive vitamin pills our expensive diet of junk food prepared in labour-saving kitchens and grow neurotic about the value of our lifestyle: would it not be nicer, nobler, nearer to what God intended, to be shipwrecked like Robinson Crusoe ... well, just start again?

Nowhere but in the tiny scattered garden islands of the South Seas are the ingredients of such dreams found in such full and honest measure. Colour, beauty, good weather and a bountiful Nature. A handsome, gracious people fond of music, dancing and the good life. Above all, no group of islands is more remote from any continent: the whole Pacific Ocean, covering sixty million square miles would be your insulation against war, pollution, plague and economic strife. This is the refugee's dream.

But the single most potent force in the image of the islands as an earthly paradise, the one which turned the cultural establishment completely on its head two centuries ago and has delighted and titillated the popular imagination ever since, is the South Seas promise of random free love. The beautiful, graceful, fun-loving island maidens considered fair skin a mark of beauty and their indolent comfortable lifestyle in never-ending summer in a Garden of Eden encouraged a

[7]

style of free and easy sexual gratification that made starchy Christian senses boggle. Captain Cook, the first white man to spend considerable time in Tahiti and the Society Islands, electrified the drawing rooms of 18th-century England with his accounts of love games he observed. Sexual play was indulged in from early childhood, he reported, and there were few constraints. With only faint surprise he related how he witnessed a girl of about twelve being "initiated into the arts of Venus" by an older man, while more experienced women sat around offering advice on how to please him. Small wonder that Cook and his men returned there frequently for spells of "r and r" and that the whalers, traders and other maritime adventurers who followed in his wake hung their morals on Cape Horn as they sailed into the Pacific. Even Captain Cook, on his boat trip round the island, woke to find his breeches had vanished along with his dusky companion of the night.

Ships commonly sailed into shoals of naked nymphs who clambered aboard bearing gifts of fruit, scores of them. Loud and noisy, they pantomimed gestures to the sea-weary sailors and made liberal offers of their charms. For the sake of getting rid of them, the Russian naturalist Langsdorff explained archly, some were let on board his ship.

These graces appeared in general with all their charms exposed: for though they never left the land without at least so much clothing as a large green leaf, yet this light covering was lost by swimming.

One after another, the maidens vanished below decks hand-in-hand with the sailors "while the goddess of night threw her dark veil over the mysteries that were celebrated".

A similar adventure befell the missionary ship *Duff* on its pioneer voyage to the South Seas, when a bevy of visitors swam out to pay their respects. The knavish goats carried on board, the captain reported, were guilty of a very great offence,

... for they would not leave the poor young maidens even the little clothing they had but flocked round them to get at the green leaves till most of them were left entirely in their native beauty.

The sexual ethos of the South Seas gripped northern man's imagination for two centuries and continues to be exploited as a tourist draw. Ever since Herman Melville jumped ship in the Marquesas and collected the experiences with which he afterwards put the South Seas on the literary map, what he called "lovely houris" have topped the list of island delights. His first book, *Typee*, furnished the stuff on which generations of South Seas dreams were made:

[8]

What a sight for us bachelor sailors! How avoid so dire a temptation? For who could think of tumbling these artless creatures overboard, when they had swum miles to welcome us? Their appearance
perfectly amazed me; their extreme youth, the light clear brown of
their complexions, their delicate features, and inexpressibly graceful
figures, their softly moulded limbs, and free unstudied action,
seemed as strange as beautiful. The *Dolly* was fairly captured . . . We
could not do otherwise than yield ourselves prisoners, and for the
whole period that she remained in the bay, the *Dolly*, as well as her
crew, were completely in the hands of the mermaids. Our ship was
now wholly given up to every species of riot and debauchery. Not
the feeblest barrier was interposed between the unholy passions of
the crew and their unlimited gratification . . .

Bright and high-handed adventure, sexual indulgence without the
complexities of love and marriage, self-sufficiency, astonishing natural
beauty and placid contentment: these are the themes of the South Seas
Dream as reflected in two centuries of literature between the journals of
Captain Cook and Joseph Banks, the poetry of Rupert Brooke, the
romances of Robert Louis Stevenson, the short stories and novels of
Somerset Maugham, the narratives of Charles Nordhoff and James
Norman Hall, the real-life story of the painter Paul Gauguin, the films
of *Mutiny on the Bounty*, and the James Michener fantasy of Bali Ha'i in
South Pacific. In fact the very words South Seas grew into a kind of
synonym for these excitements and I knew from my own small
experiences that they were no imaginative lie. As a young reporter
interviewing blue-water sailors who had crossed the Pacific by yacht, it
was when I put my pencil away that the talk would turn to the
beautiful girls who stopped aboard with ukeleles, of feasts offered in
return for the simple pleasure of receiving visitors, of sexual sport
under the palms, of girls who paddled out in canoes with a bunch of
bananas and stayed for a week. But when I had the chance to sail as
a deckhand in an American globe-trotting yacht from Sydney to Hong
Kong, I heard the first faint ringing of the alarm bell that was to
awaken me from the South Seas Dream. When I noticed a big stock
of penicillin in the galley fridge I asked why we carried so much. The
obese Alabama youth in cut-down jeans, who was engineer, winked
heavily and explained, "Aw, that was for Tahiti: we'd get ourselves
a girl every night and a shot of penicillin every morning."
And once I had my antennae tuned, the signals came in thick and
fast. Cruising yachtsmen told me of how, having crossed the widest and
emptiest part of the Pacific to the Marquesas Islands, they were
welcomed in beautiful anchorages amid rugged volcanic bays fes-

tooned with jungle by canoes paddled out on the blue surge by "lovely houris" bearing fruit to trade, not for the delights of Venus but for batteries. Every thatched hut had its cassette player, but batteries were in short supply.

It was clear that Pacific rim nations – with sixty-two per cent of the world population – were taking an increasing interest in the islands, especially since exclusive offshore economic zones had been agreed, giving the islands rights and responsibilities over oceanic territories vast in relation to their dry land. As they achieved political independence or measures of home rule, island countries whose entire populations were smaller than an English county town were gaining a significance undreamed of ten years before. Yet some island groups continued to be administered blatantly as colonies, and seemed content, which surely went against the grain of political progress. France was turning Tahiti into a nuclear laboratory. Tonga had been negotiating with Russia to provide a base of the Soviet distant-water fishing fleet. The People's Republic of China had opened diplomatic missions in Fiji and Western Samoa. Were Dorothy's messages thumb-nailed on green bananas now quoting Mao's *Little Red Book*? I could not tell, for the next time I returned to New Zealand, with my family to introduce them to a Down Under Christmas in the sun, the only bananas I could find were imported from Ecuador.

So it was that I began to speculate rather than dream. To wonder what the future held for these tiny countries with nothing to sell but images of a picturesque past. To doubt that carnivorous cockroaches really did eat your feet as you travelled in reeling, reeking, copra cutters. To puzzle over the fate of the gin-sozzled traders, bare-knuckled schooner skippers, and stiff-collared missionaries who peopled South Seas tales of fact and fiction. To hope that I was not too late to witness from a pitching spray-wet deck the kind of South Sea landfall at sunrise which Robert Louis Stevenson described as "the fit signboard for a world of wonders".

Judging by tourist brochures and glossy picture books alone the South Seas Dream was flourishing but I was suspicious because the geography of the imagination has always been a potent influence on the development of the world. From the very beginning, first-hand journals and even the pictures brought back by the explorers were distorted to fit the image of an earthly paradise, at that time a classical one. Tahitans were portrayed wearing loin cloths and Greek gowns in vase-like postures as if frozen in mid-tableau of some dreadful high school play. When the explorers failed to find the hoped-for Great Southern Continent those at home made do with images of Arcadia. Mercantile adventurers who followed, having swiftly stripped the islands bare of sandalwood, sea slugs dried and traded to China, and pearl shell, also made do with cargoes of dreams. The missionaries looted the islanders of their heathenish laughter, music and easy lifestyle, and distorted the same picture to emphasise the primitive and dark sides of the South Sea character. In modern times, the boundless promise of the islands of love was deliberately exploited as a means of attracting tourists. Brochures and guidebooks implied, without stating it as bald fact, that your queen-sized bed in your air-conditioned room equipped with sanitised lavatory seat came complete with reclining native houri. States one contemporary guidebook about Tahiti:

> The *vahines* of Tahiti have dispensed their pleasures upon visitors from the first seamen to the modern day tourist – all strangers who arrive in peace can expect the fullest of local hospitality.

It was during the Christmas holiday in New Zealand that the suspicions which had been festering in my mind took an urgent twist. I was sailing with my father in his little ketch into the port of Opua in the north of the country, when we spied an interesting but ungainly black ship at the wharf ahead. Flying a faded *tricoleur*, she was clearly a cut-down sailing vessel of some kind, though now she looked like a cross between a lighthouse tender and a gravel barge. She had a sawn-off stump of a bowsprit, a tarpaulin slung over the fo'c'sle, and a tea-caddy of a wheelhouse atop the deckhouse aft. In small white letters on her transom was written her name, *Hawk*. And below, in smaller letters, her port of registry: Noumea.

As we sailed down her side a hawk-faced, bearded man leapt on her rail, waved exuberantly, and shouted, "Hey, you jokers, that's *my* boat!"

Jacques Sapir took our lines as we swung wonderingly alongside and he explained that fifteen years before, soon after he had emigrated to Melbourne from Paris, he had owned the trim little ketch that now belonged to us. She had been first of a long line of different craft that had led to his owning *Hawk* which he had bought in the New Hebrides and now sailed on a trading route in New Caledonia between Noumea, the capital, and the Belep Islands to the north-west. The old ship had been built nearby in New Zealand, ninety-nine years before, and he had brought her back to be re-rigged and restored as nearly as possible to her original condition.

As I swung my leg over her broad, scarred bulwarks I entered the dimension of my South Seas Dreams. Under the shady awning forward I saw a flash of white, like sun winking on pearl shell, as Hake, doing the washing up in a tin bowl, beamed a shy welcome. The ship's pet, a turtle called Lady Hawk, paddled listlessly in her glass-fibre bathtub on deck. A thick sweet odour, the heady perfume of a multitude of copra cargoes, rose from the open corner of the hatch. In the little cabin where Jacques and his wife Robyn made a pot of strong Noumea-grown coffee, shell necklaces hung from the light fittings and polished cowrie shells gleamed among the books where they had been thrust to stop them rolling about at sea.

Here was a South Sea skipper in the flesh, a man who lived his dream, setting his own course by his own compass and collecting cargoes where he could. The sights and smells of the old trading ketch, and the skipper's yarns and bright enthusiasm, stirred the pot of my lifetime's imaginings and suddenly, as if struck by lightning, I realised how they could be distilled into a single, realisable adventure. I had no wish to commit my wife and four children to a years-long blue-water voyage by yacht. I had no real yearning for shipwreck and a lonely life on a desert island. I would be no refugee, not even from nuclear holocaust. The allure of lovely houris had been a youthful fancy, perhaps also a fleeting fantasy of the seven-year itch, but in truth I was contentedly, loyally hitched. Nevertheless, I burned with curiosity. Couldn't I test the South Seas Dream in its various forms without actually committing myself to it? Couldn't I wander through the South Seas, from trading cutter to hospitable verandah, from beach to riff-raff reef town, testing the image against the reality? I would encounter the islands as the old-time sailors did, as green oases in a vast dark-blue wet desert. I would commit myself to the vast leisure of the ocean's embrace, investing in what Joseph Conrad called "all those hours of staring, boredom, tediousness ... all those hours spent *between* rather than doing ..." I would make my South Sea landfalls as did the characters of history and romance, with sea-weary and land-hungry eyes.

Jacques neither scorned nor mocked. In fact I barely had to explain. "God, matey", he said at once, "you'd better be quick. Everything is changing so fast, even the kids don't dive in the lagoon any more, unless they've got flippers. But I tell you what ..."

He had a government contract, he explained, to make a voyage every six weeks and in between he picked up what charters he could. Now Jacques closed his eyes and counted on his fingers. "Say six months from now," he proposed, "which makes it early September, around the tenth ..."

So it was that back home in London I spun the globe and for the first time seriously comprehended what I was in for. The Pacific Ocean is the largest area of the world under one name. It covers one-third of the planet and you could drop into it all the world's dry lands. It has

25,000 islands, of which 1,500 are individually habitable. Of these, half are in Oceania, the broad belt of islands scattered loosely parallel with the equator and becoming ever smaller and more fragmented as you look east.

As geographic discovery extended, scientists after Charles Darwin had settled on the term South Pacific for that field of ocean more or less south of Hawaii and stretching from New Guinea, Australia and New Zealand, across the baldest area of the atlas, to South America.

But my own interest focussed on the South Seas, a term which missionaries had borrowed from the romantic imagery of the dis-coverers and applied not to the ocean but to the tiny and remote specks of land scattered over it. Starting in *Hawk* I would cadge, buy and work whatever passages I could and voyage through a constellation of islands spanning 3,000 miles. But consider the perspectives. Put all eight countries together and they add up to only 21,000 square miles: half the size of Iceland, smaller than Tasmania, one-third as big as Florida, about the same as Costa Rica or Benelux. Total population 1.3 million, about the size of Birmingham, England. But the land is not in one easy-to-manage piece. It is scattered in crumbs over a carpet of ocean rather larger than the USA. The individual crumbs are meagre beyond imagining. The Samoas are smaller than Long Island. Tonga, spread over an area as large as England, is one third the size of the Isle of Skye, in Scotland. The Isle of Wight is 147 square miles, a mere pin-prick on most maps of the world, but the Cook Islands, fifteen of them strewn over an area as large as Western Europe, together total only ninety-three square miles. Just to look at the map, even with the aid of a magnifying glass, was mind-numbing.

South Seas! What words could make the blood pump faster, I wondered, as I plodded fruitlessly round the London travel agents. The first shock came when I learned that steamers which formerly criss-crossed the Pacific by way of the islands had long ago been put out of business by over-flying jumbo jets. Even the few Russian cruise ships had been chased out of the South Pacific by anger over Afghanistan. Had I wanted to voyage to the South Seas as a romantic must – by ship – there was only one sailing in the whole year.

So it had to be by DC-10 that I made my rendezvous. At 7.28 pm on 10th September I found *Hawk* in pitch darkness, loaded and ready to sail, at the *Quai des Caboteurs* in Noumea. I had written to Jacques during the intervening six months but received no answer. Tele-phoned, but his line was dead. Nevertheless I flew halfway round the world to keep a date calculated on fingers and thumbs because, I reasoned, sometimes dreams simply had to come true.

Crossing the quay in the warm, sweet darkness I saw the ship's new rigging silhouetted against a velvet sky blazing with stars but the deck was in total darkness. As I fumbled my way over the bulwarks, swinging my kitbag, I all but collided with a figure coming the other way. "Ah, it *is* you!" Jacques exclaimed, glancing at his luminous watch. "I was giving you until seven-thirty. Lucky you made it. We sail first thing in the morning."

Trailing a perfume of strong coffee, *Hawk* sailed out into the broad Pacific at dawn, just ten minutes after the *croissant* shop had opened its doors. Dear Dorothy, I thought, here I come . . .

2

HAWK

Copra Ketch
in the Black Isles

The first passenger to go ashore was the Kanak with a withered arm and a double bed. He lived on a low, flat island separated from another larger island by the shallow channel in which *Hawk* cautiously anchored. The route into the beach was marked by a withy flagged with a worn-out Adidas shoe. Jacques lifted the outboard and let the long glassfibre canoe coast into the shallows. The bows rode up on the carcass of a large shark entangled in a net, its guts hanging out like a blown-away line of washing. We carried the double bed over a path of crunchy white shells to four or five thatched huts in a clearing. Fences of brown beer-bottles pushed neck-down in the sand made neat enclosures in front of each one, and I thought of my own garden in London which the children had edged with shells. I could hear people in the huts but nobody came out, not even the children. The passenger ducked into the gloom of a hut and never reappeared. Two engineless fishing launches, new but dilapidated and uncared for, were lying in the sun. It was a furtive, eerie place and we zoomed away as soon as our Tahitian crewman, who had pornographic doodles in Biro all over his T-shirt, had walked up a palm and kicked down a score of coconuts which we collected in a sack. There were bush limes to pick, too, so I knotted the cuffs of my shirt and filled the sleeves.

It was a relief to weigh anchor and steal away from this sullen place where the crew of a French survey ship had been killed and eaten in 1850, prompting France to annex the island. Jacques put a tape on loud, to cheer us up, and with quadrophonic stereo blasting *The Sugar Plum Fairy* at the silent brooding shore the ketch turned her bowsprit towards the sparkling open sea.

As we picked our way out through the reef the old ship shook her head in the beam sea, a jib was hoisted and sheeted home with a Cape Horn heave. Jacques ripped the skin from one of the big fish and cut the grey flesh into tiny cubes. I squeezed half a pint of lime juice into a jug. Hake sliced the tops from half a dozen coconuts with a wicked bush knife and when we had drained the sweet, cool, juice he split them open and scraped out the slithery flesh. This he heaped on a dish cloth then squeezed out the cream into a bowl. Then we put it all together in a large tin bowl, along with a heap of chopped onion. Stung by the lime-juice, the oily fish meat withered and cured before my eyes, becoming delicious, firm, non-fishy white meat. George, an American lone yachtsman who had left his yacht in Noumea and signed on for the voyage, had made a side-salad and we had a stick of crusty French bread. I sat on deck in the narrow strip of shade cast by the wind-tight jib and devoured the fruits of the South Seas.

Hawk had been transformed since I had last been on board. Jacques told me how he had sailed her into the forgotten port of Dargaville, where she had been built as a Customs cutter nearly a century before, to a breathtaking reception. Hundreds had lined the riverbank to watch and cheer and wonder. There was a civic reception. Teams of volunteers orchestrated by the local newspaper had done the restoration work under Jacques' direction. In 1922 Alan Villiers had sailed in her as a deckhand when she traded in Bass Strait. "She had once been a fine vessel but had fallen on evil days," he wrote later. "The fight with her gaff tops'l stands out in my memory as one of the worst experiences I ever had in the rigging of a sailing ship." Subsequently, the story goes, an Australian skipper had taken her into Vila, in the New Hebrides, where the harbourmaster had taken one look at the long and unused bowsprit spearing dangerously beyond her clipper bow and screamed "You can't come in here with that bloody barge-pole!" So the skipper had scratched his head, rowed ashore, borrowed a chain-saw, and dropped the bowsprit into the harbour.

Now the ship sported two sturdy masts, an elegant new bowsprit, lots of bright paint, and she was shorn of the ridiculous wheelhouse perched up high. *Hawk* breathed character. She was a ship with a glint in her eye, an elderly lady not quite certain she had tried everything once. Jacques' love of the old girl did more than shine from his eyes: it absorbed him body and soul and sucked in every person who stepped aboard. But this alone had not been enough to fire the imagination of a remote rural farming community in New Zealand. Nor had it been just the love of an old ship that spurred them. It was the call of the sea, perhaps, the beckoning of isles with their dazzling sea days, star-lit anchorages, and thrillingly frightening reefs. It was the spirit that

Jacques personified, the footloose sea-rover with the wind in his hair and a star to steer by and a fish stunned on deck for lunch.

Veiled by blue haze, the high main island of New Caledonia filled the horizon to starboard. Although it is the largest South Sea island it is not typical. It is more like a piece of Africa cut out of a map, crumpled into a long thin twist – 250 miles long and 50 miles wide – and dropped in the sea. The gaunt ranges rise to 5,000 feet along the spine of the island and are splashed with the ochreous colours of iron, manganese chrome, cobalt and nickel which rains wash into the sea and trucks carry to the smelter in Noumea. The coastal plains are narrow bands of savannah with spiky grass and stunted knuckly eucalyptus. Here there are extensive cattle ranches owned by settlers and the only cowboys (*les stockmen*) in the South Seas. It is a shoreline of mangroves and tussock, with few palms, and in the south grow the tall sentinel-like pines with short branches that reminded Captain Cook of Scotland and inspired his name for the place. It is hard to see anything of the mellow ruggedness of the Highlands in the jagged, flinty rawness of this strange tropical island of black history and black repressed natives.

The Beleps are an archipelago of five hummocky palmy islands thirty miles off the north-west tip, and they are a native reserve. The sun was low and the wind had dropped when *Hawk* sailed into a large bay and sounded her whistle. There was an outcry, like the shrieks of many birds, and within moments a horde of shrilling people were sprinting along the beach. Thatched huts were visible between the palms. High on the hill was a white-painted Roman Catholic church with a red roof. Happily Jacques conned his ship to the T-shaped wharf. Warps were passed over to the throng. Quivering, the black puppy was manhandled over the gap and dropped roughly on the wharf where it shook itself and its bell jangled like an old alarm clock.

When I strolled along the red dirt track behind the first rank of palms rimming the bay, it seemed that I had made a landfall in Robert Louis Stevenson's *The Beach of Falesa*:

> It was good to foot the grass, to look aloft at the green mountains, to see the men with their green wreaths and the women in their bright dresses, red and blue. On we went in the strong sun and the cool shadow, liking both; and all the children in the town came trotting after with their shaven heads and their brown bodies, and raising a thin kind of cheer in our wake, like crowing poultry . . .

Real poultry, too. At the far end of the beach a tiny chicken detached itself from its mother and followed me, cheep-cheeping all the way, to the wharf. Some youths in old army clothes and rakish head-bands stuck with feathers sat on the bollards staring, their faces orange in the ruddy glow of the sunset. With such longing I too, as a boy, had stared at the liners and freighters which linked New Zealand with the wide world. When I gestured at the stupid chick, thinking that one of them would take it home, they laughed and threw a hail of pebbles at it.

I poured shots of rum sharpened with fresh lime, took ice from the galley fridge, its door lashed up with string, and when I reached the deck again with the drinks the sky was a deep black pricked by stars that speckled the quiet water like a fall of bright dust. I smelled the cooking fires on shore. The sound of a dog-fight came over the water, then a cock-crow. Well may the dreamers dream, I thought, sipping my rum. Next morning I started to discover the nightmare.

No romantic articles of commerce spiced our seventy tons of cargo. No bêche-de-mer, pearl shell, ambergris or sandalwood. Unloading started in the cool shade of dawn and was finally completed when the sun stood right above the mast, blazing directly into the dusty hold where Hake and the boys toiled in the slither of their own sweat. A mountain of concrete building-bricks, timber, roofing iron, bags of sugar and outboard motors stood on the wharf. Among it waited the missionary, a tall fleshy individual with a pink face, flip-up sunglasses clipped to his spectacles, a nylon trilby and a blue plastic raincoat buttoned up to his neck. Although visitors were scarce in this part of the world, and he had been here for three years, the American made no attempt at conversation or contact. The natives got the missionary they deserved, I suspected, or was it the other way round? The Kanaks did not strike me as likeable. Meet a Tahitian's eye and he grins, winks or responds in some human way. But these people did not look you in the eye. Their laughter had a cruel edge, more of a cackle. Many were drunk. Interestedly I watched two burly natives set about the task of loading a neat stack of bricks into the back of a small truck. It seemed to pose something of an intellectual quandary: instead of taking bricks from the edge of the stack they were trying to get them from the centre, which required an awkward lifting posture and it was difficult for the bushman's big fingers to fit into the cracks between the bricks and get a grip.

That was nothing, Jacques laughed, when the ship was still and quiet and we were eating the last of the *poisson crû* in the cool of the cabin. He claimed he had often seen islanders trying to pick up objects on which they were standing. The trouble was that the men were so strong that the thing usually broke. Later he demonstrated his point. I was on the cabin top with my camera and he was driving the donkey engine when he caught my attention with a finger to his nose as if to say, Watch this! On the wharf were three wooden pallets which Hake and his boys were roping up for him to swing aboard with the derrick. "No, no!" Jacques shouted, "Just *one* pallet!" The islanders lifted two pallets off the pile, which they put to one side. They lifted the bottom pallet on to the rope, thus manhandling all three pallets when they had needed to lift only one.

When he owned my father's yacht, Jacques told me, he had watched an old fisherman single-handedly berth a seventy-footer with one warp. The bight had flowered perfectly over the bollard, he had taken a quick turn on a cleat amidships, then it was slow ahead and hard over, and the big vessel had fallen neatly alongside. "I have been using that method to come alongside in all the three years that Hake has been working for me, but I have to explain it every time," Jacques said. "Why is it that a White man sees the neat trick of the week and never forgets it, but the Melanesian sees it every day and never remembers it?"

Jacques took my arm and said he had something to show me. George was busy with the frying pan in the galley, cobbling a fry-up of frozen steak, tinned sweet corn and fresh green peppers. "Don't be long, guys, it's nearly ready," he said.

Beached under the trees and shaded with planks of plaited palm-fronds that had blown awry was one of the prettiest little sailing hulls a sailor could imagine. It was clinker-built, about twenty-five feet long, with a sweet sheer and a broad beam. But its paint had blistered, the timbers were cracked, and a stagnant pool nourished mosquito-larvae in the bilges. Several similar boats were to be seen along the shore, all of them designed, Jacques explained, by a Breton missionary who lived here for years and taught the natives how to build them. "These boats sail like witches, carry a fair load, are good for fishing and the wind is free," he said. Then he slapped the planks so angrily that slivers of paint wafted like Technicolor leaves to the ground. "But the administration introduced an aid scheme. A native had to put down only a 10 per cent deposit to get a big new launch and an outboard engine of sixty or eighty horsepower. Nobody knows anything about servicing or maintenance, the engines bust and have to be sent to Noumea. How many did we bring up with us on the deck, eight?"

Along the red-dirt track was a rusty yellow bulldozer overgrown with grass. It was the only heavy machine on the island, invaluable for many purposes. Four years ago the battery went flat. The native council ordered a new one but it took a while to come and nobody put a tin can over the vertical exhaust pipe to keep the rain out. The cylinders rusted up. The administration categorised it as a workshop job but to get the bulldozer back to Noumea would be a $10,000 tug-and-barge job. Jacques suggested that the machine be traded in for a new one: he would bring the new one up in *Hawk* and use it to dig the old one out. The native council agreed but did not have the money, and the administration said the old machine had to be brought in and taken off the books before they could claim a grant for a replacement. But why couldn't a mechanic have flown up in the twice-weekly plane, dismantled the parts needing repair, and shipped the parts back to the workshop? "That's just it," Jacques responded with righteous glee. "The bureaucrats despise the Kanaks for their lack of initiative and dumbness, but doesn't it make you wonder?"

On the way back to *Hawk* I told Jacques about the chicken that had followed me. He ignored the appetising dinner George was in the process of dishing out, snatched his briefcase from his bunk, and waved the manifest in my face. "Look, twelve cases of deep-frozen oven-ready chickens we brought up here. And crates of eggs, scores of them . . ."

Did the natives really have deep freezes?

Jacques glared scornfully. "How else do you think the natives keep the bloody fish they have to catch to pay for the bloody boats that don't work and the bloody engines they forget to put oil into and the bloody petrol to make them run . . ."

"Dinner's on the table, you guys," George announced.

Jacques snapped the clasps of his briefcase like pistol shots. "Two years ago a man here could sail out in his trim little cutter and in a couple of hours catch enough fish to feed his kids and trade at the mission for a bit of flour and sugar. Next day, if necessary, he went out again. Now he has to work for the one thing his island lifestyle does not provide. Money."

But hadn't the world moved on? I argued. For all his noble sentiment for sail, Jacques himself was happy enough to keep his Gardner diesel thumping below deck. Why should a native hack a canoe out of a treetrunk when a better one could be stamped out of glassfibre?

"But it's moral sabotage: you blackmail the people into being cash dependent but give them no opportunity to earn it. Instead of giving the Kanaks a lot of picks and shovels and telling them to get on with building an airstrip, so they can earn money to pay for their boats, the administration sends up a lot of Frenchmen with heavy machinery. Then the Kanaks are given hand-outs if they remain living in their reservation so the problem of their existence is removed from Noumea. In other words, money is given to the Kanaks to keep them quiet by the same people who despise them for their lack of drive."

Jacques continued, his eyes blazing, into a catalogue of administrative idiocies that put native dumbness in the shade. Like the automatic bleeper that *Hawk* was required to have by French law, to transmit distress messages if she went down, despite the fact that the

Ingredients of a South Sea voyager's feast of *poisson crû*: Hake (right), Solomon Islander fo'c'sle hand in the trading ketch *Hawk*, diced fish caught over the taffrail then cured it in juice of wild lime and cream of coconut.

Hawk, at anchor in New Caledonia on her last voyage as a South Seas trader: finally it was bureaucracy, not reefs, that sank the dreams of her adventurous skipper and owner.

Ship day on the tiny island of Mataso in the New Hebrides (now Vanuatu). Signalled to come in by smoke on the beach, the *Konanada* drops anchor. Copra is bought for cash, the cash is spent in the supermarket in number two hold.

At Bongabonga in the New Hebrides bagged copra (dried coconut) is paddled out through the surf by outrigger canoe then loaded aboard *Konanda* and traded for the modern necessities of island life – roofing iron, tinned fish, pink tissues, ribbons, toffees and Christmas decorations.

Parents celebrate an international event at a school on Tanna, New Hebrides: the pidgin English written on the wall says "yia blong ting abaot ol pikinini" – Year of the Child.

Bob Paul, South Sea trader, visits the "custom" school near his store on Tanna. Education is a male-only preserve, and pupils wear traditional straw penis wrappers.

The South Seas diet, laid out in Suva market: coconut, taro, kassava, chili, pineapple, sweet potato, mango.

Deck passengers of an inter-island cutter in th Yasawa Islands, Fiji.

No dream but a South Seas nightmare: relief supplies are brought to Kadavu Island, Fiji, by the government ship *Cagi Donu*, following Cyclone Meli that virtually stripped the land bare; from here, whole houses were whirled away.

transmitters at Noumea were switched off at night to save electricity. Like his project to go commercial fishing, which would have employed half a dozen men, but under French law only a local man could take out a licence. Officials told Jacques they would turn a blind eye if he wanted to employ the licenced man as cook or deck hand. "But why should I be the fall-guy in what was technically a frame-up? Like everything here it's a case of the tail being swung by the cat."

Not long before, the New Hebrides had been paying heavily for Australian rice while Solomons rice was half the price. Also, the New Hebrides was over-producing meat which the Solomons were buying expensively from Australia. It would have been an ideal two-way trade for a little ship like *Hawk*, freighting meat to the Solomons and rice to the New Hebrides. "But there was no way I could get them together on it: all I wanted was two cents a pound but nobody would budge."

At last Jacques started his steak. "This is great, George," he said.

"It was better fifteen minutes ago," George muttered.

"You just wouldn't believe it," Jacques began, after one swallow. George lifted his eyes to the lamp, as if to say, He's off again! "I know I'm a prickly son of a bitch and the administration hates me because I make them look stupid. It used to be the drunks and the beach-combers and the White riff-raff who caused all the trouble in the South Seas, but now they've all got jobs in the government. Adventure in the South Seas . . . Ha!"

"Eat your dinner, Jacques," George pleaded.

"Honestly, you'd think an energetic man with his own ship could earn a decent living in a country of small islands absolutely dependent on ships for transport," Jacques sighed, his anger fading into bitter disgruntlement, "but I'm afraid I've had enough, I'm giving up. This is *Hawk*'s last trip."

I was at the wheel, having taken my turn at galley duty, when I heard a thin, plucking sound tunefully distinct from the wet rippling vamp of the sea. George took over so I could investigate. In the shelter of the awnings of heavy canvas flapping thunderously around the stern, the deck passengers had contrived a skiffle group. One had made a ukelele from a soap-powder box, using four strips of nylon fishing line, a piece of wood, and some wire. Another had taped two spoons together which he rattled like a tambourine. A kitchen knife with a half-filled box of matches taped to its blade was jammed into a crack in the timbers so that it made a strangely melancholy buzzing noise when it was twanged. Overhead, the milky way made a brilliant arch but clouds were gathering and the waves were beginning to curl, driving spray across the deck and dashing water against the wheelhouse windows. In the light of a hurricane lamp swinging wildly in the bows, Hake and his mates sat round a cassette player accompanying the music with guitars. A mile or so to port lay the reef, dangerous and invisible. Soon we would have to turn towards it, navigating through the tricky narrow passage and Jacques was on edge because of it.

The chart showed two wrecks of merchant ships high and dry on the reef. Both were called *Edward Prosperity* and both, it was commonly believed, were wrecked within thirty miles of each other by the same captain. "Don't laugh!" George warned me, "It's only too easy go up on a reef in this part of the world," a remark that later proved to be remarkably and sadly prophetic.

Looking haunted, Jacques took over the con at around ten and switched on the radar, searching for the passage. Hake and the three seamen pressed into the small wheelhouse attracted by the electronic magic of the radar, or perhaps the skipper's evident anxiety had triggered an instinct to stick close to their leader. The wind was cold so I dressed warmly and strolled back and forth on the pitching hatch cover, watching the moon and the hard-grained waves through which *Hawk* chiselled a nervy furrow. Framed in the wheelhouse windows I saw a line of tight faces weirdly tinted with the blue of the radar. *Relax, go boating*, said a sticker on the glass.

The motion changed to a heavy roll as Jacques took his courage in both hands and turned the ship for the opening in the reef which was visible only in the saucer-sized radar screen. The skiffle band in the stern became demented. Clouds covered the moon and it became very dark but for the distant sky-glow of Noumea. The only light came from a fisheries research ship anchored just inside the reef: on his previous trip Jacques had seen it on the radar, assumed it was the navigation buoy, and turned for the entrance at the wrong moment, nearly wrecking his ship.

Then a strange thing happened. The sea all around began to bobble. The waves formed little splashing peaks going nowhere but bouncing in one place. Water thrown vertically into the air was blown over the deck. I sheltered in the lee of the wheelhouse and, looking in, saw that the radar screen was a mass of white as the scanner picked up the echoes of the dancing water. *Hawk* plugged on: Jacques looked worried, George was busy with the chart.

Later, when we were safely inside, Jacques explained that the passage was safe at night only with radar, and when the radar had "snowed" he was frightened for his ship. "I'm not superstitious, but ships do look after you, just as the sea looks after idiots and beginners, and everyone else has to watch out. This ship is trying to tell me something. Twice I have made this passage in the dark and each time it was nearly disaster. I would never do it in the dark again, never." At dawn when I went ashore to collect *croissants* for breakfast the baker told me of the earthquake that had shaken the town late in the evening, which explained the weird dancing of the sea.

Noumea is a blown-away French provincial town, with the only casino and the only heavy industry in the South Seas. Its character is coconut Provençal. The town beaches are cluttered, boutiques are filled with sports gear for tennis, windsurfing and diving, and Kanaks squat on the pavements at night to watch television in the shop windows. There are some run-of-the-mill French restaurants which excite Australians and New Zealanders who come here for the *chemin-de-fer*, and one excellent one, *L'Eau Vive*, not listed in tourist literature but packed with the *metropolitans*, *colons*, and *pieds noirs* who flocked here with the nickel boom in the early 1960s. The restaurant is run by nuns who ask guests to join in singing the Ave Maria at precisely 10 pm.

Across from the mineral smelters belching smoke, and overlooking the orange dust of the raw ores trucked out of the ranges and dumped into the holds of Japanese freighters, is the bald and hummocky island of Nou, now joined to the town by causeway and developing into a new dormitory suburb. For forty years this was the prison of the Pacific, an islet of misery and despair where 40,000 convicts, many of them socialists deported after the 1870 Commune, were sentenced to terms far beyond the course of a natural life.

The penal settlement ended in 1896 but the indigenous Kanaks have become the new prisoners. Until the Second World War the island was left pretty much alone, then nearly one million Americans passed through to the Pacific front line in the Solomons. Guadalcanal was fed and munitioned from here, with as many as one hundred ships in the harbour. Then came the boom in the nickel, chromite and manganese. Colonials displaced from Algeria flooded in. Natives were enticed out of the bush to lift shovels. There was no urban infrastructure: people of all kinds lived in tents. The blue sky rained dust. And cash. In 1967 a native could earn $200 a week for breast-feeding a shovel, an undreamed-of figure for a man who needed no money and had no commitments.

Then the world decided it had enough stainless steel for the time being and nickel crashed. When the bubble burst the Whites at least understood why, though they were dismayed. But the natives had no idea why the tap had been turned off. They found themselves outnumbered by outsiders with all the best land occupied by settlers and only twenty per cent of their country designated for their own use, mainly in outlying island areas like the Beleps. The Kanak Front, an independence movement much encouraged by protestant churches and Australia and New Zealand, turned a suspicious and disgruntled native population into a downright hostile, anti-White one. The French settlers desired independence too, but not at the expense of relinquishing their French citizenship and munificent aid that comes to about $750 per head, whether black, white or pale brown. They were furious when, after a referendum in which sixty-six per cent voted to stay with France, the Australian newspapers reported the result the other way round, and equally angry when a native threw a brick through the window of a bank and the press reported people lying on the pavement in pools of blood. The legacy of bitterness and repression that exists here, I thought, was nearer the troubled Caribbean ex-colonial Africa than the image of a sunny island in the South Seas.

After sipping a *pastis* (banned until recently because the Kanaks could not be persuaded to dilute such strong stuff with water) I strolled one evening across the *Place des Cocotiers* (Coconut Square) in the centre of the town. Here, in the bad old days, a chain-gang orchestra of stricken men in straw hats and brown calico, guarded by prim *surveillants* who were also prisoners, would mount the elaborate pagoda every afternoon to play for the gentlefolk. I was musing on this spectacle of misery when suddenly there was a heavy roaring noise and with shrill cries the natives sitting around in the dust leapt to their feet and ran for dear life. I looked over my shoulder but saw nothing. What was the panic?

Then it struck. Not your average English downpour but the collapse of Heaven. Drumming filled my ears. I gasped, breathing water. Protecting my eyes with cupped hands I staggered like an exhausted soldier into the shelter of a shop awning. The natives neither laughed nor commiserated but refused to look at me; it made my skin crawl. It was my first lesson that in the tropics at night you listen for the rain.

In *Hawk* Jacques had Tommy Dorsey turned up loud on the stereo and he was sitting in his rattan chair making new lures for his trolling lines. The old ship stirred uneasily at the quay, as if she knew her days were numbered. Jacques looked unhappy, I was miserably wet. I had known from the beginning that it would be impossible to travel the next step eastward to the New Hebrides by sea. *Hawk* could have got me there in a couple of days but there was no freight and I had to take a plane. It was much later, when my mail finally caught up with me, that I heard news of *Hawk*'s last ignominious departure from Noumea. Jacques had decided to sail her to Melbourne, where she had worked for much of her long life, in the hope of getting backing to make her some sort of museum ship. All the family belongings were swung into the hold. He had pushed some rotten cargo pallets to one side and told Hake not to use them. Which the luckless seamen remembered until it came to the task of loading the last and most valuable item, minutes before they sailed: Jacques' new pick-up truck.

The skipper was coming back from a last check of his mailbox when he saw his white Datsun swing into the air. At the same moment he heard an ominous splintering of timber. He sprinted. The truck swung high over the rail then began to slip. With a thunderous dusty crash it nose-dived into the hold and landed on top of all their worldly goods, totalled.

3

KONANDA

STOP THE SHIP
AND BUY ONE

On the Sunday I landed by prop-jet the great event at Port Vila had been the snail hunt. The large round-shelled Great African Snail, brought to the New Hebrides seven or eight years ago by some French chef, or as passengers in a cargo of timber, attacked anything tender and green. Cannibal snails had been introduced from Kenya but they could not keep pace with the rapid spread of the pest. In some countries Boy Scouts, Girl Guides, youth clubs and fund raisers collect bottles or newspapers: in the New Hebrides they hunt snails. That Snail Day 30 tons of them were being dumped in the sea. Meanwhile, a rusty airport bus driven by a huge bare-footed native wearing a tattered vest and rugby shorts dropped me at an old-style travellers' hotel with a broad, cool verandah open to the tradewinds, and a view over the crooked sea-inlet hemmed in by tangled bushy hills and islands.

On *Rue Higginson* (of all names!) the main street, half a mile of sun-shuttered buildings faced the water. Cruising yachts were tied up to railings. Woolly-headed black men and Frenchmen in short shorts and espadrilles played *pétanque* in dust under the palms. The market, a complex of butterfly cement roofs that might have been a test bed for the Sydney Opera House, was deserted. A Methodist choir under a tree sung hymns to a flock of taxis parked as if they were listless ducks in a muddy lake surrounding a single red telephone kiosk that contained no telephone. Teenagers against the windows of Mother Barker's Steak House, across the street. Car number plates were still in four figures and the town was small enough to have a notice saying "Home wanted for two ginger kittens" pinned to the door of its department store.

The dollars, the hairiest legs and most of the commerce, I discovered, were Australian. The lifestyle was French on the surface but the bias was British. When the price of copra fell after the First World War most British planters had pulled out but the French remained with the aid of subsidies. But it was British political values that were disseminated throughout the native population of 112,000 scattered over thirteen large and sixty smaller islands. This was due to the strong influence of Presbyterian missions, and it was the leading native ministers who formed the core of the new government that was soon to take over the country on independence.

In wandering the scattered confetti of empires across the Pacific I had landed suddenly in a bad joke from a Christmas cracker. For the joint English–French administration of the New Hebrides, known as a condominium, was on both sides acknowledged to be pandemonium. The two countries had joined in an atmosphere of mutual distrust to stop black men from killing and eating white men, and to keep out the Germans. When Americans arrived in hordes to fend off the Japanese, the black men thought they were gods and built model aerodromes in the bush, complete with carved landing lights and control towers, to lure out of the sky the great winged machines laden with tools and trinkets. As they departed, the Americans had pushed jeeps, bulldozers and heaps of equipment into the sea so nobody could use it, a place now immortalised as Billion Dollar Point, and the military occupation had been the basis of the musical *South Pacific*.

Soon the New Hebrides condominium would become independent and be named Vanuata. Meanwhile, the comic opera was in its final act. The English policeman wore a black visored cap with a checkered band and voluminous shorts; the French policeman wore a snazzy red forage cap and tight short-shorts. They patrolled in pairs and if you were arrested you had to opt for one judicial system or the other; most chose the French because the French prisons had wine with meals. The Bench comprised French and English judges presided over by a Court appointee of the King of Spain who spoke neither English nor French but this didn't matter because he was deaf. The native was hardly disadvantaged, because in any case nobody understood the 200-odd languages in the group. French and English issued their own currency and postage stamps and there were two school systems. Although they used the same drugs, English and French doctors could not agree on the doses so they built separate hospitals. Ships flew two flags. The English conceded that traffic should drive on the right, the French conceded that a hackneyed form of English could be permitted as the means of universal communication. Called bislamar (a corruption of

[27]

the French word *bêche-de-mer*, or sea slug) this "pidgin" English is now the official language of the new nation. A helicopter is "mixmasta-blong-Jesus-Christ", thonged sandals (*claquettes* to the French, Chinese army boots to the Australians) are sensibly known as "no-walkim-backwards."

The country was grotesquely ill-prepared for independence. Many of the men in the islands still wrapped their penises in straw sheaths, guying them with string to stop them wobbling, and wore nothing else. The English were irritated by the suddenly lavish splashing around of French money, the French planters were haunted by the choice between losing their nationality or their estates. Later I was to read of how the French backed a bearded ex-bulldozer driver with a boar's tusk round his neck and a bow-and-arrow army, who persuaded the island of Santo to secede. Finance came from an American foundation wanting to establish a tax haven, its last effort to build a republic on stilts on a coral reef near Tonga having recently failed. When Papua–New Guinea troops went in to nip the rebellion in the bud and the luckless rebel leader was sentenced to 14 years, the French Commissioner was expelled. But for the time being all this was merely written on the wind.

Tonight the sky was turning golden by the second as I sank into a large cane chair and ordered an ice-cold Australian beer. Ah, the island nights, I thought happily. The lone traveller was poised for the mystery and magic of South Sea islands where – as the story books promised – faces were black and hearts were blacker.

Hugh Rundle was a friendly Cornishman with thick black spectacles who inhabited a glass cage in the dim Burns Philip warehouse. "Yes, we have a trading ship and it sailed last night and we take no passengers," he said brusquely. But after a few minutes he softened. "Well, for a writer, maybe, I might be able to fix it ... Bloody telephones, never work when you need them! René? René, where's *Konanda*? Yes, I know they're bloody pirates and switch off their radio. You think Tikilasua, eh? Can we catch her? *Merci* René. You're in luck. Pack a bag in twenty minutes. Better buy some books because the days are slow and long out there. I'll fix a truck."

The little Toyota bounced like a ping pong ball on the rutted dirt road round Efate Island. The country was wildly beautiful, a tangle of great trees and vines, and shrubs with large fleshy leaves. Natives squatted in little groups awaiting the "bus", a yellow pick-up lurching like a log in a seaway under its load of roosting passengers. The one real bus was filled with Australian tourists alert for cannibals.

We swung off the road to a dazzling beach where a water-ski boat was being loaded with a couple of fuel drums; a sticker on its windscreen said *Album Erotica*. A squat and huddled cone, the island of Nguna lay a few miles out. Scarcely distinguishable against the dark purple of its trim was the distant silhouette of my ship. A native agreed to take me across for $12. On the wet jarring ride, the overhead sun fried all the secret white creases in my bare legs braced athwartships.

Konanda made the very picture of a South Seas tramp. She was a 500-ton coaster, built in Holland a quarter of a century ago. The hull was shabby grey, the upperworks a dark shade of buff which was mostly rust. The squat black funnel wore the company's black and white checkered band, as if it was policeman's cap. A large wooden awning shaded the fo'c'sle like a coolie hat. I scrambled across the small boats crowding her lee side, walked precariously along a plank, climbed a ladder to the deck, and stepped on a kitten. Its squeal froze the busy scene on deck as effectively as a smoke-oh whistle.

"Cap'n asleep," said a large ball of a man, wearing a yellow T-shirt and red shorts. He was Kenny, the mate. He opened the door of a wooden box like a workman's hut on the deck. It had two tiny portholes, a pair of sagging beds, a Formica-topped table and chair, and a reek of vomit. The kitten followed me in, mewing, and added to its stock of trademarks under the bed. What looked like large brown splashes of tea on the wall suddenly took fright and scurried away. "You sleep here," the mate said.

The old Dutch *schuyt* was a floating supermarket. She sailed with her number one hold empty and her number two hold packed with 170 tons of trade goods. When the for'ard hold was filled with copra, or the store was getting low on stock, she put into the nearest port, either Vila or Santo. On her last round trip she had made eighty-four stops in twenty-six days; this was her second stop of the day and I had been lucky to catch her. Her twenty-eight men were now sitting round the stern eating congealed rice and fatty meat boiled in a drum. Soon they would hoist the workboats aboard, raise the anchor, and *Konanda* would make her way slowly northwards, following her captain's nose for cargoes through the chain of islands extending in a Y shape 450 miles. A boy touched my arm. "Cap'n say you come 'long lunch."

Captain Tunidau Osea was a Fijian on the far side of fifty. His lean ascetic face with soft jowls, merry eyes, balding pate, thin arms and long artistic fingers, gave him more the appearance of a professor or a pastor than a pirate. Flurried by my unexpected arrival he greeted me courteously and led me to a panelled mess-room. The table was just large enough for four place settings. There was a varnished sideboard, its glass-fronted cupboard filled with bottles of sauces. "I have to tell you that the food is not good," he said gravely. "Some days we have boiled meat and rice, other days it's rice and boiled meat. But it's so hard to get a good cook. I point my finger at the youngest crew member with clean hands. Here, you'd better have some Maggi."

The captain had put on a clean T-shirt in my honour and it showed a map of the islands framed in the outline of a sea-shell. Pointing at different parts of his bulging belly with a long finger, he speculated on our route. "We go where the business is," he explained. "When we see smoke on the beach we go in and take the copra, that's our signal."

Keep your eye on old Osea, Hugh Rundle had advised, he's got a sixth sense, and when you see him closing up his suitcase get ready to swim. Twice, as a ship's engineer, Osea had been wrecked. He was in the *Koro* which hit a reef in Fijian waters in 1952. "I guess the captain was an overlander," Osea explained mildly. The captain had not realised he was aground but looked down the engine room skylight as Osea climbed out with a suitcase. "Why did the engine stop?" he demanded. "Very simple," said Osea marking the level of his chest with the flat of his hand, "water up to here."

As we listened to the English news broadcast from Fiji, the mate showed himself on the bridge and went away again, his presence being the signal that the ship could sail. The main engine started with a sooty cough. The quartermaster, a Solomon Islander with eyebrows like doorsteps, settled his massive frame in the wooden armchair stuck on a brass spike behind the tall varnished wheel. It was only a couple of miles to the next village and as soon as the engines stopped the crew mustered on deck. As the anchor splashed into sixty fathoms the shovel-shaped wooden motor boat flopped on the water, followed by the two double-ended punts made of plate steel. I jumped in with half a dozen crewmen, all strongly muscled, dare-devil young fellows with skin that shone like the toes of guardsmen's boots, and a strange array of tattered, sun-faded clothing. Most wore necklaces of coloured beads, and charms of various kinds on knees or ankles. One had a turquoise vest with LOVE IS TURE [*sic*] printed across the front, and a coupling that was scarcely missionary position on the back. One carried a docket book, its blue carbon papers rattling in the wind, and had three ballpoints stuck in the tight curls of his hair. Another carried a set of Roman-style cast-iron weighing scales.

Alerted by two blasts of the ship's siren, a few people strolled out of the trees and sat on the black volcanic rocks as we approached. The launch did a smart U-turn as a coral head loomed under its keel, then cast the punt adrift and we drifted on into the shallows. "Yu fela got copra, yes or no?" the clerk shouted, and was greeted by blank or puzzled looks.

Two young men waded out and jumped aboard. "Me lookim shop," one said. The launch creamed in, took our rope, and jerked us out to the ship. An uncanny stillness settled. The freezer motor in its frame outside my bunkhouse door rattled and clattered. Crewmen and kittens sought the dim shady interiors. The steelwork radiated heat like a hot oven and to touch it with bare skin was like being splattered with fat. Osea snoozed. There were no seagulls, or any sign of life, only the stubby motor launch dementedly going round in circles at full speed while the two villagers prospected for goodies. Eventually they were taken ashore, one clutching a brown paper bag with some sweets and fish hooks. Then Kenny appeared on the bridge and disappeared. The engine was cranked into life. The anchor was winched up. A welcome breeze flowed through the ship as the captain rang for Full Ahead. "The other trip we saw a native in a canoe paddling like blazes and waving," Osea said. "I watched him for a bit, then altered course and stopped alongside in case he was in trouble. He came aboard and do you know what he wanted? Masta, me wantim buy one ice cream." With a gesture so subtle that an eye unaccustomed to the routine of years would have missed it, Osea ordered the quartermaster to put the helm over.

"So what did you do?" I prompted.

"Sold him one, of course. It's company policy to do business. Twenty cents." The captain saw my surprise, and added, "Well, you never know, next trip he might have twenty bags of copra to sell."

For several days I wafted leisurely from one oceanic greenhouse to another. Captain Osea scanned the beaches through binoculars for signs of smoke. The whistle whooped. The workboats would splatter on the water like coconuts thudding into long grass. Natives flocked to the shoreline to greet the visitors. Sacks of copra were weighed and tallied on the spot, the value computed, and cash handed over. Then, crowding on the sacks heaped into the punts so they looked like floating bowls of flowers, and rocking dangerously in the swells, the people came out to shop. In number two hold Adam Vui, supercargo, sat at his calculator, cash box ledgers and docket books. He stocked 3,000 lines of goods that covered all the necessities of island life, just like a country store. There were spades, coconut knives, leaf rakes, films, cassettes, baby baths, umbrellas, sanitary towels, guitar strings, boiled sweets, scotch tape, garden hoses, pumpkin seeds, sewing machines, tinned mackerel, sugar, tea, flour, swimming masks, pink tissues, barbed wire, timber, floral-scented odour purifiers, Christmas decorations ... On one of the long glass counters a sign read: YU NO NEL AGAINST LONG – THIS FELA GLASS – THANK YOU SUPERCARGO.

After a long and patient wait some signal was relayed to the crew lounging on deck and the chant went up: "Last boat! Ho-hup. Last boat. Quick!" Shoppers rushed out of the store, cotton frocks billowing in the breeze, long coloured ribbons streaming from their shoulders. Parcels were handed over the gunw'le to people in the punts. Brown faces were buried in soft cornettos. The tug circled in, its diesel smoking and hammering, to take the strain. A panicky shout: somebody was still in the store. The tug let go and resumed its mad circling. The ship waited . . . and waited . . . as a native woman selected ribbon then climbed down the ladder, clutching as the wind got under her skirts and everyone screamed with mirth. The punt lurched soggily to the shore. There, in anything of a sea, getting ashore dry was a delicate exercise. With waves breaking over their heads, crewmen tried to hold the punts off. Women waded ashore, wet to the armpits and holding melting ice creams above their heads. Men formed a chain gang to pass the parcels ashore, chanting the contents of each one as it came out of the boat – "Shoo–GAR! Shoo-GAR! Bag-a RICE! Box-a NAILS! Tinned-FISH! New-ray-DIO! One-new BROOM!"

From dawn to dusk, three or four stops a day, the trade went on. Every morning Captain Osea reported in by radio, using code to mystify the ship's five competitors. I had bought some disinfectant in the store so my bunkhouse smelled sweeter and the cockroaches had felt the sting of fly spray. In the middle of one night I walked along the deck to the lavatory, a ghost-white figure in my drawers, and the dark-skinned watchman coming the other way let out a nervous scream. Every evening Captain Osea showed me on the map on his belly where he thought we would be on the morrow. Bongabonga, a name out of a faded *Boys' Own Paper* found in a jumble sale, where the copra was paddled out by the outrigger canoes that had to spear through the surf and fuel drums were pushed out by swimmers. Mataso, a 1,500-foot cone as perfect as a witch's hat, where the village had been wiped out five years ago by a tidal wave. Lopevi, an active volcano that was another perfect cone reaching nearly a mile high and smoking gently. Ambrim, also smoking quietly, where a great cone had collapsed inwards leaving an ash crater six miles across.

Often I went ashore to be greeted by warm smiles – "Sure, you fela mak big fela tour of village." Dogs snarled at my long white legs. Women cackled in the deep shade and told their squawling toddlers that Whitey was going to eat them up. Larger boys, never girls, followed at a safe distance. The villages were beautiful but it was the raw edge of existence: thatched huts in the bush with dirt floors and open fires. These coastal villages were open to the breeze, the land was fruitful and the climate benign. Life was basic but not poverty-stricken. Money grew on trees in the shape of coconuts. Working diligently for a couple of weeks a man and his wife could make a ton of copra currently worth about $280. "You might say the people here live under the tyranny of colonialism," Captain Osea remarked pensively one day, "but they are a lot more free and better off, in simple terms, than my people in Fiji where we have been independent for ten years."

The rhythm of the voyage was hypnotic and timeless as Osea followed the smokes, the crewmen toiled, and down in the store Adam counted the money and viewed with alarm the rate at which the diminishment of his stock was outstripping the accumulation of copra. At one anchorage the plantation had been taken over by natives whom I found squatting round a black iron pot boiling green bananas for lunch. They gave me one but it glued up my mouth. When I asked about the slogans daubed on the tin walls of the drying sheds and workshops, one told me hotly, "Me sorry mister, this not your business!"

"This very fine thing," another chipped in excitedly. "We have to get ready for Independence so last week we take our land back. This land blong American white man but when we make big demonstration, and we tell him whiteys stole this land for a stick of tobacco from our grandfathers, and we tell him this is Custom land and we take it back ... well, he went away very fast."

I watched the copra being weighed and humped down to the punts. I saw many hands but few workers. And I wondered how much copra would be produced from that plantation in the future. A hundred years ago unscrupulous men had sailed these seas to recruit labourers for the Queensland sugar plantations. Known as blackbirders, they lured innocent natives aboard their vessels by dangling trinkets before their eyes, by dressing as priests and promising prayers, by resorting to every foul conceit and means of kidnapping. But were politicians preying on an innocent people's naivety any different? These people were in danger of waking from their dreamland into an independence of a most spartan kind: when the great African snail ate their crops in the future they would not be able to play one mother country off against another, and get liberal hand-outs of cash and aid. They would be on their own. I held no brief for colonialism, but I did not envy these fervent misled young men their futures.

At Lunalea on the island of Tangoa the shore was steep grey boulders, shiny and black where they were wetted and rattled by the waves. Getting ashore was a nervy business. The boatmen had laid out an anchor with a long floating line which they grabbed as the launch towed us past it. Then the launch cast off and two boys swam ashore with another rope with which the laden punt was hauled into the beach while the anchor rope acted as a brake. A four-foot wave steeped out of nowhere and seethed around us. The steel boat clanged like a Chinese gong on the stones. A boy spitting sea water and steadying the punt signalled me with a nod. I jumped over the side, collected my *no-walkim-backwards* as they floated to the surface, and scrambled up the beach chased by the next big wave.

The undersides of my arms pulsed with the heat rising off the rocks. The air was filled with the sickly toffee smell of copra, the horizon a mass of mirages. Bright lorrikeets flitted in the trees. A flock of little boys collected behind me on the copra sacks but when I turned they fled, chirping and squawking. The first to speak up, in perfect English with a BBC accent, said his name was Roy and he was sixteen. A wooden catapult with long latex slings was tossed over his shoulder. He used it, he explained, to shoot parrots and to sting pigs when they got in the garden.

"We are in a good place here in the sun," he mused. "We have everything we need and when we want to buy something we just cut copra. We have plenty of vegetables to make our *laplap*, and a nice hospital to go when we are sick. We need nothing else. Only a river. A river would be very nice . . . And, oh yes, it would be a jolly fine thing to have our own biscuit factory."

The houses, he assured me, were the best. "Some people have a cement house with the toilet inside, you know. In fact, my father, who is chief of the footballers, has made a house for us. It is a fine cement house but the toilet is not inside. I don't mind because I like to look at the stars. And I have many penfriends. I send them shells. I will send some shells to you in England and you will send me some shoes. You do have shoes in England, yes? I would like very much to walk along the shore in a pair of shoes, oh yes. Goodbye Sir!" And abruptly, like a dog whistled away by its owner, he loped away.

The swell was increasing all the time and I regretted bringing my new camera ashore. Waves were bomb-bursting round the workboats. A long line of saturated store goods was drying on the rocks. "You have to take a fairly light-hearted view of life here – if you worry about these boats and what could happen you would be a nervous wreck," said Don, the young New Zealand farmer doing voluntary work on the island, whom I met on the beach. I watched as the next punt came in, the boys making the anchor rope fast too soon so the people jumped over the side and came up swimming, their precious purchases bobbing around them on the waves. Then the empty punt drifted in a bit and I saw my chance. I waded out rapidly, passed my camera bag inboard, and scrambled in after it.

Then I saw a horrified look cross the face of the young pirate who should have been tending the anchor rope. He had let it go. I looked over my shoulder and saw an enormous wave poised to break. The punt fell away, exposing its broadside to a cliff of water that crashed like a landslide into the boat. The three-ton hull was thrown on its side, clanging and vibrating. I was enveloped in warm, soft milk and found myself flat on my back in the bottom of the boat. As I stood up shakily, another wave struck but I thought it would be dangerous to leap out and risk being struck by the heavy steel.

At last the crew got the bows facing into the waves. As the launch towed us out, one of the village leaders, dressed in neat blue slacks and white shirt, holding a French handbag and a packet of Rothmans, all wet through, asked me kindly: "You not killed?"

"No, I not killed . . . yet." Everybody laughed. But I thought I had cracked a bone in my big toe and soon my foot was swollen and stiff. Adam sold me a kitchen sponge with which I carefully wiped down my camera with fresh water but the damage was not as great as it might have been.

At Larmen Bay, on Epi, Kenny dropped anchor for the twentieth time in seven days and I left *Konanda* because here there was an airstrip. The surf was mercifully calm as I limped ashore with my luggage and slung my sleeping bag with Tom and Mona Boyd, New Zealanders who had retired early to do voluntary work. He was a thick-set, freckled man with heavy spectacles and funny beach hat. He was teaching building at the red-roofed senior primary school but in six months nobody had managed to get him any timber and nails. She was thin-faced and practical, with a decidedly pragmatic turn of phrase. "Surprised!" she exclaimed, telling me that the ship had finally delivered their luggage from Vila, "God, you could have buggered me dead!" Both were hospitable but sour. "Look at that, bloody typical," Tom had grumbled as he stood with his hands thrust into his shorts watching the boys on deck apparently filling diesel drums with petrol and petrol drums with diesel; it was a possibly catastrophic muddle which he seemed content to watch without intervening.

Two miles up a dirt track, I learned, there was a Presbyterian hospital which I hoped might do something for my toe. "Mind how you go on that hill," Mona warned, "you can flog your tripes out." At first it was easy going among shady palms, then the track broke out into direct sunshine, the bush an impenetrable mat of vines and creepers on either side. Little flies flicked everywhere, and settled on my sweat if I stopped. The sheer weight of the heat gave me the feeling that I had to do breaststroke to swim through it. At last I reached a red hibiscus, like a beacon, where air wafting over the ridge cooled my face and I found the neat, pink-walled hospital and Sister Kath. Stout and jolly, with greying hair and gold-edged teeth, another New Zealander, she made me a cup of coffee, cut me a slice of banana cake, and said that if I could walk up that hill there couldn't be much broken in my toe. In the gardens round the hospital, people from different villages were cooking meals for their own people who were patients. None would eat food prepared by a "foreigner", Kath explained. Relations between villages were prickly. Usually they spoke completely different languages. A person paddling over from another island to catch a plane was often prevented from landing because he had no rights. Now that they were going to be one nation weren't the problems formidable? "Too right," said Kath, "and I'm going home."

Next morning I reported to the air terminal, a thatched hut under a palm loaded with yellow coconuts. The runway was a grass strip between the matted creepers flowing over the bush and the ice-green lagoon. Other passengers waited for the twice-weekly flight with suitcases of plaited palm-fronds. Sister Kath parked her Land Rover under the banyan tree in which scores of little childen squatted like bats, and waited with the mailbag open in her lap so people could post letters. Then, crabbing in the stiff wind, the yellow Trislander bounced down on the grass. I was locked in with twelve others. A rich musky smell like that of a locker room without the body rub filled the plane. Flies buzzed against the windows, and in the clip where you would normally expect to see a fire extinguisher, there was an aerosol can of fly spray.

At Lamap, on Malekula, we landed on a grass strip, taxied to another thatched hut and switched off. Nothing stirred. The blond French pilot started up and a young man appeared on a cross-country motorbike. The pilot beckoned. The youth propped his bike, scratched lazily, and walked away into the shade. The pilot beckoned again. The youth took one step forward. Thirteen of us in the plane sweltered. The flies buzzed. Finally the boy came. "Speak English?" the pilot asked.

"No."

"Parlez français?"

"No."

"Passengers?"

The youth shrugged. So we took off again, locked inside our own buzzing tube of b.o., and winged over the chain of wild and beautiful islands back to Port Vila where I had fixed a date with an old-timer.

It was early evening when the taxi let me off at the foot of a steep concrete drive leading up to a large modern bungalow. A score of dark-skinned children playing on the concrete shouted, "Masta, man come!" A little fellow solemnly took my finger and guided me to the front door where I was greeted by a jovial, husky, pot-bellied, grey-haired white man who drew me into the sitting room. It was brightly lit and draped with yellow-tasselled banners of black velvet on which the Sydney Opera House was depicted in glitter and gold paint. "G'day, I'm Oscar Newman, I'm seventy years old and I was born here, that old time enough for you?" The old planter was adorned with gold: a heavy gold ring, an elaborate gold cross on a heavy chain round his leathery neck, an expensive gold watch, a gold bracelet. Behind gold spectacles his blue eyes were obstinate, pugnacious and vain.

Scotch and Perrier seemed the decent sort of compromise for a hot evening in a Condominium. The native girl who poured it from bottles on a silver tray was elegant in a green and white, home-made ankle-length gown. I was struck by the calmness in her black eyes and the quality of her mahogany complexion. Tall and slim, she diminished the stout and blustery old gent. "This is Lily," he said with a dismissive wave. She bobbed her frizzy head and smiled shyly, showing perfect pearly teeth. I was not expected to shake hands. "She's my native girl and the mother of my kids." Oscar went on, adding, "the ones in Vila, that is."

Oscar Newman was a conversational bulldozer. I could pull a lever from time to time to twist him in his tracks but there was no brake. His father had come here after the Boer War to find gold but did not find so much as a shovel with which to dig for it. Oscar had gone into trading, established a chain of stores which were bought out, then he went back to manage them and run his own plantation at Tisman, on Malekula Island. There he had greeted Douglas Fairbanks Senior who had come dashing into the cove in a Chris Craft from his gorgeous yacht anchored outside, and ripped out the bottom of the speed boat on a coral head. David Attenborough had picked up one of Oscar's parrots and been seriously bitten. "Then there were the American generals who came in with the beautiful Red Cross nurses we could have. It was Bali Ha'i for planters in those days, old sport."

Not long before, like many other planters, his land had been re-claimed and his store ransacked. The administration had done nothing. "I've made a bloody pile of money in this country, by God I have, but if I'd known we were going to have this much trouble with the coon I'd have raised my own bloody army. I pray to Christ there will be a revolution because I want to notch my carbine with a dozen fucking native heads before I go."

His wife had left for Sydney twenty-six years before with their two children but they were firm Catholics and had stayed married. Twelve years ago he had taken Lily, then aged fifteen. "The customary thing is to wait until they are a couple of years older but her mother said if I didn't take her then she would be spoiled so I did, and I have never

[37]

regretted it." His mottled hand reached out and the tall girl put her own brown hand in it.

In fact he had fourteen other living children, not all of them by Lily. They all lived with him and were playing in the yard, beautifully turned out and bright-eyed. The youngest was Brian, aged four, who had guided me up the steps. When Oscar caught the drift of my tentative questioning of his ethics his voice rose to an autocratic boom – "You know what they say, an erect prick has no conscience, eh, but at least I'm open about it and I don't skulk around back streets having black girls on the sly as so many Englishmen do. I really love my girl."

Lily stepped lightly over the polished lino in her bare feet. "Dinner ready, Masta."

"You'll eat with us, won't you? Of course you will, come on, let's go."

The meal was lightly curried chicken on rice, and sweet potato garnished with coconut cream, impeccably served. It would have been delicious at any time. After *Konanda*'s corned beef and rice for seven days it was a feast. Oscar rumbled on, telling me how he had taken Lily to Singapore on a trip. "Me and Lily went round the parlours watching the guys getting massaged, it was a great trip, eh Lily?" Lily shot him a demure, yes-Masta look, and dropped her eyes to her plate.

Then he had gone to Fiji on business but his guts felt full of ground glass and he was terribly ill so he flew to Sydney where doctors diagnosed liver cancer and gave him three days to live. The story that he then related through mouthfuls of curried chicken was so disjointed that it took me a while to piece together in my mind, and when he said Lily had been slipping him massive doses of thallium, I thought he had said valium.

"No! Fucking rat poison!" he shouted. "The stuff we spread under the coconut trees to kill the rats. Rat poison. Lily wanted to save me from the Fijian girls so she tried to kill me off. The medics said I was one of the few cases ever known to have survived."

Lily looked up shyly. Oscar spoke gruffly and waved his fork at me. "Give the man more *kaikai*, go on, feed him up."

Lily had been arrested and sentenced to twelve years. Oscar appealed on her behalf and got the sentence reduced to three years. *Gateau* was served, left over from the children's First Communion the day before. Every Sunday for five months, Oscar went on, he had stayed with Lily in jail. Then came the magic surprise: Lily was released. "We got home that night and drank seven bottles of champagne."

While this amazing tale was in full spate I couldn't help noticing the legs of a native girl stretched out on a bed in another room. At one point she strolled languidly through the dining room, a small square-shouldered creature with a headscarf tied gipsy-style over her low brow and that slack, graceful native stride that seems to go nowhere but eats up the miles. Now, as Oscar paused for breath and Lily cleared the plates, the girl returned to her room, saying as she passed, "Good night, Masta."

"You know," Oscar said, holding up one mole-speckled gold-jewelled hand with the pudgy fingers crossed, "I can't believe my luck that Lily and Honoré get on, just like that . . ."

I said I didn't understand. Was Honoré a house servant?

"God no!" Oscar roared, regarding me as if I had come down in the last rain shower. "That's my second native girl. She's only eighteen, you know. I got her for 450 bucks while Lily was in the cooler".

So the old-timer told it, at any rate. A few weeks later he died.

That evening I had just dozed off when I was woken suddenly by a clinking noise, and a strange feeling of having been shaken. I looked out of the window, breathing the steamy air. In the moonlight under the palm I could just distinguish the stack of ceramic lavatory bowls that had rattled in the earthquake.

$$\Longrightarrow 4 \Longleftarrow$$

KING OF TANNA

THE TALE
OF A SOUTH-SEA MAN

Tanna is a high, bushy island about thirty miles by twelve. It lies south of Port Vila, a little more than an hour away by small plane. There is a live volcano and its ash plain at the southern end; grassy heath roamed by wild horses in the north. The shoreline is a wildly hostile, jagged hem of black volcanic lava crocheted with razors of white coral. The surging blue swells do not peak, topple, and roll grandly shorewards but die in explosive bursts in the fissures, tunnels and overhangs. Spray fountains hiss like geysers out of blowholes. Waves bouncing off the shore meet incoming waves head-on and clash in seething pinnacles. The countless nooks and crannies are inhabited by thousands of crabs that bolt sideways with a chilling rattle, the instant a shadow crosses their hot ledges. But here and there are crescents of sand, some white, most black and hot, tucked behind out-thrust arms of lava or reef. At one of these coves, hardly big enough to anchor a small ship, Bob Paul had established his trade store.

I had first heard of Bob Paul when, soon after arriving at Port Vila, I had telephoned another old timer. "This is the war office, d'you wanna fight?" was the greeting.

"Mr Discombe?" I asked faintly, nearly dropping the handpiece in fright.

"Depends who wants him."

Beneath the bluster Reece Discombe was a kindly man who had once been a midget-car driver racing on cinder tracks in Australia and New Zealand. He had come here with one of the first aqualungs to see what he could collect of the thousands of tons of machinery the Americans had dropped in the sea. Besides thousands of tyres, tons of scrap, and oil from the tanks of a wrecked troopship, he had even brought up fourteen bulldozers and sold them to the Australian Coal Board.

"If you're really looking for South Seas characters," he told me on the verandah of his home overlooking the harbour, "there's one man you've got to meet. They call him the King of Tanna, though he doesn't much like it. In the old days I was walking along the harbour one day when I saw five men having a terrific wrestle in the shallows. There was just one fair head among four black woolly ones. It was Bob Paul with two natives under each arm. I offered to lend a hand but he told me not to bother. It would be okay, he said, as soon as he got their heads under the water."

I heard more about Bob Paul from Robin Barnes, a giant of a man with iron girders for bones, who was general manager in the New Hebrides of Burns Philip, owners of the *Konanda*, an old-time trading company known variously as Bee Pee, Bloody Pirates and the octopus of the Pacific. Sprawling in a deck-chair on his lawn, sipping cool beer and watching the lingering flames of a sensational sunset while the big man lit flares around the barbecue and stoked up the charcoal for grilling steaks, Robin told me how Bob Paul had first won a foothold on Tanna.

It had been just after the War, he related, and the island was pretty much sewn up by a cartel of traders who were fleecing the natives, paying £35 a ton for copra which they sold in Vila for £80. Bob Paul was running a little boat and paying the natives £50, so he wasn't popular with the other traders. One trip he went ashore on Tanna and found his way blocked by one of his competitors who, wearing blue jeans and a big hat, stood with his feet wide apart on the road and a shotgun across his chest. He told Bob to shove off and never set foot on the island again.

The young Australian had collected a rusty Smith & Wesson from his boat, walked up to the trader, spun the chamber of the revolver in a deliberate way, and said, "Okay, you can have first shot. And if you miss by Christ I'm going to blow your head off."

We heard a car stop in the drive and a man carrying a briefcase cut through the light spilling out of the house. Though diminished by the burly figure of my host he was another big-boned, strong figure. In the light of the flares I observed thick, straight, sandy-grey hair, a sailor's blue eyes, nostrils that flared under his nose like the bows of a clipper ship, and a grey military moustache that broke along his lip like a thin bow wave.

"John, meet Bob. How do you like your steak?"

"You know me, running round the paddock thanks," said Bob Paul.

He looked tired and bothered as he balanced his plate on his knees. He told us he had been laying poison for stray dogs that nested under the floor of his house, but he had just found spears hanging out of his cattle and supposed it must be natives taking revenge.

Then, handing along the salad bowl, he said, "So you want to come to Tanna."

"I'd like that."

"Can you fight? We might have to knock some heads together down there this week."

Now, as the Islander taxied up to the hut at the end of the grass airstrip, I glimpsed the so-called King of Tanna. In a half-buttoned white shirt and blue shorts, he was swearing like a trooper and brandishing the chocks at a bunch of dogs that started a fight under the wing as I alighted.

"Come on, let's find Kath and put the kettle on," he urged. His blue Range Rover, dented by falling coconuts and encounters with trees – "Everyone drives by braille on Tanna," he claimed – was no doubt the only vehicle ever to have seen both the Scottish Hebrides and the New Hebrides: the Pauls had made a trip there to see where their mail kept going to. In the back two Australian blue heelers, cattle dogs called Giggles and Shadow, farted excitedly as Bob drove fast along the dirt road, flapping his door to clear the air.

The trade store, its cement walls and ceiling cracked by earthquakes, was gloomy and busy. In front of it the bare earth was rutted by Land Rovers and Toyota Land Cruisers and shaded by canopies of densely foliaged cotton-wood trees. These are a kind of hibiscus with flowers that blossom bright yellow in the mornings, become orange by afternoon, and die by evening. The bark stripped from the tree's long slender shoots is beaten, dried and sun-bleached for the soft feather-light fibres worn in "grass" skirts. Out back, one tin shed was the abbattoir where a beast was butchered twice a week. Another was the bakery, where peanuts bought from the natives were roasted as soon as the bread was cooked, and sold back over the counter by the handful. There was a hand-operated petrol bowser and a litter of fuel drums and gas cylinders. Open ground sloped a hundred yards down to the black spiky shore where the glittering ocean shredded in roaring white billows. A large banyan tree shaded half a dozen men picking over a mound of coffee, bean by bean, which had been soaked in a rainstorm. Under a lean-to, a home-made roaster filled the hot air with a rich aroma. Bundles of knobbly sandalwood, pinkish yellow and fragrant when you scraped a piece with your thumbnail, awaited shipment. Bags of trochus shell, to be made into buttons in Japan, stank of dead fish.

This South Seas enterprise was more than just a trade store. On Tanna it was Oxford Street and Fifth Avenue in one, a place of metropolitan excitement where you never knew what might happen next. Not long ago Bob had primed his boys to close the store's front door when it was crowded on market day. Then he threw into the middle of the floor what looked like a stick of dynamite, with a fuse burning. In fact, wrapped in the distinctive yellow-and-black oiled paper was a banana. There was a stunned silence as the fuse hissed, then a terrific surge as people dived over the counter and climbed up the walls. One man leapt straight through the big window, trailing from his neck a string pegged with T-shirts, and disappeared into the bush. "The locals thought it a great joke," Bob averred, "and they keep asking me to do it again."

A wicket gate in a wall of flowering shrubs led to the house, a wooden, ready-cut frame building of the kind supplied to Australian outback stations in the 1920s. Its core was two rooms, each twelve feet square, with high ceilings and a pyramid roof. Around them, wide verandahs had been built on all four sides to create living areas: kitchen at the back, lounge at the front, dining room on one side, office and extra bedroom on the other. The tin roof was piled with tyres to spoil the lift effect of tropical storms. Heavy wooden hurricane shutters were propped open with Glenfiddich boxes, so the house was cooled by the breeze off the ocean. Spears and artifacts decorated the walls, including rare ceremonial feather ornaments, eight feet high, used when Bob was inducted as honorary chief of the local tribe. He had to wear a *pampus* (straw penis sheath) as the occasion demanded and survived a nasty moment when the elders produced sharp bamboo splinters with which to circumcise him, a ceremony defined in pidgin as *kutm kok*. On the bar was the heavy brass diving helmet Bob had used in one of his enterprises, and the steering wheel of one of his trading ketches. But a frame of large beams between the living and dining areas of the verandah, which was hung with bamboo sticks and ornaments, was not for decoration. "In hurricanes," Bob explained, "we sit underneath the beams and watch the walls bulging inwards."

Tall, slim, grey-haired, freckled, her reading glasses on a cord round her neck, Bob's wife Kath exuded an air of calmness and capability. She was the eye in her husband's storm, the shrouds to his rigging. In the evening, when we changed for dinner, she wore a long gown printed with brilliant flowers and ear-rings in the shape of large hoops of fine gold; in one was perched a jewelled parrot and in the other a bee. Bob invariably held her chair as she sat down. We drank chilled white *Liebfraumilch*. *The Trout* played loudly on the stereo but the record was scratchy because housekeeping was a constant struggle against abrasive dust floating in from the volcano. "Life can be pretty raw here," Kath admitted serenely, "what with eruptions, hurricanes and tidal waves."

Just how raw I discovered in three days of royal hospitality during which I collated the different fragments of the Pauls' story: it made the storybook adventures of the South Seas pale by comparison. First came the account of his ships. Such as the schooner *Resolution* in which Bob sailed as supercargo just after the War. The engine seized as they rushed for shelter at Port Vila with a hurricane building up, and they were in sight of the wharf when the wind reversed with a bang and blew them out to sea. Two weeks later, bruised and battered, they fetched up in New Caledonia. Bob sent two telegrams, one to Kath which never arrived and one to the woman from whom he had been in the habit of buying flowers for his young bride. Kath was packing her bags, certain that Bob had been lost, when the flowers turned up.

His first boat was a harbour launch with a sun awning for a cabin and bags of copra for a bunk. One trip to Tanna he was plodding down the track with a sack of copra on his back when he glimpsed the shore through the palms and realised with a shock that the sea had disappeared. Water poured in amazing waterfalls from the high walls of the exposed reef. Fish jumped all round his boat, which was stranded on the dry sea-bed. Then he saw a mountain of water gathering in a greasy slope and on its way in. Tidal wave.

A lesser man might have taken to the bush, but Bob sprinted over the sea-bed to his boat and was easing the anchor chain when the roaring wedge of water boiled around him. Sitting in his boat he was carried 100 yards inland, bouncing off the palms. As the impetus of the wave died he threw a rope around a teak tree. Three times the water drained away and surged in again, each time its power diminishing. In twenty minutes the sea was calm. "It was a funny situation – there I was sitting in the boat, in the bush, with two anchors out and birds singing all round me."

In his next boat, a forty-foot ex-army launch, he was making a trip with labourers recruited for work in a copra plantation when a whale surfaced under the bow. The vessel stood on end and its skipper, standing horrified at the wheel, saw sixty natives rolling down the deck towards him. The whale sounded, whacking the hull with its tail, and as a result of the hull's flexing the gearbox broke. Bob joined all the ropes together and threw them over the bows and told his frightened passengers: Swim!

They swam for thirteen hours, towing the launch through the darkness. Bob took his own turn. "You'd dive off the bow and swim to the head of the rope and after about an hour you'd have worked your way to the end and could climb up deck for a spell. But by gee I had to drive 'em. Natives will just give up if you don't keep them going. When we got in, without losing a single man, the British agent gave me hell for slave driving, but they were only wet and tired and if I hadn't done it they would have been eating each other in two days."

Another boat was the schooner *Avalon* that had been an Australian Q-ship in the Indian Ocean. When the volcano on Ambrim buried villages, he evacuated 701 people from a lee shore in a smog of ash. The anchors dragged. Ash got into the diesel injectors. The bilge pumps clogged with crud. People were three-deep on the pitching deck, crying and vomiting. There was a fire. One old man died of a seizure, but a baby was born so Bob reached his destination after three frightful days with the books balanced. "The mother dropped the baby on the steps of the cabin which was crammed with about twenty people. We got her inside, I cut the cord and tied the knot and pointed to the baby and said, his name is Bob. Years later I met the lad in Vila and got the shock of my life because his name was George. Funny, that."

Ash had so scoured the engine cylinders that only four of the six were working but when the schooner limped into Vila Bob was asked to go to the aid of a missionary whose boat was on the reef three days away. The missionary gave him enough oil to change the gritty remnants of what was in the sump and Bob towed him off the reef. "How much do I owe you?" the missionary asked.

"Never mind, Fred, I know you can't pay," Bob told him. The engine seized up for good. Bob sailed to Tanna for repairs. The anchor snapped and his crew jumped over the side. He put her aground deliberately then used the diving helmet and went down to nail up the split planks. On the way to Vila, the pump broke and the ship filled quickly, growing more tender with every soggy roll. Bob made harbour with minutes to spare and ran her up the beach outside Burns Philip. Ashore he was handed a letter: a bill for £1 from the missionary for the cost of the oil. And there was tragic news of the people he had taken off Ambrim and landed on Epi: 120 had been buried alive by a landslide.

"By jove," Bob said, as *The Trout* scratched to its conclusion and Kath rang the little bell for the girl to clear the plates, "those were desperate days all right."

Then there was pirate hunting. In the 1960s the islands were troubled by Taiwanese fishing boats. With three or four skiffs carried on deck, and crews of divers, they swept the reefs clean of anything valuable, particularly trochus shell, and made such a thorough job of it that the ecology took years to recover. Natives in canoes could do little but watch helplessly. There were no patrols or preventive measures. Once Bob arrested a ship at the point of an old .303 rifle. He locked the officers in a shed, put the native policeman on guard, and had the villagers stake out the shoreline to ensure that none of the reef pirates came ashore from their ship anchored in the bay to effect a rescue. After checking his sentries and stiffening their backbones with a pep talk, Bob found the policeman asleep. Just for sport he grabbed him in a throat lock but did not get it quite right, the constable let out a blood-curdling scream, and every man jack of the native sentries lit out for the bush. Next day paratroopers arrived from Noumea and made a big splash of the bravery with which they accomplished what Bob Paul had done for them single-handed.

Another arrest he made, by luring the ship on a reef as it repeatedly tried to ram him while he had three of the divers' boats in tow, had a strange sequel. The officers were locked up in the cooler at Tanna while the authorities decided what to do and Bob and Kath felt sorry for the captain who seemed a decent sort so they invited him home for dinner. The captain promised Bob he would come back in six months to work for him, and he did.

One morning Bob heard the distinctive thump-thump of a Taiwanese engine and saw the ship anchoring off Lenakel. He sent out a note advising the captain to clear customs and immigration at Vila. Back came a note saying, "I got gold, I got transistor radios, I got everything." Embarrassed, Bob asked the British agent to handle it. As the ship finally sailed away Bob's young son paddled ashore in his outrigger. "Look Dad, it's terrific," he said, and out of his bathing trunks pulled handfuls of new watches.

One young Australian he employed broke his firm rule about messing with native girls but pleaded it was unfair to be sacked, and Bob heard him out. Sure, he did take Hannah out into the garden, the young man explained, and they were just getting on the job when it started to rain. This put him off his stride, as you could imagine, but Hannah reached out and plucked a banana leaf which she held over him, like an umbrella. That was okay and they were just getting started again when he heard a funny noise. He looked over his shoulder. A billy goat was nibbling the leaf. He lashed out with his foot. The goat put his head down and butted him in the arse – "You can't sack me for that, Boss!"

He was right, Bob admitted – "I was laughing too much."

Goats were always something of a menace at Lenakel. Like Claud, an immense buck who liked to sit on the seat of the outside privy. Many a visitor had to be rescued from a desperate situation, pinned to the lavatory seat with their trousers down by a sprawling billy goat. Claud liked to nibble things in the store, so one day Bob threw a firecracker under him. He turned round three times and charged out of the door just as Kath was coming in, wearing her best party hat, with the prim wife of the new British District Agent.

The privy had collapsed into a parallelogram, with Bob hollering inside it, during an earthquake. And Claud had been carried away, with 130 pigs, by a tidal wave that swept the floorboards of their verandah, twenty-two feet above sea-level.

Such extraordinary experiences were scarcely credible, I thought, lying that night in the kind of stupour that comes from drinking too much Glenfiddich in good company. Suddenly the floorboards thundered with the noise of some kind of wrestling match. There was enraged shouting and high-pitched yelping. Had Taiwan pirates landed? I ran out to see Bob with a big black mangy dog that had strayed into their bedroom. Gripping it by the scruff and the tail he hurled it bodily through the door, which was shut.

But later, as I met more people, I began to realise that Bob and Kath were modestly understating their own parts in these delightful yarns. On the following evening Father Albert Lacco came to dinner. He was a Maltese-born Marist, raised in England, who had worked his way through the ranks to be a Major in a tough Scottish regiment and had been in Tanna since the War. The hurricane that disposed of Claud in 1959 had made Father Lacco a little wet, too.

A couple of hurricanes were lurking about and he had hammered down a loose corner of his roof and gone to bed, he related. But he had not been asleep long when there was a tremendous thud and when he reached for his spectacles his arm came up wet. He switched on the light and saw water up to the level of his bed and rising. He thought the water tank on the stand outside his little house must have burst but as he waded out of the bedroom a fish swam between his legs; it had a light glowing on the tip of the spike on its forehead. It was then that he realised what was happening.

He splashed as fast as he could fifty yards to the teacher's house but there was nobody there. Then he realised he had to get his spectacles for he was blind without them. As he reached his house a suitcase floated out. Inside it were his old glasses that he had repaired with string so he put them on and saw lights as people came down to see if he was still alive. The wall three feet high across the front of his verandah had been swept away. His Land Rover was gone. He decided to rescue the generator of his new lighting system but somebody shouted "Run for it, there's another wave coming!"

The water ran up the slope then receded and his house went with it. His companion said, "Let's get that motor" but Father Lacco told him to forget it: the motor had been washed up and dropped beside them, complete with batteries. A tree had knocked down the back wall of the church and another man wanted to retrieve the Blessed Sacrament. Father Lacco was worried but went with him. They had just got into the church when a third wave struck.

It swept them inland. They found themselves swimming among the trees. The church came down like a house of cards. The Land Rover had reappeared: it was dropped into the water tank, sitting on its tail, and for some reason the headlights had come on so they beamed straight up into the sky from beneath the water. The lenses fell out of the priest's spectacles. "So there I was," he told us calmly over Kath's fried chicken and chilled wine, "I had no house, no church, no glasses, and my pyjamas didn't even match."

In 1941 a native in the south of Tanna claimed to have been visited by an unearthly being called John Frum who promised that if they destroyed all that the Europeans had given he would send shiploads of cargo from his own El Dorado. Overnight the missions were deserted, cattle killed, money thrown into the sea. When US military forces arrived the following year, men of Tanna recruited to labour at Santo were astonished at their uncanny ability to summon from the heavens great silver birds filled with objects that were wonderful beyond imagining. They decided John Frum must be American, an image which many Sea Bees fulfilled perfectly through their well-intended efforts to steer materials and supplies the natives' way. The natives could hardly be blamed. The missionaries had deprived them of all customary values, imposed false modesty, frowned on dancing and any sense of fun, and had arranged for a British cruiser to bombard them when they did not comply (the cannon balls were in Bob Paul's garden). Blackbirders had kidnapped them. Epidemics had carried them off by the thousand. When the people witnessed Europeans benefitting from great shiploads of trinkets and desirable luxuries without money seeming to change hands, they were culturally disoriented and ripe for a Messiah. The movement gathered steam rapidly, despite the arrest of the leaders. When one leader was released from prison and returned to Tanna on Bob Paul's schooner wearing a cast-off medical orderly jacket, he claimed it had been given him by John Frum. The red cross on the sleeve became the symbol of the cult. Devotees drilled in military order with rifles carved of wood and fitted with razor-sharp bamboo bayonets. They daubed military insignia on their skins with paint and charcoal. Today the cult is slowly losing impetus but many of Tanna's 10,000 people continue to live within its confines, refusing education and any degree of co-operation with the administration. The movement is basically non-violent and some Frumites are also Christian, but it falls an easy prey to any kind of manipulation from outside.

Most Frumites lived at Sulphur Bay and Port Resolution, in the shadow of the volcano at the south of the island. Captain Cook had landed there to make astronomical observations but seismic activities have since raised the seabed and altered the lie of the land. I went there next day in one of Bob's Land Rovers, in company with Judy, a lady tourist with pink knees and prominent teeth, who had come in by plane on a day trip from Vila.

The dirt roads were slippery after rain and the tyres were smooth. As we puffed over the 3,000-foot saddle and skateboarded down the other side, it was a race as to whether I climbed on to Judy's lap or she on to mine, but the driver was unruffled. At the village we collected the butcher, by the name of James, who was to be our guide. He spoke English and had the well-oiled muscles of a Gold Medal sprinter.

Yasur is one of the most easily accessible volcanos in the world. Once you get to Tanna, that is. It is a nearly perfect cone of black cinders, about 1,500 feet high. A desert of hard ash stretches away to the north-west for several miles and in the centre of it is a brackish lake where natives were fishing dourly from rafts. The rain had cleared and as we drove hell-for-leather across the ash plain the sun appeared, filtering through the thin spirals of smoke rising from the crater.

It was only a thirty minute climb but after half a minute Judy gasped for a cigarette so I rather caddishly climbed on alone. It was like walking up a giant black sandhill but the rain had formed a hard crust which steamed visibly as the sun sucked out the moisture. The walls of the crater were smooth and nearly vertical and looked no more secure than those of a sand castle so I didn't care to stand too near the fume-wreathed rim. Suddenly a shadow flickered across the crater, a flick of distorted light, and there was time to register surprise and realise it was a shock wave. Then the bang came. It was an explosion of such bass resonance that every bone in my body seemed to rattle in its socket. Then a screech of such intensity that I crouched, holding my ears. A fountain of rocks shot into the air, tumbling over and over and rising almost out of sight before they began to come down, thudding into the black cinders. After the rocks spurted a thick cloud of fumes and dust. I remained crouching, frightened, wondering if the Noah's Ark filled with everything John Frum had promised was at last materialising from Yasur's throat, as the cult followers anticipate. Nothing came out of the smoke but James and Judy. Pale and trembling, she said, "My God!" and started down again. I took the direct route, half leaping and half flying in giant strides.

In the shade of a bush on the edge of the ash plain where we picnicked there was a strange little stockade in which the Frumites had erected a cross. It was surrounded by crude wooden models of landing lights, a control tower, and aircraft lined up on a tarmac, all painted a red that had faded to pinkish silver. This was one of many shrines of the cargo cult, built with the aim of luring out of the sky John Frum and his great silver birds stuffed with goodies. But it was clear we would get no nearer to the cargo cult than glimpses over the stockades of their shrines. To win the trust of such fanatics might be possible over the course of years but to be privy to all their secrets would probably be impossible for any white man. There was one exciting moment when I saw a large gathering of natives watching women dancing. The dancers had fern leaves tied around their heads and waists. Could it be a clandestine gathering of Frumites? Not at all. It was open day at the local school, and the grannies were putting on a funny turn while the mums played handball and the dads had a soccer match and the kids all cheered from the shade of a mighty banyan tree.

But Bob and Kath had survived confrontations in plenty.

Inspired, perhaps, by French interests, the Frumites had often tried to run Bob and Kath off the island. Once, when Bob was tipped off that trouble was on the way, he walked alone up the road to meet a squad of men of the so-called Tanna Army, wooden rifles over their shoulders, dust flying from their bare feet. When they halted in front of him, there was a tense moment as Bob wondered if he was going to be skewered by fifty bamboo bayonets, then he held his breath to make his face red and bellowed, "Piss off!" This they did.

But the run-up to Independence was proving to be the most anxious time. The French were suspected of secretly backing the Frumites to cause trouble and discredit the Vanuaaka party that had been established by the British. Indeed, soon after I left a politician was shot on the island, Tanna tried to secede from the new nation, and the Frumites dug up the airstrip to stop planes landing. Two of Bob's drivers were beaten up. When a column of men marching in fours approached the store with the stated aim of running the Pauls out of Tanna, Bob and Kath walked out to meet them and Bob started taking photographs. The men kicked the fence down and sat in war council so Bob and Kath opened for business and did a good trade in Fanta and Coke. Then there was another uproar. Men marched with axes, knives and clubs and set fire to some huts. Howling and shrieking, the mob wheeled and headed back to the store. "This is it, love," Bob said to Kath, and went out to meet them.

But instead of cutting him down the leaders said, "Get your camera, we want you to take our picture." Bob was so distraught that he got the settings wrong so the pictures never came out. The mob brought fifty dollars worth of lemonade and went home.

Now the Pauls were trying to sell up. After his John Wayne confrontation in the middle of the road it had been the local chiefs who had invited him to establish a store, and had made land available at a minimal rent. Bob claimed he had always been that little bit more than scrupulously fair with the natives, and when the mood of the country changed he had been quick to return the plantations he controlled despite the fact that he held them under legal and proper leases. Besides the dourness of the Tanna people and the French who resented the success of a Britisher, the Pauls had suffered more than a fair share of viciously distorted reporting by journalists who set him up as King of Tanna, with all the connotations of feudal exploitation that the phrase implies. For this reason alone, he believes it would never be possible to begin all over again in this age of so-called liberalism. "There are thirty native co-operatives on this island, which get all kinds of financial support and preferential prices," he explained, "but nearly everyone does their shopping at my tradestore: would that suggest that I am gulling poor downtrodden natives or that I am giving them a fair crack of the whip?"

Only that day a French woman journalist had quizzed Kath about how much she paid their workers (enough to make most stay with the Pauls for many years), how many servants she had in the house (two), how much rent they screwed out of the poor innocent natives for the terrible huts in which they lived (nothing: the Pauls are not landlords). "The funny thing was, she didn't write anything down, she wasn't interested in the answers," Kath sighed. "And when I saw her sunbathing under a coconut palm and went over to warn her about the danger she said it was a free country and I couldn't tell *her* what to do."

"When a nut breaks her head open it won't be the natives she goes to for help," Bob commented dryly. But then he visibly brightened. "People like that couldn't begin to imagine some of the great times we've had in this place. Kath, do you remember that Fijian boat that sank ... ?" The record had finished and Bob flipped it over, blowing the volcanic ash out of the grooves. "Your friend Osea was the engineer and we picked them off the boat as it sank, then somebody said, where's Syd?

"Syd was drunk, sitting stark naked in an airlock in his cabin. I had to dive to get to him and he just waved me away, saying he had been shipwrecked before. I knocked him cold and hauled him out and put him in the launch. I laid him on some boxes of cabin biscuits but next time I looked he had gone. He had rolled over and was lying prone on the stern boards. But the tip of his penis, hanging down, had been worn away by the spinning universal joint of the prop shaft. After that poor old Syd had to use a tube. Occasionally he'd lose it and all of Vila had to look for it."

Through the propped-up shutters I glimpsed a brilliant moon and heard the spurt of breakers along the rocky shore. A warm wind fluttered the table-cloth. "But you're on your way to Fiji, aren't you?" Bob went on. "They're all cannibals over there. Our lives here are quite ordinary, really. Aren't they, dear?"

"Oh yes," Kath replied, folding her napkin neatly. "Nothing much happens on Tanna. It's just a backwater nobody has ever heard of."

The tourist dream of the South Pacific: white sand, limp and warm green water, gentle breeze, blue sky. In the leeward (western) islands of Fiji the dream comes true, but here on Beachcomber Island an army of islanders sieves the sand daily to remove sharp coral fragments and cigarette butts.

The South Seas sunset is a rapid, violent and poignant event. For tourists it signals time for a rum punch, but for ancient Polynesian navigators at sea in voyaging canoes it meant the start of the working day, for the stars were their signposts.

Signboard to a South Seas adventure: as the Fiji government ship *Kaunitoni* prepares to sail from Suva, the captain's family watch the bustle on the wharf.

Inter-island cutters and trading boats of all shapes and sizes crowd Prince's Wharf in Suva, Fiji. Sail has virtually disappeared and the commercial viability of the few remaining vessels is threatened by competition from small aircraft and heavily subsidised but less frequent services by government ships.

The P & O cruise liner *Sea Princess* docks at Apia, Western Samoa, early in the morning, last of the long line of great passenger ships that once criss-crossed the Pacific.

Young lads fishing the sandy shallows inside the reef in Western Samoa, where the lifestyle most closely resembles that of old Polynesia (note the tattooed thighs of the youth at right).

The wearing of a straw mat around the middle, in traditional style, is the most visible of the old customs retained in the feudal society of Tonga. Some mats, handed down through generations, are stiff, creaky, and of great age. Increasingly, younger people are devising shorter, lighter and more comfortable versions, or forgoing the custom entirely, as these two pictures show.

5

PRINCES WHARF

THE GARDEN OF WAR

A trick of the evening sun bathed Suva in sepia light. The saw-tooth ridges of Viti Levu behind the town were silhouetted against a sky of copper-yellow steam, as if the sun had plunged into the sea, and this cast the air of a faded photograph over the city. The downpour had stopped as I drove in from Naussori Airport, sharing a tiny taxi with an Australian salesman of sanitaryware who bombasted me with advice on how to treat Pacific Island natives ("They're just kids, you gotta be cruel to be kind, remember that"). The tarmac was awash with water, every gutter a cataract, and rain still dripped from every glossy leaf.

In any other tropical geography, Suva would be a small and rather quaint semi-industrial town. In this oceanic middle of nowhere, it is a metropolis of some standing. The town has the feeling of being pushed into the sea by invading bush. Its back is to a sea-wall lapped by Pacific rollers brimming over the reef where the hulk of a Japanese fishing boat is rusty monument to near-miss navigation. The city centre flourishes the only multi-storey car-park in the South Seas, and a handful of modest high-rises surrounded by an untidy cluster of seedy wooden shops of turn-of-the-century vintage, their tin-roofed curly-cue verandahs extending across the pavement and presenting a picture of what Honolulu or Singapore would have been like in pioneering days. Beyond, the suburbs burrow between tall creeper-festooned palms and trees, the dense foliage seeming to flow like green volcanic lava out of the thick clouds capping the peaks. Out in the harbour the cable-laying ship *Retriever*, shaded by tightly laced awnings, lay awash in the yellow light like an old-time steamer.

[53]

No Somerset Maughams sat in the cane armchairs in the lobby of the Grand Pacific Hotel, nor even the ghosts of them, as numerous travel books promised. It was a beautiful four-square colonial building with broad balconies, trim gardens, and the harbour breeze billowing the long white curtains and rattling the potted palms. Fans hung on long stalks from the high ceiling but only a few of them were turning. A discreet notice in gold on a little varnished rostrum said: Gentlemen are asked to wear shoes and socks in the evenings. A heap of young Australians with wet hair, and running-shorts split on each side to the waistband, sprawled noisily over the cane chairs. An American woman in a pink cocktail dress was grotesquely drunk and bothering two Singhalese WHO experts who looked as if they were discussing their expense accounts. The hotel was owned by an Indian: the bedspread and curtains in my room were exotic purple, the lino tiles had a gold fleck. The telephone was one of that old-fashioned Bakelite variety with which you could do serious damage to an intruder if you could get close enough to brain him with it. My window opened on to the balcony from which British royals had waved to the crowds, now a roar of numerous air conditioners.

Everything is wrong about Suva. It is on the windward side of the island where the tradewinds unload their cargo of moisture, the rivers run brown with silt that discolours the lagoon, and the coastline is mangrovy and fetid. The air is not light and bright, as on the dry leeward side of the island, but clammy and suffocating; even the lightest clothes hang heavily on your body as if they were wet serge. Because the sky is often cloudy, there is no shade to offer relief. Suva is like a town that has sprung up around some railway siding in the middle of nowhere and from which the rails were long since lifted and sold for scrap. Until comparatively recently it was the crossroads of the Pacific. Passenger steamers of the colonial days berthed to the barefoot stamp and *oompah* of the Royal Fiji Police brass band. Flying boats slashed the sultry lagoon with long ripping feathers of spray and passengers with ringing ears came by launch to revive their spirits with a gin and tonic on the verandahs of the "Gee Pee Aitch". The hotel was a transit camp for colonials changing planes and ships: it was the only real hotel in the town and nothing ever ran to schedule. Here, with blanco'd shoes, white ducks, collar and tie and Panama hat, the aspiring colonial reclined in a cane chair whilst awaiting the summons to the administration headquarters. These buildings, being just across the playing fields and next to the botanic gardens, have the look of a rather formidable and austere public school.

For all that, Suva is a bustling, colourful, industrious place. You can even be hustled there, another distinction that is unique in the South

Seas. The banyan tree between the hotel and the town was haunted by broad-shouldered young men carrying sports bags who hailed me in a friendly way. "Bula! Where you from? What's your name? You like Fiji? Look, we got a special souvenir custom made for you, hand-carved Fijian sword with your name inscribed – see!" Sure enough, a shabby wooden sword in which my name had been incised with a few flicks of a pen-knife was pushed into my hands. Only twenty bucks they said, special price. I asked to take their picture and they posed, grinning, then I demanded twenty dollars. They retreated into the shade, muttering. Much later, in a drawer in my room along with the Gideon Bible, I found a notice warning against these touts and a gracious apology from the Fiji Visitors' Bureau. I also encountered the Australian sanitary-ware salesman ("You gotta be cruel . . .") making for the more expensive hotel next door with a bundle of swords under his arm. Eight-five dollars for his bundle of firewood, and good luck.

In sunshine so hot and steamy that I felt I was swimming the Amazon, I prospected the waterfront next morning. Not for the first time I was struck by the lack of complexity of these Pacific ocean-side towns. There was never any need to ask directions. To travel onward was never a question of finding some bus or train station tucked away in the back-streets. There were no back-streets. In these islands the sense of sea as a highway, as front door and back door, dominates the character of every town. To find the wharf I walked to the waterfront then turned and followed the sea's edge. In some towns it was a sandy beach. In others, like Papeete, the Pacific lapped a grassy bank. In Suva it was a busy road with railings, past the car-park, towards a frieze of masts and spars of inter-island copra cutters and trading boats at Princes Wharf. What a romantic Conradian picture they made. These were the vessels in which I had dreamed of roaming willy-nilly among the Fiji archipelago, sleeping on hatchcovers and gazing at the wake glittering in the moonlight. The reality was a cruel disappointment, for the vessels were ugly, uncomfortable and unappealing.

One cutter making ready to sail was scarcely fifty feet long, beamy with two masts and a bowsprit. It carried a couple of tattered foresails for steadying, and was deep in the water already, the foredeck heaped with all kinds of general cargo. Now at least fifty people were scrambling aboard. Through the shutters I glimpsed people stretched out on every available surface, sometimes two or three to a bunk. The vessel looked as seaworthy and congenial as a double-decker bus in the rush hour.

A young Fijian sailor, built like a Greek god with rippling muscles, gleaming black skin, a sunny smile, and looking like a Red Indian brave with three coloured ballpoints jutting from his hair, caught my eye. "When do you sail?" I asked.

He glanced at his digital watch. "Maybe five o'clock, maybe tomorrow, I dunno." It would be a long day surging against the quay wall in the fetid little cabin, I thought. But when I asked what his destination was the reply came like a jungle drum. I pretended a look of understanding and went off to buy a map, but it was not much help.

The prospects of getting away on an inter-island trip seemed bleak. I wouldn't have called the promise of such an adventure romantic so much as hideous. But trying to travel with a jet-age mentality by a marine mode that depended as much on a skipper's fickle fancy as on wind and cargo was like plugging a shaver into the wrong voltage: buzzing shrilly it gets hotter by the second until the armature melts. So it was that, buzzing shrilly and melting by the minute, I trekked to the cool verandahs of the GPH. There, reflecting that none of this sort of thing seemed to happen to Somerset Maugham, I threw myself into a cane peacock throne woven in Thailand and ordered a cold Australian beer.

Feeling disgruntled I opened a days-old *Fiji Times* and the first thing I saw was a picture of the equally disgruntled cutters leaning against Princes Wharf. It headed a story about the secretary of the local ship-owner's association, Leo Smith, complaining that local shipping was run down due to lack of government support. I telephoned on spec and he came so quickly that my beer was still cold. After a hot and bothersome morning on the quay he was as disgruntled as I. His ship had come in with 1,600 bags of copra which the wharf labour, super-intended by the port authority, would unload in two eight-hour days. But the dockers had made him an offer on the sly. Give us twenty hours pay on the side, they proposed, and we will empty your ship in six hours. Even on a South Sea island there is the turn of the screw.

Leo's grandfather had washed up in the islands as a deckhand in a sailing ship, married a half-Samoan, and established estates on Vanua Levu, the other big island in the Fiji group. Leo's father, blinded at five when other boys had squirted the juice of a poisonous leaf in his eyes, ran the estates all his life. As a youth Leo had shipped out as crew in an old yacht called *Diana* in which an eccentric Englishman called Sir Norman Young was sailing round and round the world while expressing the desire to die under full sail. Meanwhile, as a retired diplomat and a former director of the Suez Canal Company, he dressed every evening in old school tie and mildewed linen jacket and had his dinner served with style in the tossing cabin by one of his crew. It turned out that as a cub reporter I had interviewed the old man on his arrival at Auckland, and Leo had been in the picture we printed. He had jumped ship there to train as a

Customs Agent while Sir Norman had sailed away, ultimately to fulfill his wish somewhere off Cape Town.

His complaint against the government was that the Marine Department operated its own fleet of Suva-built ships which were heavily subsidised on the grounds that "roads" to the islands were an essential part of the country's basic infrastructure. But the subsidies were killing off the small cutters and ketches operated by private owners. Of these, only about twenty-five vessels remained and they sailed on an *ad hoc* basis only to ports where there was sufficient cargo to make the voyage worthwhile, so the smaller islands were by-passed and worse off than before. To voyage in one was easily done: you haunted the quay, asked questions, and staked out your reservation with a good supply of food and coconuts. To travel in a government ship was easy enough too, Leo explained, but reservations were made on a first-come basis and the services were intended for islanders, not tourists. A round trip cost three times as much as a single passage, there were few hotels or lodging facilities in the islands, and the government took a dim view of tourists sleeping under the palms. The visitors bureau at Nadi Airport, I discovered later, was besieged with the arrival of every international flight by young people with back packs, especially Americans, who had little money and wanted to stay with native families. Often they turned belligerent when told there was a comfortable and cheap hotel outside the airport gates. One wonders what sort of dusty answer an unwashed and penniless Fijian youth might get, landing at Los Angeles and announcing his intention to live with American families.

In a high-ceilinged corner room of a colonial building on the waterfront, I found Captain Micky Joy, superintendent of the Marine Department. Rocking back in a creaky chair he threw a white-socked leg over a large brown knee and contemplated the Admiralty chart pinned on the wall. It showed Fiji as a milky way of reefs, atolls and islets around a close group of four comparatively large islands. About a third of the 300 land-specks were inhabited, principally the chain of twenty-two called the Yawawas in the north-west, and the widely scattered Lau group of fifty-seven islands to the east, some of them nearer to Tonga than to Suva. The waters were so dangerous that in some areas, vessels were required by law to anchor during darkness.

Besides the subsidies killing off local shipping, Captain Joy explained, every airstrip was a blow because it took away the lucrative cabin-passenger trade such as civil servants and teachers. The islands produced little, so the ships were left with only outward cargo to carry and deck passengers paying a token fare.

But there were two promising possibilities. A government ship was taking the Police band to Ono-i-lau, one of the most distant islands, three days' steaming away, and I was welcome to go along for the ride and sleep with the bandsmen in the ship's hold. Another ship was taking cyclone relief materials to Kadavu, in the south, but first she was going north to take forty geography students on a field trip. Either way, I would see an awful lot of sea and not many islands. Both were sailing that day, he said, and I should make my mind up at once. I decided to try my luck on the wharf, with a little help from Leo, but when I got there again, two cutters had sailed suddenly and the one I had seen filling up, on the day before, was deserted and knocking listlessly against the quay.

Outside the wharf gates was the large covered market, the hub of Suva life. For me the market became an oasis of shade and refreshment as I fruitlessly patrolled the inter-island wharf for a cutter going to an interesting destination and in which there was both elbow room and a reasonable certainty of a safe arrival. The market was surrounded by flame trees, curry carts and bus stops. In its dim interior the aromatic spices, turmerics and rices of India were set out in open sacks along with the muscular casava and dalo roots, bush chilis and pine-apples home-grown in Fiji. There were garlands of black mangrove crabs spitting bubbles, giant avocados, hands of bananas, heaped-up limes and bundled coconuts. Outside, amid the congregation of taxis, news stands and teaming crowds, buses with roll-down awnings instead of windows, and with exotic names (Flying Prince Transport, Maharaj Buses), waited in lines. Their rattling diesels pumped oily smoke into the wool-heavy air. Here was displayed in the raw what I slowly came to perceive as a spectacular racial miracle, for Fiji is truly two countries co-existing harmoniously in nation. To squat on a crate and suck a piece of pineapple and watch the crowd was a delight.

The Fijian man is the most regal of human beings. Tall and big with it he does not walk so much as coast, like a supertanker that has long ago stopped its engines; on big bare feet he seems to glide forward under the impetus of his own inertia. Grave of face, majestic of bearing, enormous in bulk, he walks tall as if flying a message in signal flags from his masthead. His hull is generally sheathed in a tailored skirt, or *sulu*, which extends to mid-calf. Schoolboys wear white cotton ones, Methodist ministers thick black ones with parson's collar and black coat, policemen white ones with serated edges, waiters coloured ones with cummerbunds, and Sir Joseph Rabukawqa (a name I had to practice in front of a mirror) greeted me in the Prime Minister's office wearing a *sulu* made from the kind of pin-stripe that English gentlemen wear with white carnations to Ascot. The breeze above and the breeze below is the maxim: even the Prime Minister and police constables wear brightly bulled leather sandals, and you may go bare-footed to Church but you must wear a collar and tie.

A Fijian woman, her black hair puffing like smoke from a funnel, is a big boned, big person. The capacious and beamy banana boat of the population fleet, she dresses overall in flag-bright, ankle-length cotton dress and steams in idle convoy with her friends, arms loaded with heavy baskets, head thrown back, shoulders squared and ship-shape, and smiles breaking all round like bow waves.

The dainty women of Indian origin are yachts by comparison. Silken saris billow in the breeze like spinnakers, jewellery gleams like gold scrolls rendered upon varnished skin. Sharp of feature, lithe, whippy, they cut through the milling tide-race as prettily as racing dinghies, though some are wizened or dumpy, listless hulks that have seen better days.

Slim, rakish, flashy, living on their wits and commercial cunning, the Indian men adopt Western dress: white shirt, sharp creases, snappy cuffs, shiny shoes. There are the fat and greasy ones, fleet oilers and provenders. There are stick-thin touting ones, privateers. Always they have a purposeful air of being on the make, not beautiful but busy, as do fishing boats and ferries.

Neat and officious as harbour launches, the Westerners resident in Fiji rig themselves casually. Women in cool frocks and sandals. Men in open-neck shirts, tailored shorts, shoes with long socks ("A man's gotta have a place to keep his comb and ballpoints," one Australian told me). The tramps and bumboats of this exotic population regatta are in fact the true voyagers, the tourists. Open-decked with bra straps showing and shirt-tails hanging out, top-heavy with duty frees, their paint blistering in the sun, they are the freebooters, the smugglers, the tugboats that insist on their rights of way. Their cameras go like carronades and they are cheeky enough to stick an oar in anywhere.

In the eyes of the great harbourmaster in the sky I suppose that all ships are launched equal upon the sea, but the waters, as any South Seas man knows, are fraught with danger. The big-ship Fijian natives, owning the land through family and tribal groups, steam on compara-tively untroubled by the winds of politics and oblivious of economic reefs. The little-ship Indians have the quickness of eye and education, not to mention the cunning, that makes them survivors: they must pay rent for their land but they work hard. While tourists, like Arab dhows, are here today and gone tomorrow, bringing gold and loading booty.

Little more than a century ago, however, the native Fijian was a bloodthirsty figure. While he was in neighbouring Tonga in 1733, Captain Cook recorded that "Feejee" was described to him as,

... a large and very fruitful island, abounding with hogs, dogs, fowls and all kinds of fruits and roots. Those of Feejee are formidable on account of the dexterity with which they use their bows and slings, but much more on account of the savage practice ... of eating their enemies whom they kill in battle.

Cook later did sight one small island in the group but he did not venture nearer. The first white men to filter into the islands, from about 1800, were chiefly escaped Botany Bay convicts and deserters from the first sandalwood ships. They got a warm welcome: ground ovens were heated to cook them. The shipwrecked, flicking salt water out of their eyes, experienced briefly the pleasure with which a fat turkey anticipates Christmas until despatched with a crashing blow from a spiked war club. Among the array of murderous weapons displayed in Suva Museum I saw strange objects like chopsticks with the end split into four prongs arranged in a square. These were cannibal forks. We might have been cannibals, the Fijians claim primly, but we were certainly not savages.

Though small on the map, the beautiful islands of Fiji at the time of white contact two centuries ago were a garden of barbarity and warfare that it would be difficult to equal. The old were strangled. The sick were buried alive. War canoes launched over living bodies returned from coastal raids flying victory banners called 'birds of the sail' – bodies of children hanging by the feet. Human sacrifice was common, the flesh consumed on behalf of the gods. A special plant was grown near temples so its leaves could be used to wrap human flesh for baking, and its tomato-like fruit were made into sauce to reduce the meal's constipating effect.

Today the war-drums of Fiji summon the warriors of the Lord to church. Having been all for savagery, the people came all out for God under the spell of the Wesleyan missionaries whom they had put through a grim trial by gore, throwing half consumed human heads over their garden walls. The doors which the missionaries kept firmly closed to shut out the smell of poached bodies were opened again to admit the enlightened. In losing their heathen ways the Fijians nevertheless salvaged much of what was valuable and unique in their culture: their language, national dress, music, courtesy and chiefly system. Today, more than half the breezy and amiable native Fijians continue to live in about 700 classic villages scattered along the shores of their host of islands, many of them still in the comfortable and sweet-smelling little hayrick-style huts built of cane, pandanus and palm-fronds called *bures* (boorays). These, sadly, are being replaced by more permanent but less healthy and less picturesque cement houses with

tin roofs. Communities are rich in traditional virtues though individuals are poor in cash. Cars and gadgets are rare but village
churches are fine. The custom of *kerekere* survives strongly as the pivot
of village life: instead of trading by barter Fijians share everything,
work as well as wealth. This drove the early discoverers, missionaries
and traders to a high pitch of exasperation for they saw it only in terms
of petty pilfering. The custom also wars unceasingly against mercantile
progress because any individual who betters himself must by ancient
right share his rewards, so why bother? Taking a cynical view, a Fijian
could measure his wealth by the number of friends from whom he can
beg. But it is hard to be cynical about a dignified people who remain
contemptuous of capital assets, who live simply, ensure nobody is ever
in need, and whose silent though eloquent protest against the uni-
versalism of world cultures – as the author G. K. Roth observes – is
itself a cultural achievement of the first order.

Just how the custom of *kerekere* translates in modern terms I discovered when, in the course of my quest for a ship, I encountered
Isimeli Bainimara. He told me that he had been brought up in a village
on Taveuni Island and when he passed his high school entrance exams
his younger brothers and sisters went to work in the plantations and
the family pooled resources to pay for his further education. It was
money well spent. Bai was the young army officer selected to salute
the country's brand-new sky blue flag when it was hoisted for the first
time on Independence Day in 1972. He did a spell as *aide-de-camp* to
the Governor General then joined a bank and gravitated to his present
job in the Fiji Visitors' Bureau: a handsome, ruggedly built, engaging
man of thirty-eight. Now he was ungrudgingly paying the price of the
advantages he had enjoyed. Although he had three children of his own
his duty now was to assist the children of his brothers and sisters who
had sacrificed much for his future. So far he had put three nieces and
nephews through school, paying their education fees, books, clothing,
travel and lodging them at his home. "You can see why there are no
rich native Fijians in Fiji," he said.

When Britain took Fiji under her wing in 1874, partly to ensure no
other country got a leg in, partly to protect the people against the
blackbirders and speculators (a business syndicate in Australia was
trying to buy the islands) and partly because there might have been
a future for the place in growing the cotton which was then in short
supply due to the effects of the American Civil War, it was agreed from
the beginning that native land should be inalienable and to this day
the natives own eighty-three per cent (compared with ten per cent in
New Zealand, very little in Hawaii). But it was clear that there was
no hope of getting a day's work out of the easy-going natives. In the

event it was not cotton but sugar that proved to be the most promising crop, and between 1879 and 1916 more than 60,000 Indians of mainly agricultural caste were brought in as indentured workers to develop what has become the country's staple industry. After ten years in the cane fields they were free to return but few did so because they saw an opportunity to break out of the caste system. During the 1920s Punjabis and Gujeratis arrived under their own steam to found what is now a merchant class. The result is that Indians now outnumber native Fijians. Four out of five farmers are Indian, but Indians as a whole own less than three per cent of the land.

Although Indians have no land as a base, and worry about it, they have made themselves independent and indispensable through education. Especially strong in commerce and the professions, they are the businessmen, contractors, speculators, clerks, doctors, lawyers and graduate teachers. In contrast to the family-oriented Fijian, the Indian fends for himself in a fiercely competitive way. The suburban house with cars in the driveway is invariably Indian. One evening after a fruitless search for a boat I found the suburbs magically transformed. Strings of lights like jewelled cobwebs draped the houses and trees. Candles in coloured paper tents were spaced over the lawns. Lines of flickering candle-flame bordered every path, step and sill. Patios were grottos of soft, yellow light. Rockets blossomed in the night sky and the air was filled with the reek of gunpowder and hot wax. Hindu families were in their best clothes, sitting out in the warm Fijian evening to celebrate Diwali, the festival of light.

Late into the evening, as I walked the enchanting spark-lit streets, I realised I was not alone. Native Fijian families were out strolling, too, enjoying the spectacle, some of them strumming guitars. But in a genuinely plural society in which mosques, temples and churches rub shoulders, and the rights of ethnic groups are as protected in the country's constitution as the rights of individuals, it was hardly surprising to find people enjoying each other's festivities. Native Fijians might be outnumbered, out-moneyed and out-educated by some 260,000 acquisitive Indians, as *Time* reported in 1977, but compromises and concessions on both sides have resulted in a remarkable harmonising of cultural differences. Prejudices do exist, and are certainly exploited for political advantage, but they are not as noticeable as the tolerances. Both sides benefit from the fact that English is the mother tongue of neither. "There is no question that the Indians have sharpened us up, we think more quickly and are thriftier because of their influence," one Fijian manager of a hotel told me, "but the Indians tend to mistrust everyone and be furtive: we don't want to be like that, but if you trust everyone as the Fijians do then others trample all over you."

After three days of lurking on the wharf I made up my mind to be a beachcomber no more, and to take the first boat out, to anywhere. But a long and hot morning on the waterfront merely confirmed that the boats which came in at the start of the week did not sail for the outer islands until late in the week. Dispirited, I walked beyond the big-ship wharf with its high wire fences and stacked containers to a cluster of jetties where I had glimpsed Japanese fishing boats, a deep-sea tug, naval minesweepers and other assorted craft. Jutting high above them, piratically raked, were two tall spiral-welded masts. Beneath them I found a pretty little ship. Dark blue, with a low single-deck superstructure aft, a wide flared bow and a bowsprit, she was a brand-new government vessel about 100 feet long and called *Cagi Donu* (pronounced thangy-donoo, meaning tradewind). As I watched, a crowd of students clutching kitbags and geography books milled aboard and I saw Captain Joy sitting with a contented smile in the narrow band of shade on the steps of a little hut. "I thought you didn't want to sail," he said.

I made an instant decision. The waiting around Suva was getting tedious and the cut of this little ship interested me. "How long have I got?"

"Twenty minutes, no more."

Three hours after I had swept into the hotel like a tornado, thrown a few clothes in a bag, left the rest at the desk, paid the bill and scooped up some paperbacks, the little ship pulled away from the jetty. There were no sails to set on those elegant tapered masts because they were still being made in Scotland but it was doubtful that the ship would ever sail. As the Lau Islands which she was intended to service were up-wind of Suva, her designers had made a brave attempt to build a fuel-efficient vessel that could plug against the wind under power but spread her wings and sail home. The mast made her so top heavy, however, that the hold was half filled with tons of concrete blocks for ballast.

My cabin was bright and clean with a silent-running fan and a romantic scuttle that did not open, but the cistern of the lavatory constantly overflowed, drenching those who used it. The wall of the shower-room was part of the funnel housing and too hot to touch, and the six inches of water surfing back and forth with every roll, because the drain was blocked, was nearly too hot to stand in. But I was at sea at last and on my way, by the most circuitous route imaginable, to an island where the people had suffered the reality of the worst of South Seas nightmares, a cyclone (hurricane, cyclone, typhoon, all are the same thing).

For the first two hours we slid around the coast inside the reef, navigating by eye from beacon to beacon and following the dark blue colouring which indicated, as if it were a dye, the canyon of deep water wending through the pale green plateau of coral. A seaman cut me a large wedge of water melon and I blew the pips to leeward.

With the young mate hanging in the rigging and bellowing steering orders to the helmsman, the *Cagi Donu* turned hard a-starboard and made for the gap in the reef. Hastily I swallowed a Kwell, from my stock of seasick pills, and the forty students ranged along the side-decks swooned with a loud "O-o-oh!" as the ship rose slowly over the first swell, and like a roller coaster switch-backed down the other side. Further out the swells were smaller and we rolled along, a mile off the reef, taking them on the beam. What a pity we had no sail, I thought, as the damp wind braked in mid-air somebody's projectile of vomit and sprayed it back over the faces of all those crouching greenly to windward. Churning hillocks of white water beneath it, and touched by the sun at high altitude like an Alp at sunrise, a towering squall blotted out the island. Another was gathering to seaward, trailing a black curtain of rain, but it crossed the bows and left us dancing the billows in our own private spotlight of silver sunlight.

Dinner was an oily steak with sweet potato, followed by tinned fruit salad in orange jelly, which I forced down in company with Mamasa Navunisaravai. He was a young clerk of the Prime Minister's Hurricane Relief Committee, wearing a blue sports shirt, black *sulu*, one striped sock and one blue sock. Our cargo, he explained was largely the month's rations of staple foods such as rice, sugar, powdered milk, tinned fish, tea and soap donated by the EEC and neighbouring Pacific countries following the disastrous destruction by Cyclone Meli a few months before. Our destination was the island of Kadavu, south of Suva, but first we had to take these students to Savusavu, to the north, adding two long days to the trip.

The students, from the University of the South Pacific, were a mixed bunch from different island countries but most were Fijian and most of these were of Indian race. The young man who took up station beside me was Kini Marawi, a native Fijian with a heavily muscled bare torso that did not raise so much as a goose-bump in the crisp sea wind. One bulging bicep was tattooed with the outline of a fist and the words, *Omnia Vincit Amor*. In the small of his back, less elegantly, was inscribed *Historia Me Absolvera*. His black hair was a stubble scarcely a quarter of an inch long and his eyes were the colour of the night. At intervals he broke loudly into song, or jumped to his feet in a sudden whipcord spasm of muscle without using his hands and patrolled the deck to cheer up the girls swooning under thin blankets. Then he would return to berate me, with more enthusiasm than animosity. His politics were incomprehensible but his images were quaint once I got my ear tuned, for he had a way of spitting his words, accentuating the *brrs* and *grrs* so everything else got lost in the echo. It was like conversing with a bongo drum. "Bolly digs is a gabe of Bodopoly," he asserted gravely. The gist of his reasoning for saying that politics was a game of Monopoly was that small countries like his kept on passing Go without collecting their two hundred bucks. Some countries could play the game with a counter in the form of a racing car, a motorbike, a wishbone or even a top hat. Little countries in the Pacific had the old boot, he thought.

At 3 am the ship slipped into smooth water and discharged the students at the end of a wharf lit by one streetlight. Nothing else was visible in the total blackness except the myriads of tiny, brilliant fish finning languidly in the green pool beneath the light. Kini carried the luggage of three different girls, which he set carefully on the pier then stood to attention and mocked me with a crisp colonial salute. I returned it with equal sharpness and he grinned, shaking his head dismissively: "You moved the wrong man, Whitey: you fellas chose the racing car and it's running out of gas."

6

CAGI DONU

CYCLONE,
SHIPWRECK AND SALVAGE

Near sundown after a long day's bashing through sunlit blue seas and a fresh wind, I slid back the lee door and found the wheelhouse crowded with as picturesque a band of cut-throats as a Gilbert and Sullivan imagination could conjure up. All were native Fijians. The captain, grey-haired with a hand-rolled cigarette hanging in the corner of his mouth, stood by the corner window gazing at the edge of the surf-pounded reef a few ship-lengths to starboard. Beyond, streaked with colour like the marbled end-paper of an old ledger, spread a lagoon. Soon the reef would curve away from our course and *Cagi Donu* would have a clear run, encountering no hazards through the night.

Captain Illai Raivoka understood a little English but did not speak it. His face had the grave immobility of an Easter Island statue and he adopted a strange pose, knees pressed together and body hitched slightly forward like a man holding himself in. Much of the time he stared down at his unlaced shoes, as if puzzled by them.

The chief mate Saiasi Buliruarua was an ebullient muscular young man whom I called Sai. He sported a thick black moustache and was for ever shadow-boxing, feinting and shamming fights with the older men. "Live hard, man, that's the sailor's life. You make yourself at home here, John, and live hard and play hard with us, you're welcome." Though Sai might have passed his formal exams it was clear that the Second Mate was the real boss of the ship. Vaitia Sibo was a man of voluminous girth, every limb shaped like a funnel. His face had the wave and weather-cracked look of a ship that had resided for a long time under the water. For most of the day he had tended the trolling lines towing astern but had caught nothing. Now he sat on the wheelhouse floor, his thick legs splayed around a large draughts board, plywood with crayoned squares; the pieces were cross-sections of a sawn-up branch. His opponent was Yavala, the old cook with a gummy smile and thick black spectacles, whom I had talked to as he cleaned vegetables with a wicked instrument he called his "all weather knife". The game was fast and noisy, the pieces on the board jumping and rattling as the players, chuckling thickly, slammed their men down.

Emosi the cabin boy, who through the day had been making glass mugs of hot tea thickened to syrup with lavish helpings of sweetened condensed milk, stood around playing with the Polaroid camera he had bought with his first pay packet and clutched the pictures he had taken. Now it was out of film, a contingency that left him sad. George, the hugely built young engineer, had exchanged his green overalls for a purple *sulu*, running shoes, and a double-breasted brass-buttoned ship's purser jacket with gold stripes on the sleeve; beneath it his torso was bare but for a black necklace, and the black furze that radiated from his head like an explosion of soft Brillo was thrust into a red and blue knitted ski cap. Now he sat on a high stool strumming a guitar softly and thoughtfully, his mind miles away, as he loosely accompanied the music coming from a transistor radio lashed with cord to one of the bridge windows.

During the voyage I had observed the ship being run in a Bristol sort of fashion. On the hour and half-hour the watchman rapped the little brass bell. Helm orders were given in a seamanlike way, the flag was lowered at sunset and raised at eight bells of the morning watch, the deck log was kept religiously. But there was no bull, no yessir-nossir. Officers and crew were informal and affable and beneath the bureaucratic dressage of certification and official rank I fancied the existence of a rather different structure of authority (or non-authority, depending on how you looked at it). There was certainly a loose-limbed atmosphere in the wheelhouse of the little ship that would have given your average hard-line shipmaster fifty fits, but it took a little while for the cause of it to dawn.

I had found a comfortable elbow-leaning position from which to watch the rise and fall of the bows over the steep waves licked by a raspberry-flavoured sunset. At some signal, Emosi the cabin boy checked his Polaroid in a corner and picked up the blue plastic bucket which Mamasa, the clerk, was holding in place against the binnacle with an out-thrust foot as he sprawled comfortably against the bulk-head. The captain indicated me with a tilt of his head and the boy came over. The bucket was half filled with a liquid the colour of milky tea, on which bobbed a bowl made from the half shell of a coconut. It was *kava*, the universal narcotic of the South Seas.

The men watched me out of the corners of their eyes as Emosi stirred the *kava* around with the bowl, then he filled it to the brim and held it up to me. The men clapped softly with cupped palms as I took it, and muttered "Bula!" which means Hello, Have a Happy Day, and *Geshundheit*, all in one. For one ghastly moment I thought I was the victim of a practical joke. Was this gritty horrid stiff out of a muddy river truly *kava*, or was it the water with which they had been swabbing down the deck? Rapidly I searched the expressions of the watching men for a twitch of a smile, but there was none. The stuff had a peppery taste and a chalky consistency. As I drained the bowl and handed it back the men clapped again, and again muttered the word "Bula!" Now came a most curious sensation. My mouth and tongue tingled as if I had been shot with Novocaine, and turned faintly numb. The taste was refreshing and cleansing and the effects were subtle: *kava* is not a bit alcoholic but like a mild narcotic it makes you tranquil. You become disconnected, silent, sleepy and lose appetite for food. Every ten minutes or so the ceremony was repeated, the bucket and bowl being taken to each man by turn. Men drifted in to have a bowl or two, then went out again. It was a harmonious social routine and the warm feeling of togetherness was generated more by the fact that twelve Fijians and one *palagi* drank from one cup than from any warming effects of the kava. The draughts board changed hands several times. The *kava* bucket was replenished. The ship hammered and swayed through the darkness.

While killing time in Suva I had made a lucky strike at a little white office behind a Shell service station which I discovered by accident. As archives go it was not much larger than a high school library but the dainty Indian girl at the desk had shown me some of the material and by chance my hand had fallen on a manuscript which I scanned quickly. Late in his life, a trader called Edward Turpin had recorded in a journal his memories of the savage South Seas. They were bloodcurdling accounts of the era of club rule, so rivetting that I had made a photostat of the whole thing. Now, wedged in a rocking bunk while the kava bowl did the rounds of the wheelhouse and worked its glum magic on the crew, I settled down to read it. Soon, as I turned the pages of the old journal, I was hypnotised by the horror of it. I became as dry-mouthed and round-eyed as a small boy reading of ogres and if it hadn't been such a sweaty night I would have been under the bedclothes afraid to look out. But it was no fairy tale. These ogres who cooked and ate *palagi* – whites, known throughout the islands as "men from under the sky" – were real people, the great-grandfathers of the piratical bunch up there in the wheelhouse.

In 1834, I read, the American brig *Fawn* was caught in light winds and carried by strong currents on to a reef near Savusavu (where we had landed the students). The sailors manned the boats and landed on the nearest beach. Hooting and yelling savages armed with clubs and spears surrounded the castaways, bound them hand and foot, and carried them to the village. The chief had a head of hair measuring seven feet in circumference and a face painted red, blue and black. Round his neck was a necklace of whale's teeth and over his shoulder he bore an immense pineapple club.

One of the minor chiefs had been to the Tongan Islands and he spoke up for the castaways, pleading that they should be made slaves because they were good mechanics, could make many planks from a tree from which the natives could make only one, and could show them how to make the black powder that carried death in its grasp. The sailors could build canoes and help in wars and the village was not short of *vuaka balavu* (long pig, the name given to men to be killed and eaten). In any case, he concluded, the sailors were too thin to be worth the effort.

A scar-worn, one-eyed warrior had then argued that the castaways did not belong to the people but to the gods.

The issue was decided by the chief priest who chewed and swallowed twelve inches of a red-hot stick and went into a trance. "What I am about to tell you must be obeyed ... It was I who commanded the winds and the waves to surrender these prizes. The white men's gods were weak but I alone was strong so all of them must die save one, and he shall show you the knowledge of the white men ..."

The survivor was one Jim McGoon who had told Edward Turpin all about it. First, drums were beaten vigorously to inform those at a distance of the transaction, then there was a kava ceremony. Jim McGoon related:

"We were not left long as to what was to be our fate. Many skulls and half-eaten heads were stuck up on spears. Young men came with large quantities of taro, yams, bananas and other leaves. The women also came back from the bush, where they had been sent, and we needed no telling that a great feast and holiday was to be held. In a short time the town was crowded and the priests appeared busy on one side of the square near large circular holes eight or ten feet in diameter in which were a great number of boulders. These were the ovens.

A short consultation was held among the old men and the chief. Suddenly the chief who had been our advocate jumped up and came over to where I was and cut my bond adrift. Oh! the blessedness of that moment. The relief was almost overpowering. My hands and feet were black with being bound so tight, for I could not stand, and whilst in this condition I heard a sudden crushing blow followed by cries from my comrades. I instantly looked up and saw to my great horror that a naked savage had just clubbed one of my poor comrades. Faster than I can tell you this they were all massacred. The last one was poor Jack Shute, my chum, who was a schoolmate and townsman of mine, being clubbed within three feet of me.

I can truthfully say I felt no fear, I could not realise the atrocity. The moment before, the world appeared so calm and quiet, and now . . .! Women and virgins now appeared, gorgeously dressed in flowers, otherwise perfectly naked. They deliberately and obscenely insulted my poor dead friends who had been stripped naked. Then a man took hold of either hand of each body and dragged it face downwards to the beach where they were disembowelled. Some of the bodies were then put on fast canoes and sent to different towns in the district as presents."

After the feast, which lasted more than two days and nights, Jim McGoon was given eight wives, a house and a workshop where for two years he made weapons and tools from the brig's ironwork. He was finally exchanged for half a dozen muskets and a bundle of assorted trade goods collected by other white men living in the nearby pioneer community of Levuka.

With my skin crawling I took a turn round the deck to shake the images out of my mind before I turned in and found the descendants of the cannibal warriors having a party on the stern deck. It was not kava, now, but rum and whisky. "Live hard, play hard, John!" Sai muttered tipsily, and handed me a good shot of rum in a tumbler. The captain's knees were pressed even more firmly together and he stared down at the deck, magically standing perfectly upright when all around him was tilting drunkenly as the ship corkscrewed southwards. All through the night Vaitia, the Second Mate, stayed on watch.

The schedule seemed uncertain. The clerk told me we were calling at thirty-six villages on the island. The captain said two. It turned out to be five. Later, I discovered that the ship had arrived at Kadavu (*kan-dar-voo*) too early so we had proceeded along the northern shore, a distance of some twenty-five miles, to the other end of the island. This totally reversed our schedule and was a classic case of the way in sailing the South Seas that the tail wags the dog. Don't stop the ship: if you arrive too early change the timetable.

A long, thin, bush-covered mountain ridge jutting above the ocean and surrounded by broken reef, the island had the profile of a sleeping sea monster. Later I was to find its nearly identical twin in Tutuila, the main island of American Samoa, even with a similar fiord-like harbour that nearly cuts it in two. As we rounded its western tip in the early morning, the rising sun was still low over the water and directly ahead, the colour gradients that are the signposts of navigation in coral seas were obscured by a blaze of glittering reflections. The captain, with the second mate at his shoulder, had much trouble picking his way into the lagoon.

It was only when I could see the land from up-sun that the full horror of a tropical cyclone grew larger by the minute in the lenses of my binoculars. I saw the coconut palms along the shore of crunchy coral sand flayed and worn out, like old dish mops. Stripped of leaves, the bigger trees thrust silvered branches skywards like a forest of driftwood. I saw entire hillsides scalped clean by a battle-axe wind, their red soil dissolved and carried away by days of cascading rain. All vegetation, where it remained, seemed abraded nearly to death as if the sky had rained weedkiller.

Then, as we sailed closer, I saw whole trees up-ended, houses standing without roofs, concrete foundations swept clean of everything but lavatory bowls. Cooking fires smoked outside army tents air-dropped as a relief measure and now, six months later, still serving as homes.

On Tanna Bob Paul had shown me the stump of a coconut palm cut clean through by a sheet of corrugated iron that had blown a distance of only twenty feet. Here, on a brightly sunny morning with not a cloud in the sky, I saw what a cyclone could do to an entire island.

Cyclone Meli had been vicious from the beginning but nobody was unduly worried because she was moving eastwards, out of the Fiji group. These revolving killer storms travel fast across the South Pacific between November and late March, and this was the last few days of the season. But suddenly, on a Sunday night, the storm-centre had turned south. By Monday morning it was heading down through the scattered islands of the Lau group and by Tuesday the outlook was very different: Meli was heading nearly due west, plunging back through the Fiji islands. In Suva yellow flags were hoisted, schools and government offices closed early so people could prepare their homes, hurricane shutters were erected. A Nauruan freighter decided to ride it out in the open sea and left the harbour. Weather bulletins were broadcast every half hour: people were concerned but not frightened.

On Viti Levu during that Tuesday night three people were killed. The freighter was thrown high and dry on a reef. A Korean fishing vessel went missing with all hands. By 2 pm on Wednesday all warnings were cancelled as Meli curved away to the south-west and dissipated. Not until the weekend did reports of disaster begin to trickle in, for it was not realised that radios and aerials had been swept away. A Fiji Air pilot circling Nyau Island saw neither buildings left standing nor vegetation: the storm surge created by Meli had coincided with the highest tide of the year and capped by terrific seas had swept to the top of the island. Two schoolteachers had packed their tiny babies in suitcases and scrambled to a cave at the highest point when the in-rushing sea chased them out of their homes. Six people were killed and the islanders had only hot water to live on for five days until their plight was noticed and they were all evacuated.

On the small island of Ono within Kadavu's lagoon, the Methodist Church had been the first building to crumble and the people shelter-ing within it had crawled across to the more solid Catholic Church which had served as a reliable hurricane shelter for sixty-nine years. Its heavy limestone walls collapsed inwards, crushing and smothering twenty-one people. Survivors lived for days on a bag of rice and a tin of biscuits, all that was left of the village shop, and did not have the strength to dig out the bodies. An American yachtsman was washed up on the beach from his trimaran that had been anchored in the lagoon but his father and fiancée were never seen again.

At Vunisea, the principal village of Kadavu where we landed from the *Cagi Donu* in a blue and yellow surfboat piled high with bags and cartons of rations, I walked up the bare-earth track with Mamasa. The village sprawled over the knobs and hollows of a valley a little back from the shore. There was a lot of springy grass so the village – like a camp ground – had a pleasing, sunny aspect, the more so now that the crowns of so many palms had been torn off or mutilated.

When we reached the government station Waqu Naivalururua, the district officer, despatched messengers to inform the surrounding villages that the rations had come. He was a grey-haired, dignified man whose bare feet padded silently on the steaming earth as he walked through the village of tents and bare foundations and told me the story of Meli. He had himself lost both his elderly parents, carried away in their house which was picked up bodily in the mighty wind and whirled out to sea; four other relatives had slipped through the open door as the house began to glide from its foundations and lived to tell the tale; a baby two months old had fallen out of the flying house and landed head-first in some rushes, and located next day by the sound of her crying.

The other sixty-four households in the village had crammed into the five strongest buildings. Like forwards in a rugby scrum the strongest men had put their shoulders to the walls to stop them caving in, and clung to the purloins to hold down the roofs. A genial middle-aged man checking the rations as they were carried into the copra shed on the shore was one of those who lost his house. "Nature made a split-second decision and she took my house, just like that!" he explained, snapping his fingers to illustrate the speed with which his wooden bungalow had launched in the air leaving only a few suitcases scattered in the long grass.

The agricultural officer, St Paul Tikoicolo, told me that his water tank had simply disappeared although it was weighed down with 800 gallons of water. The noise of the wind was so great, he recalled, that when the concrete chimney fell on the roof he did not hear it. His office had flown away like a Wright Brothers aeroplane and crashed on the next hill.

Next to the copra shed was the school where the roof of the classrooms was ripped off and Esala Masi, the headmaster, had pushed his twenty-seven boarding pupils, his teachers and their families, under the floorboards. Crawling into the two-foot gap they spent nine hours until daylight, the headmaster ceaselessly scanning the nearby ground with torches in case a tidal wave swept in and drowned them all.

The islanders were rebuilding the school first, then would tackle their homes. They worked hard, streaming with sweat, but walked with a light step. Then a procession of women came down from the village, massive motherly figures in bright ankle-length dresses and head scarves. They came in pairs, each couple holding between them a fishing net rolled up on stout sticks. Stately, almost in slow motion, they waded shoulder-deep into the lagoon. When the procession had formed an arc of nets out from the beach, children ran splashing into the shallows to chase the fish out to the waiting nets. With deft fingers and loud shrieks, the women picked the tiny fish flickering in the fine mesh and put them in plaited baskets hanging from their shoulders. Then they filed ashore and, in the same slow motion, repeated the beautiful aqua-ballet not once but a dozen times. The scene was timeless and heartening, a demonstration of indomitable spirit. Hurricanes may come and hurricanes may go, but there are always fish in the lagoon. Then I realised all the fisher-women were middle aged or elderly, as were the men rebuilding their village and unloading the ship. Where was the youth of the island? They were in Suva, I was told. Their dream was discos, bright lights, and wage-paying jobs, even if it meant labouring for Indians.

That the raw beauty of the islands is periodically fed into Nature's shredder is a feature of South Seas life which few romantics remember but no sailor ever forgets. All the blue-water dreamers in this part of the world have but one aim, which is to get the hell out of here before the cyclone season begins in November, and most head south to summer in New Zealand. Most cruising yachts represent the total of their owners' worldly goods and they are seldom insured. But the harvest of the hurricane which means death or disaster to some, brings opportunity in true adventure-book style to others, as I discovered. After the *Cagi Donu* berthed at Suva I headed south myself for an interlude in New Zealand, and on my first morning back was shopping in the market for a handful of dangerous-looking bush chillis with which to revive the hotel's pallid sauces when an eddy of the human tide threw me against a familiar Kon Tiki of the population fleet: George Budd, the American lone-sailor who had shipped with me on *Hawk*'s last voyage.

George was a slightly built, grizzled, sun-wrinkled bachelor just short of sixty whose wide and easy smile reminded me of Fred Astaire at his best. He had been wandering the Pacific in his 32-foot ketch *Spindrift* since an apartment block was built across the road from his house in California and blocked his view of the ocean. He had surrendered the honorary post in the Boy Scouts which had occupied him since his retirement from the military, and set sail for the wide blue horizon. His yacht was the only one I ever saw equipped with a brick fireplace, a miniature one installed as something of a joke to set off the tiny pot-belly stove. The stove actually did operate and was the origin, indirectly, of his nastiest moment in three years of cruising. A customs officer in Papua-New Guinea had searched the boat for dope and found a miniature Presto log (made of compressed sawdust and kerosene) for burning in the stove. He kept sniffing the log, wrinkling his nose, sniffing it again until the sweat stood out on his forehead. "This is making me sick," he told George angrily.

"Stop sniffing it then," responded the skipper. The log was confiscated for analysis and three days later George was arrested for importing marijuana. After a few days charges were dropped when it was found the customs officer had falsified the scientific report. George had sailed away fast. "If any dope had been put in that log I could have lost my boat, been locked up for ten years and, in some countries, I might have been beheaded, for God's sake. It makes you very choosy about places you put into, believe me."

Now, George was listing under a heavy load of shopping. We took a bus the five miles out of town to the Tradewinds Hotel where cruising yachts anchor off the swimming pool, sheltered by a pair of tiny islands. Before getting into the dinghy he spread the vegetables on the grass, put the wrapping paper in a trash can, and searched every item for cockroaches and creepy-crawlies. In the market he had bought five big carrots, five red-hot peppers, six bananas, three cucumbers, twelve tomatoes, six egg plants and a pound of green beans, all fresh, cost: $1.32. Then he had gone into a grocery and bought a small packet of cornflakes, cost: $1.50. Here was the South Sea dream in another guise, the ultimate contrast to the savagery of Meli.

But I was in for another shock. As we rowed out to *Spindrift* I saw with growing horror that the stout little ketch was a wreck. Her rigging was a slack tangle. One side of her hull was scraped bare and there were big gouges in her planks. The main hatch was stove in. "What the hell happened?" I asked.

George rested on his oars and glanced over his shoulder to check his course. "Took a short cut getting here," he explained. "Went up on a reef. Got off again. Survived. And here we are ..."

The neat cabin was heaped with junk as if great hands had picked up the entire boat and shaken it. Which was pretty much what had happened. Making for Suva from New Caledonia, George had struck the tail end of a storm. For five days he had not been able to get a sextant fix of his position and had sailed by dead reckoning. At a quarter past ten in the evening, dodging along under plain sail with his dinner in the microwave, he was in the cabin talking on his ham radio, gassing to somebody called Bruce in Sydney, Australia, when there was a bone-jarring jolt, the yacht was thrown violently on its side, and water poured over the deck. "My God, I've hit a reef!" George yelled into the mike. "But there isn't a reef, not out here!"

"Okay, George old mate, keep calm," the far-away voice responded. "Tell me, where *are* you?"

Scared, horrified, dazed, George was learning how it feels to be among a mouthful of cornflakes. Molars of coral gnawed at the timbers of his little ship. The roar of smothering water was loud in his ears. Walls of milk-white spume spurted over the yacht and cascaded down the open hatch. George reasoned that a current must have set him to the north. He could only have hit Viti Levu, somewhere on the southwest corner. So this was the information he passed along the line. George located the dangling mike in the darkness and informed Bruce in Sydney. Bruce telephoned the rescue centre at Canberra which called the airport at Nadi which advised the Marine Department at Suva, and it was scarcely 45 minutes after *Spindrift* had hit the reef that the telephone rang beside Ian Lockley's bed. Where most people have blinds on spring rollers Ian Lockley has Admiralty charts. He located the reported position on the chart and within the hour his salvage launch *Salmar* was under way.

All night George sat by his radio in his canted cabin listening to the cruel grating of planks on coral as the yacht was pushed 150 feet over the reef. At the time of the incident he had been speaking on one of several recognised ham radio networks in the Pacific. Called the Gunkholers' Net it was orchestrated for the benefit of lonely yachtsmen by an American woman called Joyce in her Chinese junk in Honiara, Solomon Islands. All over the hemisphere gunkholers tuned into an unfolding drama and they took it in turns – Joyce in Honiara, Bruce in Sydney, Gordon in Mooloolabah, and others – to keep the chat going and George's spirits high. When daylight came the tide had left the yacht high and dry. By ten the *Salmar* had arrived and two salvage men came in by rubber boat but *Spindrift* was too big to be hauled off so they radioed the big salvage tug *Pacific Salvor*, on standby at Suva. Scarcely sleeping as he camped in the canted cabin of his stricken ship, George spent another twenty-four hours talking to his friends until the big tug arrived and a hawser was made fast to the yacht's mast. With agonising noises she was dragged across the coral but when she was on the edge of the reef two giant waves more than fifteen feet high fell on the deck. George was all but washed overboard in the flurry. When he spat the water out of his mouth he saw that his boat which had survived so much with hardly a leak was now a pretty mess. Everything had been wiped off the deck. The foredeck was depressed an inch and a half. Fifteen ribs were cracked.

"But it might have been worse," George said, as I passed up his groceries from the dinghy. "So far this season ten yachts have gone up on the reef in the Fiji group and I was the only one to get off, so you have to count your blessings."

The image of a man with a rolled-up chart beside his telephone triggered a vision of a bucko South Seas character if ever there was one. When I set out to track down Ian Lockley, whose tugs had pulled George off the reef, I did not have far to look. His bungalow with its broad verandahs and garden of tropical flowers sat on a knoll overlooking the anchorage where *Spindrift* and twenty or thirty other cruising yachts were lying. Ian had the kind of jaw that characterised the hero of every adventure story, though his was disguised beneath a half-frame beard. He had the shoulders of a rugby lock-forward, the handshake of a steel erector, the balding pate of a clever physician and the heavy black spectacles of an accountant. He also had a sweet wife, two lovely children, and a tale to tell, not for the faint hearted, about how he had recently been "laid up and put off m' breakfast a bit" when a steel wire between a wrecked ship and the big tug happened to part. The end of the wire cable had whipped through the air, catching him across both legs and bending his knees – backwards. He showed me pictures of the Nauruan freighter, high and dry on the reef after Cyclone Meli. In the photographs Ian himself was standing barely knee-deep in water at the big ship's bow. Yet he had hauled the vessel bodily into deep water. How on earth was it possible?

"Well, it's not that hard," he said modestly. "All you have to do is get hold of some old hulk and wire it up with lots of blocks and tackles to the tug. You sink the hulk outside the reef, in very deep water, so it acts as an anchor. Then you give a heave-ho with the tug. And off she comes. If there aren't too many holes in her bottom she stays afloat, and you're on a pig's back. How about a 'Cardi and Coke?"

This piece of masterly understatement took an evening to explain, as we sat with dogs and children and long, dewy glasses of Bacardi watching twilight settle over the distant jagged skyline of Beqa. Ian had served an apprenticeship repairing heavy engines in Brisbane, then been engineer in a launch conducting seismic and mineral surveys in the little known corners of the Western Pacific. In his free time he had dived on ships and aircraft wrecked during the Second World War and collected various kinds of machine-guns which he restored to their original working order. With a weekend to fill, ten years before, he had dived on the wreck of the big freighter *Ragna Ringdal* which had hit a reef in Fijian waters and slid off into deep water, scattering 700 tons of aluminium ingots over the ocean floor. It was the chance Ian had been waiting for. "There was all that metal lying around and I thought we may as well go and get some of it. The bank manager thought the idea was so crazy he might as well back it. So we bought the *Salmar* and did the job in the hurricane season, because that's when the sea is usually calmest – as long as a hurricane doesn't come along."

When the weather did turn bad they worked on two ships on another part of the reef, a US Liberty ship and the naval tug that had gone to salvage her. But here they had a problem. How to get the ship's propeller boss, five tons of solid brass worth about $5,000, a quarter of a mile over the reef? Then Ian thought of hitting it like a golfball with a drive from "a good sock of jelly." It was a hole in three. Ringing like a huge gong, the massive propeller covered with barnacles described a perfect parabola and on the third shot splashed into the sea from where it was retrieved with the salvage launch's lifting gear.

Having established themselves and paid their bills, Ian and his men took every job going. At Ono-i-lau, one of Fiji's furthest islands, they dived for an anchor lost by an inter-island ship and found thirteen others which they collected and sold for scrap. They blew channels through reefs to improve access for small boats, using explosive made from fertilizer and diesel fuel. When a bulldozer fell off a barge into seventy feet of water Ian dismantled it (a month-long job in a workshop) in eight days flat – underwater an engineer can hang in liquid space to get the job done, and force reluctant nuts and bolts with a judicious plug of gelignite. Then came Hurricane Bebe.

While most people dived for shelter, and mariners hid their vessels in the mangrove swamps, Ian and his mate put on wet suits and went for a ride round the harbour. It was one of the worst hurricanes Fiji had ever known. As the eye of the storm passed over, Ian pulled two yachts off the reef. On one of them, a schooner, the crew were too blotto even to take a tow-line when he swam over, and they told him to go away. Two years later, when Ian learned from the harbour-master that a yacht was on the reef, he found it was the same schooner which had sailed on round the world with a different name and a different owner. When Ian asked for a contribution towards expenses the skipper paid him double, saying, "I believe this boat owes you."

The same hurricane delivered a barge of some size to the main door of Naussori Airport, which is on the banks of a river. The Marine Department wanted to cut the barge into pieces small enough to truck to a shipyard for reassembly. One night of very heavy rain gave Ian a bright idea. Would the river flood again? He hired two bulldozers and waited by the airport. The river did overflow its banks and before dawn the barge was tied up at the town wharf. Ian put on his best shirt, shorts, long socks and shoes and paid a call. "What's it worth to deliver your barge in one piece?"

"That's a silly question because it's quite impossible."

"Okay, so what if I do all the cutting and trucking and deliver the sections to the yard for reassembly?"

'Say $4,300?"

"I accept: it's a deal," said Ian. Adding, after a moment, that the barge was tied up at the yard already. He got $3,700 of the money.

As Betty set dinner at a large round table on the verandah, Ian was still sunburned from his last sortie to the Solomons where three oriental fishing vessels had run up on the same reef within sight of each other. When a fourth ran aground a few miles away a government minister broadcast a message saying that a team of native warriors were to arm themselves and prevent Ian's team from removing the wreck. Ian radioed his tug urgently, telling the skipper not to mess about. 'While the bushies were doing their war dances," he said, "we were quickly putting the wires on the wreck and we pulled her off just as the first canoes arrived, filled with black men in war-paint and waving bows and arrows. Usually, when a ship slides off the reef, we round up and sort things out. This time we just kept on towing and didn't stop until we were over the horizon."

7

BLUE LAGOON

BEACHCOMBERS IN BLIGH WATERS

The canvas tore from my grip, splitting a fingernail, and whipped thunderously. Wedged by both knees on my lurching perch, I grabbed the flogging canvas in both arms and flung my weight on it, taming it. The violent motion made me queasy and I clung on for dear life while the imprisoned canvas rippled, flexing its muscles for another escape. Stinging rain drove into my eyes. My hair streamed in the wind. But this was no passage around the Horn by windjammer, however. I was riding in a Fiji bus.

The buses in Fiji are like mobile balconies, with no glass in their windows. In rain the passengers spring for the furled tarpaulins like sailors for the yard arm. As the studs or straps along the bottom of screens are invariably missing, those sitting nearest the outside must hold the thing down with their arms. If one person in front relaxes his grip the wind gets under the tarpaulin and the whole thing runs amok like a t'gallant in a gale. Rain sprays in, with jets of muddy water thrown up from the front wheels on the corners. The driver keeps up his reckless swooping pace round steep blind bends in the gravel road. You never know what will scatter in your path – rooster, buffalo or mobile library.

The seats are narrow benches upholstered with Formica and so close that even diminutive Punjabi women, their silken saris billowing in the slipstream, sit sideways. At one stop we bought bananas, ten for ten cents, from a roadside stall. At another there were large slices of water melon, five cents a piece. The real benefit of the rolled-up screens now became apparent, as we clattered beneath sunnier skies spitting volleys of pips over our shoulders.

Facing the prospect of a lonely long weekend, for Monday was a public holiday, with little to do but sit by a hotel swimming pool or cruise in a glass-bottomed boat, I decided to be marooned on a desert island for the duration and to get there – the first stage, at any rate – by bus.

Viti Levu is nearly round, about eighty miles across, and encircled by one diabolical road. Lautoka, the main town on the western side, could be reached in about five hours by the Queen's Highway, which follows the southern shore known in the tourist brochures as The Coral Coast. Or the more adventurous could take the King's Highway, the longer northern route. When I enquired about it I thought the Indian clerk at the bus station had said the trip took seven hours. It was when I had been soaked by rain, choked by dust, and rattled until my teeth felt loose, that I realised the clerk could not have said seven hours but eleven.

The Fiji archipelago lies midway between the Equator and the Tropic of Capricorn, and straddles the 180th meridian. Until the international dateline was kinked to give the whole group the same calendar day, one canny Chinese whose shop was bisected by the meridian, kept ahead of Sabbath closing by moving his stock from one end of his counter to the other. In Fiji, remarked W. S. Gilbert, if you could not kick a bore into the middle of next week you could at least propel him a considerable distance in that direction. But it is a surprise to find on a South Sea island a river all of 120 miles long. The Rewa twists out of the high spine of the island behind Suva, where rainfall is measured in metres, and swoops seawards in wide, serpentine loops through a delta of marshes and mangroves. The road which follows its valley halfway across the island is even more of a snake but suddenly it crosses the watershed. From thick, tangled bush and muddy roads you emerge on rolling open farmland where roads are dusty, the soil is a vivid orange, and the fields are silvery green with a tall spiky grass that I realised, on noticing the faintly sweet smell in the dry air, was young sugar cane. Often the highways are lined with majestic mango trees that have sprung up, it is said, from pips dropped by travellers. Narrow-gauge railways criss-cross the canefields, baby locos hauling long trains of little trucks loaded with cane stocks. With only a fraction of the rainfall and little run-off on this side of the island, the water is clean and beaches white. From the blue sky blazes the kind of heat in which you fry rather than steam, but the nights are pleasanter.

Thick smoke, from fires lit to clear the mature cane of undergrowth and snakes prior to cutting, filled my room during the night. I had switched off the noisy air conditioner and opened the windows wide, which was my usual practice because the body seems to cope better with heat during the day if it is not refrigerated at night. A sick buffalo grunted all night like an English Channel lighthouse in fog. Cane engines rattled along nearby, hooting mournfully. In the morning every level surface in the room was covered in specks of black ash and I smelled like the perennial bonfire in my father-in-law's garden.

The holiday weekend was being launched at the sugar-mill town of Lautoka with a hockey tournament. Scores of tall, lithe Indians dashed about like antelopes in short pyjamas, earnestly hitting white balls with curved sticks and occasionally hopping over the dry brown grass grimacing and clutching their shins. It was here, only slightly bemused by the kava he had been expected to drink as the ceremonial opener of the proceedings, that I found Dan Costello.

A seventeen-stone, blue-eyed and grey-bearded giant of Irish stock, Dan was a *kai viti* (European born in Fiji) who had made something of a fortune by marooning people on desert islands. The son of a cattle rancher, he had started in 1965 doing weekend cruises in a shark-fishing motor launch called *Bulumakaw*, the universal Pacific word for anything to do with cattle, be it cavorting round a paddock on four legs or sliced rare-medium-well on a silver dish. Popular calls on these weekend trips were the tiny sand cays, capped by groves of palms, an hour's cruise out on the sheltered lagoon. So he leased two of them from native chiefs and established a resort business that is something between Robinson Crusoe and country club. Each five-acre spot – it is hardly big enough to be called an island – is rimmed by a broad fringe of dazzling sand. The "island" is tufted with palms shading *bures* joined by coral paths. Beachcomber Island has two twenty-six-bunk dormitories and no social graces but the rate is $17 a day with all the food you can eat. Treasure Island, less than a mile distant over the water, is more up-market: it has a restaurant with a menu, and its thatched *bures* are as well equipped as standard motel rooms. There are other variations on the theme along the Coral Coast and on other islands nearby – Mana, Castaway and Plantation – where tourists can find every level of accommodation from luxurious hotels to self-catering grass huts.

Diversions on a desert island are few, so quite a crowd stood on the shore as Dan zoomed in from the anchored launch, his bright red *sulu* flapping in the breeze. As King Beachcomber splashed regally ashore a strange figure, roaring like the buffalo in the smoke, clasped him in a bear hug and lifted him off the ground. This was Jerry, five feet tall and nearly as round.

I glimpsed a moon face decorated by a short black beard turning grey on one side only, and a floppy straw hat with its broad brim pinned up at the front and sporting a wilted red hibiscus. Jerry was in the rag trade in Sydney and this was his fourteenth three-week holiday on Beachcomber Island.

For a moment the stout men swayed and strained, each going redder in the face by the second and smacking kisses on the other's forehead. Then Dan lifted Jerry off his feet, danced round in a full circle, and with a triumphant bellow dumped him in the sea. "Lovely man, that," he told me, puffing only slightly as we walked bare-footed up the sand to the thatch-shaded bar. The manager who met us there, wearing sun-glasses, a *sulu* and an impressive suntan, was Max, also a Fiji-born European. In mid-conversation he suddenly cowered, then screamed. All at once there was a rattling noise behind me, a loud woosh, and a distinct chill around my neck as a bucketful of water and ice cubes went past my ear like a projectile and caught Max full in the face. Beachcomber Island is that sort of place.

But even on a "desert" island in the South Seas you cannot escape the long reach of the public health inspector. He was an Indian gent who insisted, Dan told me, that the sandy space of raked sand that served as a dance floor should be tiled from bamboo wall to bamboo wall. "You see, Sah," he had explained, "everybody will be spitting." To save his face Dan agreed to meet him halfway, which explained the foot-wide spitting trough, like a brown-tiled urinal, that surrounded the bar. The dining area on the island was nothing but picnic tables under straw hats, but regulations stipulated that every hotel dining room must have a tiled floor measuring at least eight feet by thirteen. And there it was, that odd bit of pavement scattered with sand, the footprint on this desert island of a public health inspector.

The worst thing that could happen to you on this island, I discovered the hard way, was to catch a squirt of lime-juice on your sunburn blisters. The visitors were mostly young Australians and New Zealanders, especially airline staff on cheap tickets. The girls were languid, toasted and dressed like a salad in half a pint of oil. Their boy friends had gold bars swinging from little chains in the hair on their chests and when they weren't as somnolent as lizards in the sun were forever playing volleyball: Fiji v. the rest of the world. Only Max looked as if he had a pulse in his wrist as he organised his army of beaming Fijians to rake the sands for coral fragments and cigarette butts. Another daily ritual was the arrival of the water barge, towed by the old *Bulumakaw*. A gas-masked figure with an engine on his back daily blew clouds of pesticide smoke into the sand. Almost I could hear Robinson Crusoe flinching in his grave. But there was a lovely sense of humour in the place, thanks to Dan's Irish touch. He would greet Australian arrivals gravely. "I'm terribly sorry, the beer is rather cold because some idiot put it in the fridge. Wait just a minute and I'll put it out in the sun for you ..." Lunch was a fiercely hot curry with mountains of fresh pineapple and passionfruit as large as oranges. As we shuffled through the sand, heaping our plates, Jerry pulled the bow lacing up the modesty of the beautiful girl in front. Instinctively she pressed her arms to her sides to keep her scrap of bikini in place, then she turned around to see what was happening. Whereupon Jerry nimbly re-tied the laces in front. The girl was helpless and the little round man nuzzled her breast with the tip of his button nose. "My old man always taught me," he said, "to keep my nose to the rhinestone."

All next day I swam, lounged, ate, swam again. It was, as one Australian described it, another shitty day in paradise. In the late evening I circumnavigated the entire island, wading calf-deep in the shallows. The moon twinkled on the calm sea and was bright enough in the purple sky for the overleaning palms to cast crisp shadows on the pearly sand. The distant beat of disco music emphasised my loneliness. Like Alexander Selkirk, the real-life model for Robinson Crusoe, I was growing dejected, languid and melancholy. For me, paradise could never be the equivalent of indolence. For the first time I became truly homesick, not out of sentiment for my family, although that played a part, but out of a sense of neurotic need for activity. I thought of the lawn which would need mowing, the potatoes in the vegetable garden which needed heaping up. I might have been more content had Max asked me to help rake the sand, or to dry the dishes. The island was like a cruise ship, detached from land, disconnected from any sense of responsibility, poised between befores and afters. But unlike a ship this island was aimless, going nowhere.

When I climbed aboard the glass-bottomed boat after a relaxing but inconsequential couple of days, Max's protagonist in the water fight – a QANTAS chef on honeymoon – was also leaving. The manager waded out to shake his hand and as soon as he had a firm grip dragged him overboard into the sea. There he submerged, fully clothed, with a satisfactory howl of rage. The two of them wrestled in the waves, the trippers cheered, and the launch tooted. Steaming contentedly, the honeymooner left to catch his plane and I took the Air Pacific shuttle back to Suva.

Trevor Withers was a crisp old man living alone in a back room of the Defence Club in Suva. He met me at the top of the stairs in a white safari tunic with a top pocket full of pens, a batik cravat, and his thin white hair parted down the middle and stuck down. He walked badly, shuffling with two sticks, and as he lowered himself painfully into a deckchair he pulled up his trouser cuffs to show both legs scarred, swollen and discoloured from the knee down. "That's what coral does to you," he explained. "Ten years ago I was diving under my boat and was chased to the surface by a barracuda. On the way up I banged my head on a coral ledge and ripped my legs open trying to get clear. My legs became allergic to sea-water and have never properly healed. I had to sell my boat and now I'm on the beach waiting to die. Well, almost."

I remembered how my own small coral cut, inflicted in the New Hebrides, had taken three weeks to heal. What I should have done, Trevor Withers reckoned, was grit my teeth and scrub the wound with a sterilised toothbrush.

A peppery old chap with a sense of humour, he was a New Zealand lawyer who had come to seek his fortune in Fiji soon after the war. After an unsuccessful venture in tuna fishing he had bought a crash boat, fitted it out with accommodation for four, crewed it with two handsome Fijians, and gone into the cruise ship business. That was in 1950, when the world knew of South Sea islands only what it had seen in *Mutiny on the Bounty*. The area he chose was the seventy-mile chain of twenty-two beautiful islands, half of them inhabited, called the Yasawas. He stole the name from the film being made there at the time, called *Blue Lagoon*. And to add panache he signed himself Captain Trevor Withers KCMC. The initials, he admitted with a blimpish guffaw, fooled most people most of the time. They stood for Kindly Call Me Captain.

For four months he sailed from Lautoka every Monday and returned every Thursday without carrying a single passenger but he had to keep going to show his flag among the islands where he had made special arrangements with the village chiefs to provide feasts and dances. He was down to his last shilling and preparing to sell out for what he could get when an old friend in Suva offered a proposition. An American colonel and his wife were coming out for a visit. Would Trev give them a royal good time, best fishing, best champagne, best of everything, but get them out of the light?

It was the life-saver he needed. He went through his boat scrubbing and painting everything in sight. He stripped and re-assembled the engine, and stocked it with liquor and supplies. Three days before the guests arrived everything was ship-shape but for one detail. He told his crewman, Peni, to put a nice coat of pale green Dulux paint on the wooden seat of the lavatory. Then he went to Suva to collect the Very Important Persons.

When he returned with the colonel and his wife, Trevor put his head into the WC compartment and the seat winked at him, gleaming with gloss. "You're a good and reliable boy, Peni, I'm going to give you another ten bob a week," he said.

They hit a school of tuna in the first ten minutes. The colonel caught a fish. His wife caught a fish. The colonel caught another and had a bourbon. His wife had a bloody mary. The sea twinkled, the sun shone and the high Yasawas beckoned. After a time the Colonel contentedly left his game-fishing chair, picked up a copy of *Time* that was in the wheelhouse, and went to the lavatory.

Fifteen minutes later Ratu Veniasi, the mate, took Trevor's arm and whispered, "Come quickly, Cap'n, colonel in trouble." Putting his ear to the ventilator of the foredeck Trevor heard angry shouts. "Get me out of here! Help!" He rushed below, knocked on the WC door, and asked what the matter was. "For Chrissake get me out, I can't move!"

"Listen, colonel, just slide back the shiny bolt on the inside of the door, and . . ."

"I know what a goddam latch is but I can't reach it!"

The mate took the colonel's wife to the bow on the pretext of seeing some dolphins, Peni brought a mallet and smashed down the door. A big man, red-faced and in pain, the colonel was sitting on the throne with his shorts around his ankles and the magazine screwed into a ball between his feet. A thin trickle of blood ran down the outside of the pan.

The colonel was very angry and very stuck. When the skipper, standing no nonsense, took the colonel's hands and tugged, the old soldier yelped and the flow of blood increased. "Look, sir, I can't understand what has happened. We will have to undo the seat. You must lean back and suck your tummy in so I can kneel on your thighs and reach over your shoulders to release the pin."

The trick required two expeditions. First to unbolt the nut on one side, then to pull out the pin from the other side. Both men streamed with sweat as they struggled in the small lurching compartment. When at last the seat was detached, the colonel kicked off his shorts and was led to the stern deck while Peni found some turpentine and a pad of cotton-wool.

At the polished table in the Defence Club Trevor paused in his tale, pensive as he poured his beer into a glass. Then he leaned towards me and dropped his voice to a confidential whisper. "There is one piece of practical advice I can offer you as a result of this experience," he went on. "Never – I mean never, John, old friend – *never* apply raw turps to a pair of naked balls."

The colonel had let out a mighty scream and kicked out. His foot skidded on the blood on deck and he fell. The lavatory seat clipped the fishing chair and was torn off, leaving two matching crescents of raw flesh gushing blood.

Hearing the scream, his wife rushed aft. The colonel was laid tenderly on his bunk, face down. Trevor had already turned the boat around but now he radioed for a doctor but none was available so he contacted a pharmacist friend and arranged for dressings to be rushed out by speedboat. The colonel sipped a bourbon through a bent straw. His wife had a bloody mary. The colonel had another bourbon. Then she started to giggle. The colonel was peeved. "I don't see what's so goddam funny!"

"Darling, I was just thinking," she told him. "When you step out of the shower at the golf club and they see your scars, what are you going to tell them?"

"Why, that I was attacked by a toilet seat in the South Seas. What else?"

"Oh no, my dear, you'd never dare."

After collecting the parcel of dressings Trevor turned his boat round again and the two-week voyage was completed smoothly. It was only when the luggage was being handed ashore, and the colonel tipped each of the boys with a five-pound note, that the skipper's complete mystification was resolved. Peni had been getting strangely agitated and now he spoke up. "Colonel, sir, one thing I must tell you, excuse me. You think your accident was all the captain's fault, No sir, it was my fault. You see, the captain told me to paint the seat but just before you arrived I saw a mark so I opened the Dulux and put on just one more thin coat with the paintbrush. Sir, the captain was very pleased and raised my pay ten bob a week but I am a Christian and Christ tells us to confess our sins, so . . ."

The colonel flung his arm round Peni's shoulders and said, "Well, son I'm a Christian too, and the Bible tells us to forgive trespassers." And he pushed another fiver into Peni's top pocket.

For obvious reasons my first check, when I boarded the Blue Lagoon cruise vessel in Lautoka a couple of days later, was the lavatory seat. The 450-ton *Oleanda*, one of six in the fleet and built locally, was like a miniature liner and carried forty passengers. Skipper Rob Southey reversed the pretty little ship nearly beneath the overhanging rusty bow of a Japanese trampship loading logs, Fiji's developing new export. Then we ventured out on a heat-bowl of mirrored blue, the Yasawas jutting like cardboard cut-outs of dream islands on the north-west horizon, thirty miles off.

Fiji had first been named after Captain Bligh, who had sailed through the islands, charting as he went, on his remarkable 41-day voyage to Timor in a small open boat after he was turned adrift from the *Bounty* by Fletcher Christian and the mutineers in 1789. Three years later he returned and made a more thorough survey. The name which stuck, however, was the soft-spoken Tongan pronounciation noted by Captain Cook of the word *Viti*, meaning land. Bligh's name endures on the chart of these waters around the Yasawas, where the indomitable captain in his crowded little boat was chased by a canoe filled with natives. He must have had a brisk wind behind him to have given a fast canoe the slip, perhaps one like today's I thought. At first the waves made little white surges in the growing breeze but as we ran out from behind the lee of the main island and hit the full blast of the tradewind the waves became energetic and spray cracked across the deck. As we ran through a narrow reef passage the rough sea fell dead calm as abruptly as if we had shut a door astern. Pale-faced passengers staggered to the bar to buy drinks with coloured beads. In the palm-fringed bays we saw the *bures* of little villages, their sailing cutters moored off and canoes drawn up on the sand. What could have been seals bobbing in the water proved to be young women diving for shells. Young bloods in the crew leapt on the rail, their pale blue *sulus* rattling in the breeze, and whistled and beat their chests and got cheeky signals in return. Then the *Oleanda* zig-zagged between shelves of coral that showed like dark purple mushrooms in the clear water and headed into a perfect bay. The anchor rattled down. The ship turned on top of it and reversed into the beach. Splash went the tin boat on the water. A rope was run ashore and made fast to a palm. We lay stern to the beach, hardly thirty feet from it. I dived over the side and swam ashore.

The water was milk warm, the sand lambswool white and hearth-rug soft. Out of the blue sky blazed that thick, pulsating warmth that licks up the back of your legs when you toast your bottom before a log fire. In a few moments the moisture was a dry salty powder on my skin. I followed a track through the palms to the windward side and sat astride a palm growing almost horizontally out over the water before it bent upwards in an elegant curve, like the bow of a ship. It swayed as the strong breeze tried to turn its umbrella of fronds inside out, and when it dipped my ankles were submerged into the wavelets. In my polaroids the steel-bright reflections became a carpet of vivid greens and blues. For a long time I remained there, thinking of my fellow passengers. They were a strange lot, but the mixture was typical of any tourist honeypot. Two wealthy widows with sugar-bag complexions, funny hats and heavy diamonds, who danced together; from Sydney. A tall and hairy-legged computer man whose spectacles darkened in the sun and his merry IBM wife whom he called Huggy Pair (a US brand of women's tights); San Francisco. A thick-set, moustachioed, polyester-clad marketing man with olive-skinned wife who tied her thin bones together with string instead of wearing clothes; Toronto. An engaging, pot-bellied, barrel-chested man in a surfer's hat who always had a bottle of cold beer in one hand and a high-grade book in the other, and his Polish wife in a track suit; from some red-dust town in Greater Australia. The jovial radio-station engineer and his motherly wife, whose sunburn turned third degree; Sydney. Two pink-skinned, floppy, cackling young men called Bruce and Wayne who wore athletic shorts and coloured vests and admitted they came to Fiji because they could get away with doing things they could not do at home, and whom the widows christened Bloody Hyenas; barmen from Newcastle, Australia. The stolid honeymoon couple, he a mortgage executive and she a trained nurse devouring Barbara Cartland romances as if each one were as brief as a Snoopy strip; Moosejaw, Canada. And the rest. All of us pursuing one kind of South Seas dream or another. And when at last I slid from my bucking coconut palm and returned to their company I couldn't help thinking it was a mighty far cry from Bongabonga.

A freckly girl who proved to be a newly graduated doctor had left her studious boy friend dozing on the sand and also gone off alone, as I had. But she had encountered a well muscled Fijian youth wearing a *sulu* and a shark's tooth necklace. He carried a cane knife in one hand and a coconut in the other. A true-life figment of a maiden's dreams? Perhaps. He certainly acted the part, for he flashed a brilliant sugar-cane smile and asked conversationally, "Please can I fuck you?"

"I *beg* your pardon?" I could imagine the freckled hand clutching the sunburned throat; she was a nice girl.

Again the soft voice, the smile, "Please, can I . . . ?"

The lady doctor took to her heels and fled along the beach to the picnic tables where she arrived flushed and bothered, and fortuitously was given something else to think about when one of the friendly crew asked her to lance his boil.

Knowing nothing of this at the time I noticed she had a snorkel and flippers wrapped in a towel, which she was not using, so I went over and asked conversationally, "Would you mind if . . . ?"

She shot me an alarmed look, then grinned and told me all about it. Had it been a beautiful girl stepping out of the bushes and offering herself to me, it would have been the South Seas fairy tale come true. The fact that it was a young man propositioning a woman gave the image of romance a whole new feminist twist.

With mask, snorkel and flippers I finned straight out from the beach and twenty yards out found myself looking down on a miraculous underwater garden of coral. It was like being in a corner candy store when suddenly all the brilliantly striped boiled sweets float out of their jars and hover weightlessly around you. Finned liquorice allsorts flickered among sugar sticks of coral. Humbugs with tiny eyes and dilating lips darted out of my shadow. Dainty angelfish, their thin butterscotch stripes rippling like flags, nodded tamely. Gross purple starfish lay on the bottom like congealed bubblegum. When I looked back, a cloud of tiny silver fish turned away as one, flashing like a horde of dimes. And the fish had names to match, I discovered later when I identified them in Suva Aquarium: Teardrop, Vagabond and Threadfin Butterfly Fish; tiny bright blue fish as large as a fingernail called Blue Devils; a brilliant red one, a white band just behind the eye, called the Tomato Clown; the Lemon-Peel Angelfish, brilliant yellow with a bright blue margin to the eye. Finally it was only the sheer murder of sunburn that forced me out of the water.

Along the beach I noticed a woman was cross-legged under a palm selling shells for ten cents apiece. The two widows were looking them over, exclaiming at how cheap they were. When I met the Fijian woman's eye she winked, for she knew that I knew the shells could be picked up for nothing, just along the sand. One of the women, wearing butterfly specs not unlike some of the fish I had been viewing, held out a dish-shaped clam shell for me to see. "Peanuts on the terrace, eh, what do you think?" she asked. "Or potato chips? No, they'd blow away. But peanuts would be okay. On the terrace, y'know?"

The higher islands of the Pacific, like all those I had seen in New Caledonia, the New Hebrides and so far in Fiji, are volcanic. Often, the black bones of bare rock show through the foliage as if shade were being grown as a tropical crop. The valleys contain rich volcanic soil. Their shores are steep and their beaches black except where coral reefs have formed around them, and in places white coral debris has been deposited in the corners. The volcanic action has occurred largely as a pimpling of the thin and volatile oceanic crust that has formed as the single India-Australia-Antarctic continent known as Gondwana-land split and drifted different ways. In more recent geological time there has also been volcanic uplift which has heaved coral reefs above the surface and sometimes tilted them to form limestone massifs. Such a one was Sawa-i-lau, a 600-foot sugar-loaf of white rock sparsely covered with scrub and honeycombed with caves, at the northern end of the Yasawas where we dropped our hook next day. The water was so clear and the white sand beneath so sensationally hued with shades of aquamarine that it was hard to believe you weren't stepping into mysteriously molten windows. When we landed by boat I was first ashore and first up the track into the cleft that was the doorway to a limestone grotto.

The interior was as cool as a cathedral and had the same faintly musty, bare-stone smell. Sunlight streamed through a foliage-rimmed circle high up, filtered as if by a stained glass window in which all the shades were green. The vaulted ceiling was sculpted freestyle Gothic and festooned in its darkest corners with mossy growths.

For a short while, as the old ladies and hangover-laden tourists plodded complainingly up the path, I had the place to myself. The silence was perfect. The angled light detailed every stone and pebble lying thirty feet down in a pool of liquid jade. So motionless was it, without a single ripple or reflection, that it took all my courage to dive in, and I launched myself head-first only because one of the braying hyenas was entering. For the briefest second I experienced a spasm of panic, the kind when you plunge into a swimming pool and think, my God, did somebody empty it overnight? Then the water, shockingly cool, splintered and crashed around me. With a feeling of sacrilege, as if I were roller-skating in Westminster Abbey, I struck out into the mossy gloom of the apse and found a handhold where I could float and watch, lying straight out with my toes up, like a marble Crusader on his tomb.

The crew boys greased their way by invisible handholds almost to the top of the arches seventy feet up and depth-charged the tentative swimmers with war-whoops. Like bats, only their gleaming bared teeth were visible as they winged out of the high shadows. Soon the glorious cavern was like Blackpool on Bank Holiday, and I returned to the beach, the brilliance cutting so deep into my retinas that for several minutes I had to hide my eyes. As I lay in the warm liquid of the shallows waiting for the afternoon to pass, while most of the others were shoulder-deep in the next bay playing a languid kind of pass-the-parcel with a coconut, I reflected that one part at least of the South Seas Dream is sensationally real and satisfying.

The physical comfort of the islands is glorious. Could any other natural environment be so well furnished, so exquisitely tailored to basic needs? I was discovering that in the South Seas you see and listen and think as little as possible: intellectually, you're on another shelf. But your senses operate on a dimension that for me, at least, had been forgotten since I was a boy. I was living through my skin. The differences between light and shade, heat and chill, are magnified. Crusted salt and goose-bumps come and go. The air registers on your whole being, whether it be a turbulent tradewind massage or a stillness that settles like a feather duvet. With no necessity to be cocooned in clothes, the shell you inhabit becomes a single tingling antenna registering the changing mood of every shadow, every passing cloud, every spear-point of sunshine. It was easy to imagine why islanders bathe so frequently in freshwater streams, perhaps as often as six times a day. It would be necessary to the sensitivity of your being, as blinking is to sight.

As it grew cooler, the colours thickening in the softer light, we were ferried to a village on the other side of the bay. Here was a lovely scene straight off the brochures as women set up their shell market under the palms along the shoreline, displaying beautiful necklaces and corals on spindly branches stuck in the sand. The village was neat, comfortable and attractive, with hurricane-proof cement houses built from the proceeds of the carefully regulated tourism established by Trevor Withers. On a shady beach behind the women sat Ratu Epeli, the village chief. Tall, imperious, he had a high brow with eyebrows arched over deep-set hooded eyes, a beaked nose, and a square-set jaw. A century ago the sight of such a figure would have had a shipwrecked sailor shivering in his damp breeches. Now he beckoned me over with a commanding gesture of his big hands and told me to tell the visitors they *must* go to see the school before they buy any shells. And everyone did.

In the evening the women came on board, led by the chief who was decked out in a plaited crown, grass skirt, and a battle-axe smile. He danced to guitars and hollow-log drums with a haughty stare of his grey eyes, head high, shoulders squared. The comparison may seem unlikely but I was reminded of the late Lord Mountbatten. When he conducted the women's chorus it was with aggressive swipes, as if he were wielding a chopper. And when the dancers selected partners from the passengers the old chief arrowed unerringly for the sexiest girl on board, the coloured girl from Toronto clad in more string than bikini.

From these dances, and royalties paid by Blue Lagoon, he told me later, the village had financed most of its reconstruction after the terrible damage wrought by Hurricane Bebe in 1972. The women's shell market had paid for new water tanks and now they were saving up for a generator. Such were the advantages of keeping strict controls on tourism. The Prime Minister of Fiji, Ratu Sir Kamisese Mara, had said tourism could be in the form of a dreadful cocktail party, or a pleasant dinner party in which you had time to talk with and look after each guest individually. "And we all know," he said magisterially, "what kind of occasion we prefer." Fiji was still small enough to be the dinner party, still conscious enough of its cultural heritage to exercise constraints, and is far enough away from great centres of population to be able to make its own choices. The Yasawas were a microcosm of the policy. There were no airfields. The cruise boats were small. Villagers depended on them, but could continue to live their chosen, largely traditional way. Nowhere illustrated this better than Waya Island, at the south of the chain. It is the remnant rim of a great volcanic crater, one-third of it open to the sea, so we sailed into a perfectly circular bay rimmed by massive bulwarks of spire-capped rock sloping steeply down to a shore of wide soft sands. The village is strung out beneath palms but here the houses had been reconstructed mainly in traditional style. Through the open window of one large *bure* overlooking the village green I heard a welcoming shout and out came a big, middle-aged man who shook my hand warmly and asked where I was from. He was Ratu Naloto Naivalu, paramount chief of the island. He showed photographs of his family hanging on the thatched walls. Plastic lilies of the valley stood in little glass jars. The little house smelled sweet, like a new basket. Enthusiastically the chief introduced me to his teenage daughter, Ranadi, who was hanging out washing and wearing a football shirt and *sulu*. She was an 18-year-old of exquisite beauty whose accent dropped each word into the air as precisely and beautifully as raindrops falling on an English rose. She was excited because she was soon to go to the mainland and work in a tourist hotel with her elder sisters.

In shady spots on the close-cropped grass among the houses, older women were at work washing, rolling and drying the long leaves of pandanus with which they would weave baskets, sleeping mats, and roof thatch. The Methodist church, which Ratu Naivalu ordered me not to miss, was decorated with carpet-like wall hangings depicting The Last Supper brought home from Jerusalem by the island's sons who had served as soldiers with the peace-keeping force in Lebanon.

After a time, other passengers wandered off the beach and poked around the village. I was back at the chief's house, talking with him about how he planned the week's work programme for everyone in the village, when he suddenly spotted a young Seattle couple walking by. He was wearing frayed cut-down jeans and she wore nothing that was immediately visible. "Go tell those people to stay on the beach or get themselves dressed, my island is not America!" the chief thundered, and like a lamb, I went and delivered the message, hearing the wooden door of the *bure* slamming angrily behind me.

Plunging back into Suva's swampy torpor after the crackling brilliance of the peaceful Yasawas was wearying. It was back to the milling Indians and tooting taxis, the steamy rain squalls that made my bones ache and the same sword-sellers under the banyan tree. Landing at Naussori Airport after the 35-minute hop across the island in Air Pacific's shuttle I had missed a bus by the skin of my teeth and was directed to another, standing ready to go with its engine running. The Indian supervisor told me it would go in a minute. The driver climbed in, put the bus into gear, but kept his foot on the clutch.

Three-quarters filled with people, the bus remained in that state for no less than one hour and fifteen minutes. How spoiled one could be,

I realised, by the professionalism of tourist comptrollers in starched white safari suits. But I was to be a tourist no more. Now I was to embark on a real voyage, to the islands in the central Lau group, named the Exploring Isles.

8

KAUNITONI

VOYAGE TO
THE EXPLORING ISLES

The bustle of Suva's inter-island wharf in the late afternoon now had in it the sniff of adventure. Berthed among the cutters and ketches was a smart little cargo ship, dark blue with white superstructure, called *Kaunitoni*. Aft she had two decks with lots of portholes promising decent cabins. Around the upper deck was a varnished rail where I could realise my dream, and lean on my elbow while passing the time of day with some fellow voyager. A blackboard hanging over the wing of her bridge proclaimed her schedule, mysterious names that meant nothing but made my heart sing: Cicia, Tuvuca, Katafaga, Cikobia, Vanua, Balevu, Avea, Naitauba, Taveuni . . .

We were scheduled to sail at 4 pm but I went aboard early and it was from the ship's rail that I first spotted him, weaving across the crowded wharf carrying a sack of large pale cabbages. With open shirt and khaki shorts he walked erectly and purposefully. The cut of his salt-and-pepper hair and leather sandals gave him a Christopher Robin look but the eyebrows were shaggy and nearly white, the tanned face leathery. "David," he said shaking my hand and looking over my shoulder. Then he added, "Blackley." The heavy bag of cabbages rested easily in the crook of his arm. "So you've got the Presidential Suite, eh? I've been sailing in this tub for years and never been so lucky."

He had reason to be jealous of my cabin. It was on the upper deck near the stern, spacious with two bunks, a writing desk, a window, scuttle, and a basin with hot water. A door gave access to the shower and lavatory shared with the four-berth cabin beyond, where the captain had installed his wife and two daughters for the voyage. As the first passenger aboard I had raided the other cabins for light bulbs, so the cabin had a full working set, an act of skulduggery that deprived nobody for few of the native passengers slept in the bunks but spread their mats on the floor, and none read books. Now my complete and utter satisfaction rested on just one question: with whom would I be sharing the pleasant little cabin for the next eight days or more? A member of the rucksack brigade would have been a disaster, a native who smoked cigars and snored would have been unpleasant. Then, from further along the deck, I noticed a couple standing at the cabin door. Clearly one of them was travelling but which one?

He was pale-skinned for a Fijian, with a chiefly air, a nice smile, a briefcase, and brightly bulled leather sandals: he bore an uncanny resemblance to President Nixon. She was extremely large, a pearl in each ear, a furled umbrella in one hand and a pandanus fan in the other. For a time they spoke quietly in tones of fondness and regret, then, to my relief, it was the woman who went ashore, the gangway bowing under her weight. The man's luggage tag revealed him to be Ratu W. Keni Naulumatua. "Just call me Bill," he suggested amiably.

Four o'clock came and went. A Shell truck drew alongside but now there was a hitch. The engine to pump the fuel into the ship had run out of fuel. I saw David coming aboard with more cabbages. With him were Les, a husky man with lank black hair on his head and his arms, and Gay, a lithe, neatly built girl with urchin-cut hair who presented such a picture of poise and balance that it came as no surprise to discover later that she had been a champion springboard diver. They were carrying cabbages, too.

"Have you seen a boar in a box, by any chance?" Les asked me, looking worried.

"His name is Romeo," Gay added.

"But he doesn't know that yet because we haven't told him," Les corrected quickly, "and we can't tell him unless the Ministry of Ag. pulls its finger out and gets him down here before we sail. What bothers me is that the Civil Service must have knocked off work half an hour ago."

"We're missing a dozen white pullets, too," David said. "And I'll tell you something. If we don't find that pig we'll be eating an awful lot of coleslaw between here and Katafaga." This was a small island in the Lau Group, 150 miles across the Koror Sea, which was owned by David, a fruit farmer from New Zealand. Les and Gay were voyaging out with him to settle in as resident managers.

The fuel pump was doing its stuff noisily when Uraia, the large Fiji steward in a crisp white shirt, tapped me on the shoulder and announced in a soft voice, "Tea". The saloon had one long table with an orange cloth and a cluster of condiments: crunchy peanut butter, Pick-Me-Up Worcestershire sauce, ketchup, and salt that had turned to syrup in the humidity. Tea was the evening meal, soup out of a packet spiked with bush chilis, then oxtail stew with juicy peas and sweet potato. We were just getting into the red jelly and banana custard when the table and deck vibrated. To hoots, catcalls and wild emotional waving, the ship backed away from the wharf. As we nosed into the first swells of the open ocean the engine stopped. For twenty minutes we lurched in the entrance and I wondered if Ian Lockley's tug would be called to haul us out of trouble, then the vibration started again. A loud squeak came from the cargo deck. "That's a pig!" Gay exclaimed hopefully.

"Wherefore art thou, old chap?" Les bleated. But it was only a wire cable scraping on steel as the crew battened down for the inevitable bouncy ride up-wind across the Koror Sea.

A lighthouse glimmered over to port, marking a reef. "Last time I saw that, things were a bit different," said a voice at my elbow as I leant on the rail. It was David, begging the excuse to spin a yarn. A few months before, he had flown in from America bringing the permitted two pieces of baggage, a deflated rubber dinghy and an outboard motor. In Suva he pumped up the dinghy and set out for his island but the weather was bad and the pounding was tiring so he headed for Nairai Island to rest but could not find the reef passage. He was cruising along the reef when a big comber loomed out of nowhere and he found himself in the tunnel of the breaking wave. The dinghy flipped and was carried clean over the reef with David sprawled on top of it. He could not right it singlehanded so he towed it, swimming with a rope in his teeth, for five hours until he hit the beach. He woke up a family and stayed the night, and next day flushed out the motor and got it going, setting out again at midnight, steering two fingers to the right of the rising stars.

At dawn the islands were clearly in sight, dead ahead, but as the sun rose they melted into the haze. David felt himself begin to fry. He put a towel over his head and steered to the right of the rising sun which he could see through the weave of the cloth, but at noon the islands were still invisible so he drifted until the haze evaporated and in the late afternoon spotted a familiar outline that gave him bearings.

Wasn't it a bit risky, I wondered, Pacific voyaging in a twelve-foot dinghy? Not especially, David thought. Last time he had sailed up from New Zealand by yacht he had brought a tractor on the deck, and before that some self-shearing sheep for his island. And once he had crossed the Sahara, but that was on a camel, of course. "In fact," he admitted modestly as we cowered from a shot of cold spray, "on my passport my occupation is registered as Adventurer."

The ship vibrated and rattled like a cement mixer filled with ball bearings. I went to sleep that night pondering a technical question. How did raspberry jelly set solid in a rolling shaking vessel?

In the blustery weather Captain Si Osmund abandoned attempts to land at the south end of Cicia. We steamed outside the reef to the lee side and ran ashore in the whaleboat piled high with fibreboard suitcases, huge bundles wrapped in sleeping mats with tasselled edges, bunches of plastic flowers, disassembled double beds, and bags of foam chips for making mattresses. Strangely, the sudden arrival of the ship at Tavuka sparked no excitement at all. The only reaction came from an old granny who waded into the water to meet the boat, snatched a brand-new baby swaddled in shawls from its mother's lap, and with gummy smiles jiggled it delightedly for all to admire.

The damp wind rustled the cyclone-damaged palms. Beyond the grey lagoon and smoking reef the ship nodded heavily in the lumpy swells. Meli had carried the hospital bodily through the air, high over all the houses, and dropped it on top of the school. Corrugated iron and fallen trees lay everywhere. The beautiful breadfruit trees had no leaves. Chalked on the board of the empty schoolroom was this question: "A duty-free dealer buys a Japanese radio for $20 and sells it for $28; find the gain or loss per cent." What a hollow, mocking epitaph for a place that did not have so much as a shop. But it was not all listless self-absorption. The cyclone had also ripped the roof from the church and a temporary one, built entirely of corrugated iron, was in danger of having its roof lifted by the sheer volume of magnificent singing from within. When I tiptoed to a pew at the rear I discovered that women's choirs from two other villages were competing in a singing contest. The adjudicator, sitting in the pulpit as magisterially as a high chief, was the schoolmaster's wife. The choristers were clad in white blouses and black ankle-length skirts, and they filed out to practise for the next round, one choir behind the clothes lines and the other on the beach. To competing heavenly choruses, the menfolk unloaded the cargo from the whaleboat.

As I listened to the beautiful unaccompanied voices and joked with the proud, dignified singers ("How did you get here from your village?" I had asked; "On both legs," one old dame replied crisply) I realized that what I had taken for self-absorption was also, to an extent, a certain self-sufficiency. You could armour yourself against the attractions of the outside world by deigning not to notice the arrival of a ship once every six weeks. But now a new air-strip was being built a couple of miles along the shore, and a thrice-weekly plane would be less easy to ignore. In island life the better linked you became the harder it was to be self-contained, and the sense of poverty increased with the degree of westernisation. Ratu Bill put it in a nutshell. The government was busy building roads round the islands but would it be an improvement? "Now, we walk eagerly enough," he said, "but when there is the option of riding it will be a matter of no truck, no go."

David's island appeared as a grey and bristly smear on the horizon and in the course of a couple of hours grew into a Garden of Eden. Les and Gay leaned over the rail with cameras enthusiastically explaining every feature as if they had lived there all their lives, but they knew them only from photographs. It was a humpy island covered with Caribbean pine trees that David had planted, with a scrubby coral uplift at one end. The land covered only 240 acres but it was enclosed in a large and beautiful lagoon. We anchored off the passage and loaded the whaleboat with the suitcases, cabbages, boxes of art books and tools with which the couple aimed to start the romantic island life they confidently expected to occupy the rest of their lives. With an envious glance at a pig that had come aboard at Cicia (Wherefore art thou Romeo?) they went down the gangplank and feasted their shining eyes on the splendour of the lagoon. David had invited me in for the ride but warned me he would be busy. He had to fire his manager and persuade him to pack his bags and leave on the instant.

As it happened Roger Stephens, a gnome-like man of sixty with long arms and a smile of ruined teeth, had his bags packed and was more than ready to return to the "city". His mother had been Lady St Aubyn of St Michael's Mount in Cornwall, he explained. After the First World War she had set out on a world cruise and got as far as Fiji where she met and married Roger's father, a Fijian.

The house he was leaving was straight out of a film set. Built by a German planter half a century ago, it stood a little back from a cove of crunchy white sand. In front, where you would imagine yourself sipping rum punch at sunset, were two gnarled trees with shady fleshy leaves. The stone wall around the hem of the timber walls was decorated with giant clam shells, immense pink and white dishes set in mortar. Three hardwood steps, cracked and splintered, led up to a wide enclosed verandah, its shutters propped open with struts of driftwood. The table in the simple kitchen out the back stood in rusty salmon tins filled with water moats against marauding ants. The furniture was faded and bug-eaten. Grey paint flaked off the walls like bark from a plane tree. All was splintered and faded. But a large breadfruit tree leaned its branches practically into the window: did this island of self-shearing sheep, I wondered, grow ready-sliced bread on trees? On one shrub I counted twenty-two butterflies. Chickens ran everywhere and roosters squared up to my bare legs as I strolled through the overgrown garden with a frangipani blossom stuck behind my ear and picked limes with which to freshen up my Cokes in the ship.

The new residents were enchanted. They had broken out floppy straw hats which they donned with selfconscious eagerness and I suspected they couldn't wait to be rid of us so they could patrol their little kingdom in *sulus*. I helped them carry their gear up to the verandah, much of it art books. When she ran out of things to read, Gay explained, she would gaze at the pictures every evening. Les dug out his speargun to show me. What were they going to do first, when the whaleboat disappeared round the point?

"I'm going to have a pink gin under that tree," Les said.

But Gay had other ideas. "You've got to catch us some supper, buster. Fish or something."

"We've got enough bloody cabbages," Les muttered.

The whaleboat was pushed out from the beach and the crewmen scrambled in, the engine was started, and we set a course for the ship. David gave one short wave and turned his back. Les and Gay waved their hats until we were out of sight, Les with both hands clenched above his head in a signal of supreme exultation. Here was the living, breathing, twentieth century Robinson Crusoe dream unfolding before my eyes and I tried to analyse how I would feel if it were me, waving *adieu* on the beach. The place you like to escape to is not necessarily where you would like to live for ever I decided. The island would be a dream for a long holiday, but the art books would swiftly become so much meaningless termite fodder because in this heavenly little spot the Old Masters would have no point of reference. Contemplation in such a vivid place would surely become a doze. I was content to be voyaging on. For could one be certain of finding the perfect island, the perfect existence, until the ship had called at the next one, and the one after ... ?

The kava bowl in the *Kaunitoni* was not the usual carved wooden bowl a couple of feet in diameter, nor even a blue plastic bucket, but an orange fishing float lost by an oriental fishing boat which had been sliced in half. At sunset the loud pounding of a steel crowbar powdering the kava roots for mixing with water sent its message through the entire vessel. I had a bowl while hanging over the stern, watching the wake fizzing away into nothing but a slippery skid-mark zig-zagging over the backs of the receding waves. In England you might walk the ridgeways in the footsteps of Neolithic people, or drive roads first unrolled straight across country by the Romans; in Arizona you could match your own fingers to the claw-prints of dinosaurs and in Nebraska tread the ruts of covered wagons on the Oregon Trail. But in the ocean the track of a vessel – be it canoe, sailing ship, steamer – remains visible for scarcely a whole minute. Ours caught the eye of only a cruising petrel that glided down, stiff-winged, to check a dainty morsel in the form of a discharged Kleenex. It was small wonder, I reflected, that the great migrations of the Pacific had for so long remained an archaeological mystery.

At the time of the *Kon Tiki* expedition in 1947 archaeology had scarcely touched the Pacific and Thor Heyerdahl's idea that the islands were settled by pale-skinned raft voyagers from South America was just one of many speculative theories. The South Sea islanders were descended from American Indians who had made it to Hawaii then ventured south; they had developed within New Zealand and ventured north; they were Aryans touched with Mesopotamian and Indian tar brushes; they were Aryans who had moved across land bridges that once spanned the wide ocean between Japan and Easter Island; they were refugees from a sunken continent. Ratu Bill's theory, one devised by missionaries and commonly taught in Fiji schools until the 1950s, was that his ancestors had migrated long ago from Africa; half had stopped in New Guinea and the remainder, in a craft called *Kaunitoni* which means wood that does not sink, had sailed on to Fiji. An amazing number of place names were common in both Fiji and Kenya, he explained.

It is only in the last two decades that study of the multitude of Pacific languages and pottery remnants has concluded with reasonable certainty that the two distinct racial types of the South Pacific originated in successive waves of migration from the same source, south-east Asia. The Melanesian I had encountered in the dark and jungly islands of New Caledonia, the New Hebrides, and most of Fiji, was himself a black and statuesque individual with a frizz of black hair. The Polynesian of Tonga, Samoa, Tahiti and the other islands that lay ahead beneath the sunrise were altogether gentler to the European eye, with paler skin, finer features, and straighter hair.

The Melanesians were part of a group called Austroloids who crossed to New Guinea and Australia, and ventured westwards through the nearer islands, probably 40,000 years ago. The Polynesians came out of eastern Asia by way of Vietnam and Indonesia in a much more recent wave some 6,000 years ago. Finding Melanesians already entrenched, they coast-hopped eastwards and found a promised land in the unoccupied islands of Tonga and Samoa. Over a thousand years, up to the time of Christ, they developed the cultural characteristics that were to become distinctive of Polynesians: a system of strong leadership that gave rise to despotic regimes, a mastery of the domestication of plants that enabled them to colonise distant islands that would not otherwise have supported life, and a perfection of marine architecture and navigation that enabled them to make great ocean crossings when Western man was still groping from headland to headland. Voyaging in strong sailing canoes against the wind (a strategy that allowed them to turn and run from home when supplies ran low) these "Vikings of the sun-rise" found virgin islands to the east. They created new cultural bases in the Marquesas and Society Islands, and from there peopled the remainder of what is recognised today as the Polynesian triangle. They sailed north to Hawaii, south-west to New Zealand and east to Easter Island, venturing even as far as South America where they collected the sweet potato and so laid the false trail that was later to launch the *Kon Tiki* on its great adventure. Such tracks were hard to authenticate, however. Not least because the sea records no footprints, but also because the impoverished atolls which the Polynesians settled had no clay with which to make pots and so establish clues that archaeologists in modern times might follow.

It was in the Lau Islands where we were now sailing that the black Melanesians of Fiji rubbed up against the brown Polynesians of Tonga, and the racial picture becomes blurred. In fact, a century ago these islands were in Tongan hands and the danger of the complete conquest of Fiji was one reason why Cakobau, the fierce Fijian chief, offered his war club to Queen Victoria in exchange for her protection. It also explained why several of these islands had been sold off, in a fit of pique at the traitors who had welcomed the Tongan invaders without a struggle.

Next day we entered a reef that encircles ten islands. At Munia we dropped a boat to deliver mail. At Cikobia I watched the school sports day on the beach for ten minutes while our passengers waded ashore with their luggage. Then we berthed at the new wharf in the large village of Lomolomo on Vanua Balevu, a boomerang-shaped island of which each arm is more than twenty miles long. Here, Chief Ma'afu of Tonga had established a base when he nearly became king of Fiji because he had cannon against Cakobau's muskets, spears and clubs. Many Tongans remained and today the village was divided by the drain, Tongans on one side and native Fijians on the other, though all were Fijian by nationality. Ratu Bill, it turned out, was next in line to be chief of the native Fijian side, and of several other villages on the island. Chiefs in Fiji inherit through their older brothers, and when the youngest dies his title jumps to the sons of his oldest brother. Ratu Bill's title (the honorific "Ratu" indicates princely blood) would come from his uncle, now a frail eighty and in hospital, then pass to Bill's younger brother and from him to Bill's son. "But I hope the old man hangs on for as long as possible," Ratu Bill told me. "It's not an easy post to hold because everybody relies on you, and you have to spend a lot of your money. It is expected."

The huts and gardens of Lomolomo were laid out as if a blueprint existed for suburban-style streets and pavements but the ground was meanwhile turfed with springy grass. The only real road followed the edge of the bay, under a single row of palms bending in the chilly damp wind. The two shops were virtually bare, a sign of the hard times following the cyclone. Running water was piped only to communal taps. There was no electricity. No canoes or boats were pulled up on the beach: the only fish in the place was in Japanese cans being unloaded from the hold of the *Kaunitoni*, and much of it might well have been caught in the Fijian waters. The wharf was new but the cargo went over the outboard side into a whaleboat then was man-handled over the sands to the little warehouse. Why? Because every truck on the island but one was up on blocks awaiting spare parts.

But this, I learned, was a typical result of the South Sea tradition of communal sharing, in Fiji called *kere-kere*. It made the native culturally whole and rooted his lifestyle in family and village but killed initiative. When a man earned more money than his relatives he had to share it, which encouraged people to coast. The system collapsed totally when machinery was involved. There were many fingers on the starter button, be it outboard motor, chain saw, truck or tractor, but nobody had responsibility for topping up the oil and water. Fijians were not without initiative. They took advantage of low-interest loans made available for just about any activity that could generate income, but seventy-five per cent of development funds went down the drain because the machinery packed up. Then there was no income to meet the capital repayments and the Fijian listlessly sold out for what he could get from some Indian. The custom of passing chieftainship through a line of brothers before it reaches the eldest of their sons may well be a cultural anchorstone, but the oldest and wisest man seldom had the smartest commercial instincts, and as an accountant in the Prime Minister's office, Ratu Bill knew how important this was. "The instinct for self-development must get into the blood, though it may take ten generations," he said. "Individuals must be allowed – and encouraged – to do their own thing. Those who get up and strive will live, and those who do not will go under, and that's that."

When Ratu Bill was a boy in the 1930s Lomolomo had a bakery, plenty of home-grown eggs, and fishing boats. Now the ship was unloading boxes of fresh bread and cartons of eggs. Its freezer space, for freighting island-caught fish to market, had never been used. But with an accountant in charge the island lifestyle might change. Bill was himself on a two-month sabbatical going to his land at the far end of the island to extend the goat farm he had established: the country was importing goat meat worth millions from India. For the villages a freezer for storing fish was planned, a launch for harvesting *bêche-de-mer*, a tractor and trailer for carting firewood or cargo and cultivating crops, and a portable cinema with its own generator. "But I am pushing the individualistic approach: one man must own and operate his own boat and engine, another the tractor and trailer, and the whole village must work through them. In the old days the whole village would communally build newlyweds a house and launch them in life, then they would paddle their own canoe. Now we've got to do the same in a business sense, with only one finger on every starter button and one signature on every cheque."

Next morning the ship cruised along the coast and dropped the hook off the beach of another village before I woke up. Bare-footed, I went on deck to view the dark bush of the hillside around a thin line of thatched huts, then returned to the cabin to get my brown plastic sandals. But they had gone. When Uraia came to tell us breakfast was ready – juice, porridge, baked beans, liver in gravy, egg, chips, fried taro, toast, coffee – Ratu Bill explained the problem and the steward said he would look around. Later, he brought in a good-looking lad of about sixteen wearing black slacks cut off at the knee, a white shirt, plastic beads and my sandals. Where had he got the sandals? In Suva last week. Who paid his fare? My uncle, the ship's bosun. What size were the sandals? Nine.

I looked them over but there was no way to be positive. Except that the sandals were clearly too small for his large leathery feet, because the straps had left deep impressions in his skin, and in fact they were size ten. I handed them back. A low profile seemed the answer.

Ratu Bill went round the ship asking questions. Had the boy worn the sandals aboard? "That'll be the day!" retorted the supercargo. Had his uncle paid his fare to Suva? "What I do a silly thing like that for?" said the bosun. Had the boy been on the upper deck? Yes, Ratu Bill himself had noticed him outside our door. But the boy admitted nothing. "Give the *palagi* the sandals if it makes him feel better, if it matters so terribly much . . ."

The boy was dumped ashore and told to make his way back overland and the *palagi* felt like crawling into the woodwork like a cockroach. Without the sandals to protect my lily-white soles I couldn't have set another foot on shore, but this seemed a slim justification for creating such a scene. Everybody, especially the older men, were embarrassed nearly to tears not for themselves or for the boy, but for their honour.

Now the ship was flooded with young men travelling in the large saloon, known as the pit, deeper in the ship. They were a rugby team going to Suva to play in an inter-island competition, but they numbered no less than thirty-two. And that was after the captain headed into an isolated bay to put three stowaways ashore. Why so many, when a team had only fifteen players? A century ago such a group of young warriors would have been setting off by canoe, with war clubs, to raid some nearby island for honour, glory and fresh meat. A rugby game was hardly in the same league but it served the same purpose because it got them out of their prison and over the horizon. But why, with so many educated young men committed to a nothing life of digging with a pointed stick, why did the cargo we were loading for Suva contain so many outboard motors and other bits of machinery going back for repair? Was there no trained mechanic on the island, no work-shop? Nothing. Just coconut palms and bananas, the occasional devastating cyclone, and short-wave transistor radios for listening to rugby commentaries in far-away New Zealand.

The thin woody sound of a hollowed log struck with a stout stick was summoning the dozen households of Tote to church in a tin shack decorated with Christmas streamers as Captain Si pushed the whaleboat away from the side. With Ratu Bill, Roger Stephens, and a couple of off-duty crewmen we cruised along the shore then turned in. As magically as the cliffs of Bonifaccio, ramparts of crumbling scrub-covered limestone opened ahead of us and we wended along a narrow sandy canyon. Sparks streamed from the captain's cigarette as he guided the steersman around lurking coral heads with sudden jerks of his thin arms. The gorge opened into a land-locked secret harbour. The steep hills were thick with big trees, their clinging lianas straggling down in tangled knots. Dense mangroves fringed the shore but we found a break leading to a landing place of smelly black mud that left me looking like a Fijian from the knees down. On the bush track I was challenged by a land crab that straddled the twiggy pathway with its nippers raised like a pair of bucket excavators. We pushed through mile-a-minute creeper that threatened to take over the world, clumps of Black-eyed Susie that my local garden centre in London sold in pots for pounds apiece, and the remarkable sensitive grass, a spiky, narrow-leafed, low-down creeper that curled up and played possum at the slightest touch.

Twenty leg-scratching minutes brought us out on a grassy headland jutting into the secret harbour where Cagi had established his family in a shack made of packing case timber and hacked a market garden out of the bush. Bearded and thick-set, he was a piratical gent who unrolled himself from the mat on which he was napping and, accompanied by a dozen children and as many dogs, shambled to a wooden deck a couple of feet above the ground in the shade of a banyan tree, and sat upon it cross-legged with a cheroot of home-grown tobacco. The smoke was like something that ought to have been dropped into a ship's hold to fumigate the cockroaches. Yellow chicks, a few days old, swarmed cheeping over a pile of coconuts cut open for them. Fat hens and roosters squatted on the rim of a tin bowl pecking at the washing-up water then tilting it down their throats and looking dissatisfied as if to say, this washing-up water tastes no better than soup.

Cagi and the captain were cousins and had business to discuss concerning family land which Si wanted to see because he planned to cultivate it when he retired from the sea. After a time our host called out in thick tones to a pretty little girl who took an all-weather knife and wandered into the pineapple plot where silvery, spiky leaves glittered like grenade explosions. Languidly she returned with a magnificent pineapple balanced upright on the palm of each hand and the long knife tucked under her arm. Then she sliced away their crocodile-skin armour and sliced them downwards to make pineapple spears, each with a little handle of foliage. The juice made beads of brilliant dew on the fragrant crisp yellow flesh, and the memory of it kept me going through a long day of tramping through the festooned bush, circling wild-looking cattle with curved horns and flailing my skin with palm fronds to beat off mosquitoes that seemed as big as blood-sucking blackbirds. It was hard to know which was worse, the pink polka dots rising on my skin or the stinging welts.

It was cold, grey and blowing when at last we pushed the boat out over the mud and trailed our legs in the sea to clean them off, but we went to the village beach not the ship. All the houses were of roofing iron but one small hut near the foreshore was thatched, with low cane walls. Those who had footwear removed it, then we ducked into the gloom and stretched out on a pandanus mat paying no attention to the young man who was dead asleep. The loud boom of the kava root being pounded in a hollow log with a wooden pestle brought in other men of the village. They squatted with legs folded, cigarettes and matches within handy reach, oblivious of the cold wind and drizzle whistling through the thin walls. This time the kava was mixed ceremonially, in a wooden bowl. We drank by turn, always Ratu Bill first. Soon he was yawning his head off. Captain Si, thin as a reed, floated like a stick of thistledown. Cagi let his foul cheroot go out and stared contentedly into space.

As conversation lapsed, the captain started telling stories in English of sailormen, planters and chiefs. Like the high chief at Kadavu who needed desperately to get to Suva but had no skipper available with the necessary certificate for thirty-ton vessels. So he rustled up what manpower he could and as he arrived in Suva with a heavy load of passengers the harbour-master berated him. Didn't he know the law requiring the vessel to carry a skipper with a 30-ton ticket? "Certainly but I fixed that," the high chief told him loftily. "I got two skippers. They got a fifteen-ton ticket each."

Naitauba was an attractive island where Captain Si nosed the bows up to a notch in the reef, dropped the hook on it, then let the ship fall back down-wind where it rolled awkwardly on the swells curling round each end of the island. It was the fourth port of the next day, and raining hard. When I went ashore in the whaleboat I found a story-book plantation. Handsome red cattle grazed under the palms and one was being butchered in a shed. A large airy shelter brimmed with pots of orchids being grown commercially. From the school house children waved at me when the teacher's back was turned. The island was owned by TV detective Perry Mason, alias the wheelchair-bound merchant of justice known as Ironside, alias the American actor Raymond Burr. But the "boss" had left the week before and I missed seeing him; nor did I see much of his plantation, because of the rain.

Wet and bedraggled I returned to the ship for dinner and was alerted by an unlikely noise. We had been collecting quite a menagerie and the ship was becoming more like a Noah's Ark at every anchorage, with pigs in a pen on the starboard side, goats tied on the fo'c'sle with some calves, and crates of hens among the sacks of coconuts and large yams bound up in plaited palm-fronds. Now, from the open sea, came another farmyard noise: a rather disconcerted whinnying. Approaching very slowly, its motor barely at tick-over, was a whaleboat. One of the crew leaned over its transom holding the halter of a magnificent grey horse lying listlessly in the inky blue water. Its forelegs reached out as if it were leaping a fence, its back legs trailed with its long, fanned-out tail. The crewman was careful to keep its muzzle above the surface but an occasional wave washed over its head and the horse flickered its ears trustfully. A sling was passed down and with much trouble worked under its belly, and it was nearly dark when at last the beautiful animal was lifted cleanly out of the sea and lowered to the deck.

Cargo operations continued despite the darkness and I talked with the captain as he watched from the bridge. He told me of the terrible night in 1973 when the inter-island ship *Tui Lakeba* went down in a cyclone. The ship was licensed to carry only seventy-five passengers and there were about sixty survivors who spent twelve hours in the water, but seventy-four had died, many of them jammed in the portholes as they tried to get out. One boy had made a raft of two bags of coconuts and had rescued a little pig. When he saw the wicked-looking fin of a big shark making for him he pushed the pig into the water and the shark made off with it but left him alone. What was the sea like, in a cyclone? Captain Si gestured towards the cataracts of water piling over the reef in the darkness. "See those breakers on the reef? It's like that, everywhere you look, so frothy you can hardly get on top."

The *Kaunitoni* was only five years old but there were few of the navigational amenities you would expect. Apart from a radio, a single radar set, a flag locker and the steering wheel there was nothing, no barometer, no radio direction finder, no sextant, no depth sounder. The one compass could be seen by only one man, the helmsman, so the captain could never check the course he steered. There were no watertight bulkheads in the hold, the captain complained, and no aft ballast tank to trim the ship as she was loaded, with the result that she rode tail-high and was tender and difficult to control. "But don't you smell your way round these waters," I asked. "I thought skippers like you could navigate blindfold?"

"That's all very well, until something goes wrong," he said, in a tone that suggested he was mentally knocking on wood.

There was a shout from the deck. Then a noise like a great thunder-ing of canvas. The whole ship heeled, so sharply that in the deck lights I saw the grey horse stumble. The men went into stiff, muscle-tensing postures. A blast of wind tore through the bridge, whirling papers. The door slammed with an explosive crack.

The fierce squall tearing out of the darkness caught everybody on the hop. The ship rolled upright, yawed violently on her anchor chain like a bronco rearing in fright, and dragged the heavy anchor off the reef. It dropped into the deep water and found no bottom but dangled from the bows. The men in the whaleboat alongside cast off swiftly and made for the lagoon as the shrieking wind drove the ship rapidly out to sea.

In a few minutes the engine was turning, the anchor winched aboard and the hatch battened down. The captain switched on his sole navigational aid, the radar, and the outline of the island was all but blotted out by a curtain of iron rain. On the radar I watched it wrapping around the ship then it fell on the deck like tons of chains, making the steel ring.

Quickly we were out of the lee of the island and plunging like a lame roller coaster. All night the captain stayed on the bridge, steaming back and forth along a twenty-mile track clear of reefs and islands. At intervals during the night, as I braced myself in my bunk, I heard the shrieks of the pigs as water rolled over the deck, and the wailing bleats of the calves and goats. The motion was so violent that frequently my mattress lifted off the boards and slammed down again.

At daylight the captain manoeuvred back into the calm of the island's lee and in the grey dawn took stock of the damage. Nine of the twelve goats were dead. Three calves were dead and the fourth was on its knees, the pigs fighting over its vomit. Several pigs had drowned or succumbed to exposure and one had a broken thigh. The beautiful horse was soaked and dishevelled, its flanks pink with blood, but a little blood goes a long way in rain and the damage was only a graze. The scene in the big saloon with seventy-one passengers being sick was dreadful. In the captain's cabin his wife and children had slopped back and forth on the shiny lino like wet rags in a bucket. The rugby players were hollow-eyed but squatting on the ship's rail and fortifying themselves with vast breakfasts made of the luckless goats, curried.

After collecting the boats and the rest of Raymond Burr's copra we crossed the twenty miles to Yacata Island where the horse was lowered into a whaleboat and ferried ashore. The storm had rolled a lot of water into the large lagoon and now it poured out through the cut in the reef as the whaleboat with its engine at full revs seemed to be inching up a hill of molten, cascading turquoise. The sun came out. We rounded a corner and there was the village turned out on the shore to greet us and shoulder the bags of provisions into the co-op store. The rugby team came ashore in other boats to help bag the copra and carry it down to the beach.

When we sailed again I found Ratu Bill's vacated top bunk occupied by a willowy 21-year-old school teacher called Abraham, on his way to a course in Suva. He wore a blue boiler suit, sunglasses, running shoes, and a hair style that called to mind cartoon figures of cannibals war-dancing round a cooking pot. His parents, he told me, were Solomon Islanders who had come to work in the plantations and were always poor, but as the seventh of nine children he had managed to get an education by answering an advertisement in an Anglican magazine to be sponsored by a couple in New Zealand who paid his school fees of $15 a term.

That night I was disturbed in my sleep by the flit of a shadow but I rolled over and went back to sleep. No, it was impossible for two people to share that narrow bunk. I thought no more about it until Abraham accosted me at the rail next day. He was listening to his radio with a tall shy girl whom he introduced as Jujiinua (a corruption of Georgina). He put his hand on my arm and smiled like a sunrise. "I would like to ask your opinion, kind sir, do you mind ... ? You see, this is my girlfriend. She is a village girl from Yucata where I am school-teacher for $106 a fortnight. That is the nicest way, eh? Just what God wants, a village girl for me. Do you think so?" Jiujinua knew she was being appraised and kept her big brown eyes shyly furled. She had a long thin face and close-cropped hair. She stood with arms folded and bare feet splayed on the deck, her faded cotton frock flapping wildly in the breeze. "You see," Abraham continued earnestly, "she wanted to go to Suva because she had never been to the city. I gave her $300. Never in her life had she seen so much money. I told her to look around and see if she finds somebody else to love. If not, come back to me.

"Well, that was a month ago when she went to Suva and now I have this course to attend and when I came on board the *Kaunitoni* today there she was, coming back to me. It is truly wonderful thing that God does, don't you think?' There was no chance to answer for he rushed straight on. "So you see, I bought this bed in the cabin for $54 and last night . . . last night we were man and woman become one." So that explained the funny shadow, I realised, as the teacher coughed behind his hand. "Oh, I was so worried for you. I wanted to wake you to ask your opinion, to be sure that you, too, were on God's side. Oh, it was such a difficult decision for me. Should I have woken you, *that* is what I want to know?"

The question remained largely academic, for the last night at sea was rough and although the two eager young people shared the bunk above my head they were too seasick to move. All the last day we were at anchor off Taveuni, waiting for the rain to stop so we could load copra, and it was 2 am when at last the inter-island ship slipped into Princes Wharf at Suva, to a noisy welcome. Abraham's smile was wider and wilder than ever as he shook my hand and gracefully thanked me for my "opinions". I wished him luck. "Oh, thank you very much because tomorrow we will get married, the honeymoon is over."

9

SEA PRINCESS

CRUISE TO
A CORAL KINGDOM

Steam locomotives may puff under hump-backed bridges, vintage Bentleys crackle their exhaust pipes, flying boats circle wild game en route from Cairo to the Cape. But for me, none of these nostalgic echoes of the great days of travel compare with leaning on the silky teak rail of a stately ocean liner, a cold drink in hand. A refreshing breeze streams in your hair. The pulse of the screws trembles through the soles of your bare feet. Then, shading your eyes, you sight an ever-so faint shadow in the sky ... Land ho!

Less than two decades ago, the cheapest and also the most comfortable means of travelling from one continent to the other was by ocean liner. When I was a boy, not a week passed without a passenger ship arriving at Auckland. Stately vessels flying British, American, Dutch, Italian, French and Greek flags plied the shipping routes of the Pacific, offering an elegance in travel that was scarcely appreciated until it was lost to long-haul jets. Today the great ships that churned furrows of foam across the blue carpet of the Pacific have gone, but you can fly it on any of half a dozen flights a day in twelve hours flat.

Only once or twice a year a liner on a round-the-world cruise from Europe and the US follows the old groove, and occasionally a cargo ship carries a few passengers, but in either case you pay through the nose. The only alternative for itinerant island-hoppers is the P & O cruise ship operating a regular programme of round-trip voyages of the Pacific Islands out of Sydney, Australia, with occasional excursions towards Bali and the Orient. Though irregular, the schedule is published months in advance and if the ship is not fully booked casual travellers can join the ship on legs of the circuit, even at short notice.

All you have to do is be in the right port at the right time, and be prepared to part with about $100 a day.

Now I was voyaging again on the Koro Sea, eastward bound towards the sunrise as were the ancient Polynesians casting out for new lands. But this was voyaging in style. The *Sea Princess** could have carried the stout *Kaunitoni* on her poop deck. She was a 30,000-tonner, built by the Norwegians as the *Kungsholm* but sold to P & O and converted for up-market South Seas cruises. Lolling along at slow speed, so as to arrive at Vava'u in northern Tonga comfortably at dawn, and totally unaffected by the ill temper of the waves that had rock'n'rolled us for eight days, the ship had a strangely unreal mood about her. She was part holiday camp, part luxury hotel, part sun verandah with a sea view. What was lacking was any sense of mission in the voyage. No curiosity or sense of excitement hung in the air about her destination. The island ports at which the ship paused on her round trip from Sydney were merely stationary intervals in an experience of indolence and self-indulgence.

After a five-star lunch I measured my length face-down on an upper deck, fell into a gut-stuffed stupour, and awoke sore from the prickle of artificial grass with which this part of the ship, called The Meadow, was carpeted. The pleasant Staff Captain with ginger-freckled knees was making an announcement on the blower: soon the ship would pass through Oneata Passage and there would be interesting islands to see to port and starboard.

I looked around and saw the news being greeted with total apathy. Not a muscle moved, not a nerve twitched, not an eyelid flickered. On a deck crowded with bodies grilling in oil I was alone in being unable to resist the impulse to wander to the rail, lean outward into the breeze, and look ahead. Yes. On the stainless surface of the sea gleaming in the silver light, for the sun was filtered by a skim of pearly cloud, I espied a slim short line, faint as a pencil mark ruled on a windowpane.

After I had swum in the pool and showered, I strolled to the rail sipping a Coke'n'Cuba (rum, lime, Coca Cola). The island now lay two or three miles off, a slightly rumpled pot scourer on the polished metal sea. The swell curled elegantly over the protecting reef. With my naked eye I saw the bristle of cyclone-shredded palms, and clusters of huts, but no people. Did not the sight of a great ship appearing suddenly on an empty horizon bring people running, to gaze with admiration and wonder? Evidently not. And on the deck of the cruise ship the sole indication of interest came when an elderly man in baggy khaki shorts briefly scanned the shore with a pair of heavy U-boat binoculars. The island dissolved into the distance.

* Since replaced on this route by the *Oriana*.

For dinner I was put at a table with a family from somewhere in the Blue Mountains: mum, dad, and three beefy sons. "We're in buses," the woman stated, as if it were the secret of life. She was something of a blue-rinse mountain herself, adorned with heavy gold. The sons played in the same rugby team. Had they seen the island go by?

"Naw, I was having fifty winks," said one.

"Shit, I was so chokka I couldn't move," said another.

"Oh yeah, I did hear some announcement about it," said the third vacantly.

Their mother didn't like islands too much. "The trouble is, when you go ashore there's nowhere to wash your hands, you know, and you've got to after four or five hours . . ."

"What's wrong with the Pacific Ocean?" I asked, tongue in cheek, and was rewarded with a look that would have cleaned windscreens without wipers.

Tonga is a chain of 169 islands, about forty of them inhabited and the rest very small, spanning some 500 miles. They lie in three principal groups. We would spend a day in Vava'u, the northern group, then skirt the central group called Ha'apai during the night, and arrive the following morning at Nuku'alofa, the capital, on the biggest island of Tonga-tapu in the south. Here I was to disembark and search the waterfront for a berth in some kind of island-hopper.

Sailing in from the west, as we were, out of Melanesia and into Polynesia, the Tongan Islands are encountered in two distinct bands. First there is a line of scattered volcanoes. One is a perfect cone, still active. Another is a kind of jagged doughnut, its crater filled with water, where landing by boat was so difficult that islanders sealed their mail in drums and pushed it out to passing steamers, thus Niuafo'ou got its name Tin Can Island. Another had recently popped out of the sea, like Surtsey in Iceland. Parallel and further east is the tangled maze of reefs and coral islands. They have the character of atolls but some, like Vava'u, have been lifted as much as ninety feet by volcanic rearrangement. Their soils are not nearly as impoverished as true atolls because they have been sprayed with fertile volcanic ash.

A little further east but hidden beneath the surface is the remarkable Tonga-Kermadec Trench, one of the deepest points anywhere in the oceans. Deeper than seven Grand Canyons and extending 1,500 miles, it marks where the edge of the great continental plate beneath the Pacific is bent under the continental plate of Asia and Australia. The line of volcanoes is situated along the join, when the molten magma of the earth's core leaks upwards through the seam.

Despite the lack of green fields and church spires, in the pearly dawn from the ship's bridge the Vava'u Group had the appearance of a lump of Cornwall or Brittany that had been dropped on a hard surface from a height just sufficient to scatter the thirty-four fragments and create deep channels, scarcely wider than rivers, between them. As the ship wandered among the scrub-covered limestone tableaux I thought it was the nearest thing in cruise-liner terms to cross-country driving. Breakfasting on fresh papaya and yoghurt, the teak rail for a table, I saw little outboard-driven whaleboats pushing out from white beaches where a fringe of palms shaded a cluster of huts. Converging on Neiafu, the main town, the boats were heaped with people and the handicrafts they were bringing for sale at the market. *Sea Princess* rounded up and dropped anchor in a fiord-like expanse, perfectly sheltered, the finest large harbour in the South Pacific. Here a captain of the Spanish Navy had raised a flag in 1792 and named the beautiful anchorage Port of Refuge but the gesture was never followed up. When the great colonial powers were arguing about who should have Samoa (see page 143) at the end of last century, a memo from the British Admiralty to the Foreign Office discreetly pointed out that the western part of Samoa had no harbour worth the name, and the Americans already had a naval coaling station in the excellent harbour of Pago Pago, but Port of Refuge could shelter an entire fleet. Thus the Germans were allowed to take what is now Western Samoa in exchange for giving Britain a free hand in Tonga.

As motor launches ferried the cruise passengers ashore, the arrival of each one at the town wharf was greeted by the *oompah* of the high-school band. The instruments glittered in the harsh sunlight and sweat streamed down the players' noses. Next to the band was a table with a white cloth and a sun umbrella, where a crisply uniformed steward dispensed tea and coffee: it demonstrated the self-sufficiency of the *Sea Princess*. A cruise ship made no demands for such things as large numbers of lavatories on a tiny island, and passengers could carry away with them many more handicrafts than they would as air travellers. But cruise ships were also, like chain hotels, the last lingering echo of colonialism. No Pacific country has a stake in any of the cruise ship companies.

Getting ashore well ahead of the horde, I found a hillside village of large clapboard buildings, weary-looking shutters, shady colonial verandahs and faded paint. It was enchanting. A green space around the little wooden Post Office was being set up as a bazaar where a variety of pandanus laundry baskets, grass skirts and coconut ukeleles was being arranged for sale. The dusty street was crowded as people came from all over the group for Ship Day. Far down the harbour the ship gleamed like a snowy alp in a tropical lake.

On a day like this there was no choice but to surrender. I was no longer a lone traveller seeking the gentle adventure of island landfalls, and encounters on sun-warped decks. I was a rich tourist from the ship, and the image was unshakeable. Even when I chatted with some cruising yachties on the pier, and went out with them to their yachts, I was clearly regarded as something from over the wall: a somewhat crazed romantic whose taste of the sea depended on how much salt he sprinkled on his french fries.

Scores of faces regarded me with curiosity and amusement from the dark bands and splashes of shade under the verandahs and trees along the short main street as I joined the carnival procession of pasty white and pink-skinned figures in obscenely short shorts, funny hats and cameras. We had come to see the island and islanders had come to see us and both sides were having a fine time. There was no way of stepping through the barrier.

From the yachtsmen I learned that the islands, so close together with many anchorages, are a cruising heaven. The only practical difficulty is that the shores are very steep so you have to let out a lot of chain and vessels easily drag their anchors: indeed, even the *Sea Princess* was having trouble and had to re-lay her anchors. The people were hospitable and, as you sailed in, local boats really did come alongside as they did in voyagers' tales, to invite you to their villages for a feast. Only when arrangements are finalised does the awful truth dawn: it is not natural hospitality being pressed so warmly upon you, but salesmanship. The charge is about $5 a head for singing, dancing and all you can eat. The income from a couple of hundred cruising yachts every year is an important factor in a community of only 15,000 where a clerk is lucky to earn $15 a week.

We sailed in time to weave clear of the islands before dark and I checked my morning newspaper, *Princess Patter*, for what was on. There was a choice of two films, gambling, a disco, a quiz game, classical music in the reading room and two performances of a floor show called *An Evening with Irving Berlin*, scripted and choreographed at P & O headquarters in London. The classical music was *Swan Lake* and when I flopped into an armchair there was only one other listener, a prim woman with a moustache writing up her diary. I had been on the go now for two months and had my fill of beaming natives strumming guitars and pop music on cassette players. To listen to this "real" music was more soothing on the spirit than any of the luxuries I had enjoyed in the past two days. For half an hour I lost the feeling of illusion that had dislodged my perceptions over the past weeks, and became connected again with the real world. From this moment my mood began a subtle but significant change. Up to now my wandering had been a succession of departures, but now I began to gear up mentally for an ultimate landfall. The ocean-wanderer's freedom, I was finding, exerted its own mysterious tensions. There comes a time when even the albatross returns to its nest.

Meanwhile I felt like the explorer who had crossed a watershed. I had left Melanesia behind and was entering Polynesia. A whole new romance lay ahead. Even the weather had a different, fresher look about it, as if spring were breaking.

Buoyant after listening to the music, I made the most of the evening. A large steak for dinner, then a film and the floorshow. At ten I strolled out on deck to see what I could of the island of Tofua and, just off it, the perfect cone of Kao, which the Staff Captain described on the blower. Right here, Captain Bligh had been turned adrift in a 23-foot open boat by Fletcher Christian and the mutineers. On Tofua he had landed to get water, been surrounded by natives who picked up stones and beat them together. They threw the stones as the castaways backed off the beach, killing the bosun.

Now, just one light showed at the foot of the black monolith rising blankly in the night sky. Who could resist hanging over the rail of the great white ship, floodlit from stem to stern, as she steamed down the glittering track of the moon to within a mile of the mysterious shore? Leaning a little tipsily into the stiff wind rippling along the promenade deck, I gazed forward and I gazed aft. Nobody, the deck was all mine. What were the other 799 doing on this romantic tropical night?

I wandered through the public rooms to the crowded Pacific Lounge. On stage, two bearded Australian sheepfarmers were seated at opposite sides of a small table in the spotlight. Each was swaddled in a white sheet and blindfolded with a red bandana. Between them stood a large bowl of soft ice cream. As the ship steamed through the velvet of the night, the two men were feeding each other, a comedy of hit and miss that was reducing this new generation of South Seas voyagers to helpless hysterics.

Nuku'alofa proved to be a rambling, scruffy little capital with the airs and graces of an ironed-flat Ruritania under tropical palms. Shaped like the profile of a human foot with the toes turned up, the island is twenty miles by twelve at its greatest extent but the land area is much reduced by the twin arms of an extensive muddy lagoon. It is so flat that you hardly have to puff on a rented bone-shaker of a bicycle, unless you are pedalling into the wind. The rich black soil is so densely covered by coconut palms that from the high rail of the ship the land is a sea of spiky fronds in which tin roofs are visible only on the near edge. The shallow curve of the bay does not make a dramatic port of entry, but any sense of disappointment lingers no longer than it takes to stroll a mile along the foreshore to town.

The faint speck of a sail on the horizon provokes a ripple of interest in a crowd waiting patiently on the shore. It proves to be an open, clinker-built whaler. Sail is dropped and it is poled into the shallows where a boy brings ashore strings of brilliant fish. Despite the large crowd and the long wait, nobody shows much eagerness to buy and the transactions take a long time. Another little boat comes in and a dozen octopus are laid on the sand, like thin tapered stockings filled with grey-white slime. A shark is dismembered on the rocks and people drop steaks into their straw baskets.

A pair of saluting guns gleam at the base of a tall flagpole around which old women sit beneath umbrellas making baskets from palm fronds. Beyond, over a low stone wall, is the neat garden of the Royal Palace. Its turreted iron roofs are as vividly red as the flamboyants hanging over the garden wall, its weatherboards and decorative fret-work as snowy white as the geese that hiss in its back garden and the cotton gloves of its soldiers on guard in toytown sentry boxes.

Tauf'ahau Road, the main street, strikes inland at right angles to the shore and is barely five short blocks in length. At the head of it, the modern post office dispenses Tonga's amazing postage stamps: a one-*sene* (cent) stamp is one banana, a two-*sene* stamp is two bananas, and so on up to a bunch of five, then come water melons, coconuts and a whole gallery of round, triangular and scroll-like designs. Parliament House, opposite, is a faded board-built affair like an old-time evangelist hall. The Tong Hua Chinese restaurant was formerly a Mormon church. Produce is brought to market by horse and cart. I found a bed in a nice room of a guest house that had wide trellised verandahs, a view of the sea and a rate of $7 a night. Next day was Sunday and I was clattering busily on my portable typewriter when the German who managed the place on behalf of its Tongan owners knocked worriedly at my door. He was seriously concerned that the Police would arrest me. The Sabbath in Tonga is strictly observed. Aircraft may not fly. Ships may not sail. Neither cheques nor contracts signed on a Sunday are valid. If you walk you must walk quietly. You may swim but not jump up and down. Radio stations do not broadcast. Next door an Australian diplomat had been hammering in his house, hanging the pictures which at last had arrived by cargo ship with his furniture, when the Police banged on the door and told him to stop. Not long ago, Herman told me, they had arrested a man for repairing the hospital generator. So I stopped writing, put on long trousers and a tie, and did what a good Tongan should. I went to church.

The Wesleyan Church was a vast, austere, bunker-like building that smelled as sweet as a fruit shed because most of the congregation wore flowers in their hats. His Majesty King Tauf'ahau Tupou IV came the short distance from the palace in a black Mercedes 600 flanked by two outriders preceded by a Toyota Landcruiser with a blue flashing light. A kingly figure if ever there was one, His Majesty is said to weigh about 32 stone (450 pounds). He wore leather boots, a long leather overcoat and black sun-glasses, and in his special pew at the front, spent much time fiddling with the powerful Japanese-made electric fan while the large choir sang beautifully.

With the cruise ship out of the way, I was beginning to get a feel for the people who had created this tiny capital of stagy quaintness. Now, looking at the dignified and statuesque Tongans crowding the church, the overwhelming impression was one of dignity and confidence. They faced no crisis of national identity, like the New Hebrides. They did not have to compete, as the Fijians did, with a smarter and totally different culture. The Tongans had never been colonised and their royal house, unique in the Pacific, gave them a status which in turn helped them to keep a grip of their culture and braked the slide into westernisation. The most immediately visible manifestation of this was their own habit of wearing traditional straw mats bunched around their waists. Many of these *ta'ovala* are heirlooms, generations old, and as stiff and impliable as old leather and much the same dark colour. The mats are not tailored in any way but simply doubled over, wrapped once or twice round the middle and held up with a rope or leather belt. New ones are so stiff that it is barely possible to sit down but after a time they develop horizontal creases in the right places, setting into a hard shape like that of a crinkled funnel. Even so, they adapt badly to certain modern activities such as riding a bicycle or levering yourself into a Datsun, so many of the younger people are inventing new styles of mat using strips of plastic or crochet that permit greater freedom of movement.

When the King's late mother Queen Salote made herself enormously popular in Britain in 1952 by disdaining the pouring rain and refusing to raise the hood of the open coach in which she rode in the Coronation procession, it is said that when she stood up a couple of gallons of water which had collected in the straw mat encircling her ample girth doused the Tunku of Malaya, sitting opposite. Another story about Salote at the Coronation concerns Noël Coward. Who was the diminutive gentleman with the Queen of Tonga? one of his party had inquired, Noël Coward riposted unkindly: "Her lunch."

Some coral heaps and atolls, some bits of palm-fringed beach. This was Tonga in 1906, described by the British Agent and Consul, who added unfairly that it remained a native state "by reason of its great, its regal unimportance." Tonga avoided the fate of its near neigh-bours, when Imperial countries were annexing every rock in the sea, because very early on it had a written constitution and a recognisable government that remained paternal, stable and popular. At the time when Captain Cook called, the islands were degenerating into civil war and barbarity, largely copy-catting Fiji. Traditional customs were fading and chiefs were warring with gusto but they came all out for the Lord and were wholly christianised by Weslyans within two decades. This provided the stability on which King George Tupou I built, and despite powerful outside influences throughout most of last century kept Tonga for the Tongans. Britain was already developing Suva as an important port and administrative centre, and when allowed a free hand in Tonga by Germany's renunciation of interests, was content to let the Tongans do their own thing as long as they remained friendly and did not let anyone else in. The British High Commissioner in his charming little office surrounded by flowers on the shore still has a direct telephone line to His Majesty, but Tonga has never been anything but independent.

History has taken an ironic twist, however. Although by default the Tongans are the freest people in the Pacific they are also, in a national sense, materially the poorest. So the King has consciously pandered to West Germany's odd desire to have a little pet in the South Seas. Fêted and honoured, His Majesty was given a rousing reception when he made an official visit to West Germany in 1979, and went out of his way to say on TV that any German who arrived in his country would be made welcome. It caused diplomatic pandemonium.

The Tongan High Commission in London received no less than 3,000 letters. Thousands more poured into Nuku'alofa where the tiny administration ceased sending replies after the first five hundred. This was typical:

> Please convey my greetings to His Majesty, we wish to take up his offer to come and live in Tonga. I am an engineer, my wife is an architect. We have two children and we would like to leave in June ...

Germans of all kinds, wide-eyed about paradise, arrived at the little Tongatapu Airport with all their worldly goods in a couple of suitcases and had to return somewhat disgruntled. It was hardly their fault because it had been easy to imagine from the king's remarks that he was establishing immigration on a grand scale, like Australia. Even those with a few millions to invest did not find it easy to remain, because in many cases their ideas for development would have merely competed with local people rather than created opportunity for them.

The reality of the island mystique which so entranced the Germans that the Tonga Association in West Berlin is reputed to have 2,000 members, is in fact a grim picture very far removed from the image of a sunny little isle off the beaten track in paradise.

Land in Tonga is owned by the King personally and thirty-three nobles; only unproductive areas such as uninhabited islands and urban areas are owned by the government. Enshrined in the Constitution of 1878 is the principle that on attaining the age of sixteen every male receives two allotments at a token rent of about one dollar, one of $8\frac{1}{4}$ acres out in the bush and one of about an acre in his village. On this land a man and his family could be self-sufficient in food and also earn a little cash. He could grow about 250 coconut palms, and cultivate such things as banana, breadfruit, mango, kapok, papaya, potato, yams, taro, sugar cane, pumpkin, arrowroot, pandanus, cabbage, peanuts, avocado, corn, water melon and even paper mulberry or cottonwood (for *tapa* and "grass" skirts). The problem is that with 70,000 people on its ninety-nine square miles, Tongatapu is one of the most crowded islands in the Pacific. Now, hundreds of men have no allotment and those who do must share with many brothers and uncles. While there is enough land to grow food for day to day subsistence, nobody can make any money, yet more and more cash is required to make ends meet. No kind of farming venture can succeed because the plots are too small, and to top it all the ruling nobles have seen the writing on the wall and stopped making new allotments available because they want the land for themselves.

In the Prime Minister's office I talked with Dr Epeli Ha'ufa, a large, shaggy, pipe-smoking man of forty who is Royal Historian and the first Pacific Islander to become an anthropologist. What could the Tongan people do? "Not much," he reflected. "All we can do is resign ourselves to our lot, become very religious, and pray that there will be more land available in Heaven."

Tourists came here and saw only the picture of a carefree, romantic life in paradise, he went on, yet beneath the surface Tongans were scrabbling for survival. Nobody was starving, there was no malaria, the climate was benign*, but it was not so much an economic problem as a psychological one. "Once you are educated, once your mind is expanded, subsistence on a remote little island is simply unacceptable," he explained. "We are a country of 90,000 men, women and children but nearly one in three of us has been abroad in the last ten years. Psychologically we are no longer islanders. Travel has changed our material values and expectations, drained us of talent, changed outlooks within families and transformed eating habits to the point

* In 1982 the islands were devastated by a hurricane.

that most of our protein and flour is imported. We have no future other than feeding ourselves for there is nothing else here. Our imports are six times higher than our exports, yet one-third of that import bill is for food we have to buy only because tastes are swinging away from what we are able to grow for ourselves."

While Germans set out for a new life in Tonga, the Tongans resorted to every device to get out of the place. The basic wage is only about $2.50 a day yet there are all sorts of ways of cobbling up the air fare. Church Trustees lend money freely so people can fly to New Zealand where they get well-paid menial jobs, such as factory work by day and dishwashing by night. They stay free with friends or relatives, pay back the money, and save enough to holiday in California.

Back home they find opportunity hamstrung by Custom and feudalism. In the three years up to 1976 it was reported that one-third of all the country stores in the villages of Tongatapu had closed down due to church and family obligations. In one case a storekeeper gave half his stock to a funeral one week and the other half to another funeral the following week, because he felt obliged to help his family to the best of his ability.

With only ten per cent of school leavers finding jobs the competition for scholarships abroad is intense because a university place is a passport to freedom. Young people resort to other means of escape, too. In June 1978 a freighter arrived at Auckland with no less than twenty-five young stowaways. More recently a young man died, overcome by fumes, when he stowed away with two friends in the funnel of a cruise liner. "You have to be pretty desperate," Dr Epeli said, calmly blowing smoke from his pipe, "to do something like that."

Although Tonga has had a guardian uncle in Great Britain, the little country has always lacked a patron and this is the role that West Germany seems bent on filling, though it is hard to imagine with what purpose. For years New Zealand had given minimal aid to Tonga, and Australia none, and it was only when the King started talks concerning a new airport with the Russians, who clearly saw Vava'u as a possible base for the operation of their distant-water fishing fleet, that the two rich neighbouring nations were stung into recognising that there were green spots as well as blue on the map of the Pacific. Over the past couple of years, Britain has given a hospital, a wharf, and a police training school; New Zealand has provided agricultural projects, schools, a technical institute, a hospital, runway lighting for the airport; Australia has given an automatic telephone exchange and aided the development bank; Japan has given a fisheries research centre and a dilapidated vessel. But Germany handed over a lump sum of $10 million, (more than all other aid combined) for the purchase of a magnificent new cargo ship, did the same for Western Samoa, and was now preparing to give Tonga an inter-island passenger vessel.

It was inner agonies of the kind that drove the young Tongans to stow away in the cruise ship's funnel which historians believe spurred much of the Polynesian colonisation of the Pacific, the great canoe voyages in search of new lands. For the size of these oceanic nations clinging to dry land by their fingertips is minuscule. I rented a bicycle for three days to explore the island and found I had covered more or less all of it on day one. The whole of Tonga, if all 169 islands were joined together, is less than a quarter the size of Rhode Island, but the tiny pieces are scattered over a stretch of ocean rather longer than Florida.

The outward face of Tonga, however, is a smiling and placid one. The people stay home on Sundays and entertain each other with good food, even if they have to semi-starve all week. Standards are rigorously observed: it is impolite for a man to be without a shirt, unless he is actually swimming. Erect in creaky straw mats that look as comfortable to wear as wafer biscuits, swinging a furled umbrella with bare feet splayed, a chiefly old man will flicker his eyebrows in a cheery greeting. A muscle-bound young man with wild hair, football jersey, and jeans at half mast will wink and tip his head in that macho "ocker" way of working men Down Under. Stout women in brightly coloured ankle-length Mother Hubbards grin winsomely, as if you are a familiar figure of conjecture in the neighbourhood. The pretty young teenage girls are cool, coy and cheeky by turn, and often manage to combine all three in one blushing, speculative, warning look.

I had pedalled to the south-west shore where there is no barrier reef and the ocean swells slop under ledges of coral. The waves die on the spot but the air pressure jets water upwards through blowholes, creating spectacular whistling geysers fifty or sixty feet high. I walked over the reef at low tide with about thirty Tongans "gleaning" for shellfish and octopus that crawl up from the deep water. The surface of brilliant coral was as jagged and dangerous to walk on as broken glass and it took a practised eye to see through Nature's camouflage. A quick jab of an iron spike could produce anything from a periwinkle to an octopus. Whatever it was, it went into the gunny sack over the shoulder and the sharp-eyed patrolling in ankle-deep water continued until the rising tide drove the gleaners up to the sand.

Everywhere in the neat grassy villages was heard the sound of hammering. It was a hollow, head-splitting sound of wood against wood, coming from many different sources and with the same haunting rhythm. TAP-TAP-TAP-TAP ... long pause, while further away came another with a slightly different note, Tap-ta-ta-ta-tap. Then a nearer one started again, drowning the others, THUD-THUD-THUD-THUD ... It is the sound of women squatting cross-legged in low thatched lean-to huts beating the bark of the paper mulberry tree and sticking it together with arrowroot starch to make *tapa*, the traditional paper-like cloth of the islands.

But I had not had much luck in finding a ship to take me to other islands. One ship had just sailed before I arrived, but it was bound only for Vava'u. Nuku'alofa was one of the least shippy of waterfronts. Out in the bay a small freighter was being refitted, and a fishing boat provided by the Japanese was being smartened up to take the King on his annual tour of the outer islands. A handful of yachts sheltered in a basin within a low stone wall, and there was a boat at 5 am every day to the high island of Eua, nearby, but I wanted to go further than that. Nobody had news of when the next vessel would sail. A young New Zealand scientist in my guest house offered me a ride in a sailing cutter in which he was planning a few days surveying whales, but all the time I was there his skipper's "tomorrow" never came.

Meanwhile, the mantelpiece of my little room in the Fasi Moe Afi Guest House bore a large embossed invitation the like of which I hardly expected to see again with my own name on the dotted line. In elaborate copperplate printing Their Majesties King Tauf'ahau Tupou IV and Queen Halaevalu Mata'aho bade me attend a State Feast in honour of the Governor General of New Zealand, Sir Keith Holyoake, who was passing through.

The feast was a collar and tie affair, and held on the sloping lawns of the King's country estate, in the centre of the island, on the shore of the lagoon. The arrangement of the feast typified the communal approach to social obligations that colours every aspect of life in the South Seas. The word had been passed down, from the King to his Nobles to the village elders. In Kanokupolu, Nukunuku, 'Utulau, Afa, Lavengatonga ... in all the villages of the island men and women had been busy preparing stretchers of food which were taken to the feasting ground by truck. Each stretcher, about seven feet by two, was heaped with food in a way thought to do the most honour to the village providing it. On the lawn the stretchers were laid in lines beneath makeshift thatched canopies and the guests sat facing them cross-legged on mats. Each magnificent heap of food was spanned by cane hoops wrapped in coloured paper and these supported embroidered tule designed to keep the flies off. After prayers and introductory speeches the fly screens were removed and a schoolgirl, from the village that provided the food, waved a fly-whisk. At negligible expense the State was entertaining six hundred people. It was the ultimate bring-a-plate party.

And what a feast. The tray of food confronting me was heaped with eight sucking pigs, their skins hard, shiny and crackly, as if sunburned, their eyes peacefully closed. There were yams, larger than the pigs, hands of small sweet bananas, and little leaf-parcels of gooey sweet gravy. The schoolgirl who said the food had come from Houna, near the blowholes, showed me how to break away the crackling from a little pig's back and tear out with my fingers the soft, sweet rather tasteless flesh. It was muggily hot and my knees grew numb from unaccustomed squatting but I felt I had to do some justice to the mountain of pork in front of me: only three of us were sharing it, and the two elderly people who had flown in that morning from holiday in Hawaii (paid for by their children there) had quickly dropped their chins on their chests and snoozed.

The visitor's speech was fatuous, patronising and interminable. When I caught the eye of a fellow New Zealander, we had a collective squirm. After the speeches there was a long session of formal dancing. The programme was only half way completed when the two hundred village people who had been sitting under umbrellas outside the fence received some official signal and swarmed in to collect the food they had brought. Like victims borne away on stretchers from the scene of a terrible disaster, the sucking pigs and crabs, the lobsters and bananas – little of it scarcely picked at – were carried away on stretchers draped with white, loaded on trucks, and taken home where it would be distributed. Thus the State feast at one blow satisfied national honour as well as the national appetite.

As the feast disappeared in clouds of dust I, too made my escape. For at last I had found a ship and it was going my way.

EKIAKI

DECK PASSAGE TO
THE FRIENDLY ISLES

The ship was an obsolete long-liner given to Tonga by Japan, but the engine had broken down so frequently that it was sold to a local entrepreneur who went into the inter-island shipping business. Now called *Ekiaki* and scarcely larger than a River Thames day-trip boat, the little ship was said to float on the inner of her two bottoms. Quite a lot of her passengers nodded off and rolled over the side and were never seen again, I was warned.

Fortified by a steak-and-egg sandwich, with a pocket of biscuits and apples for emergency rations, I joined the pierhead crowd an hour before sailing time. I expected that whole families would be fare-welling one or two passengers and only a handful of people would actually be travelling, but I was wrong.

At least 200 people clustered around an immense heap of gear: wooden chests, cardboard boxes, sleeping mats parcelled up with string, bicycles, double beds and mattresses, drums of fuel, bags of coconuts, pigs in crates, prams, outboard motors ... Easing my way to the edge of the wharf I gazed down at the ship. She hardly made a resolute spectacle. Deck cargo was being heaped in the waist of the ship, around the single hatch. Aft of the wheelhouse there was a deck through which the funnel and a couple of ventilators jutted, but the entire space was packed with bundles of sawn timber to within two inches of the top of the rail. It was roofed with tin on slender supports fastened with loops of rubber cut from inner tubes. There was no gangway and the vessel surged back and forth on loose mooring lines. I watched a baby swaddled in pink being passed across from one set of quivering fingertips to another. Next time the ship blew into the wharf I jumped down, landed on a roll of pig-netting, then clambered over the planks to secure an outboard position near the rail where at least I could get comfortable by swinging my legs over the side and contemplating the ocean. It proved to be a nearly fatal misjudgement.

Uneasily I concluded that the entire population of the pierhead plus their luggage was to travel with me in the overloaded and listing vessel. As more and more people pitched camp around me, I unrolled my sleeping bag beside the ship's rail and stretched out to claim the space. They came aboard with bundles of blankets and cardboard boxes of yam, taro and greasy cold pork. Already, as bits of pork gristle arched over my body to feed the hundreds of tiny fish milling in the clear litter-strewn water around the ship, my thinly endowed limbs and rump were feeling the hardness of the planks. With their ability to sit cross-legged for hours in one place, the Polynesians were content to claim spaces about three feet square while I was determined to assert my rights to the same square-footage but arranged in a coffin shape so I could lie flat. But the crowd congealed towards me like a lava flow, clotting in soft sweaty lumps of brown flesh crowned by bright smiles. I was reduced to sitting space, leaning against the sailbag in which I carried a few clothes, with my legs stretched out. To my horror I saw a man pointing to the narrow space my legs occupied. An enormous woman bearing voluminous bundles of pillows and sleeping mats picked her way to my spot. There was no point in trying to warn her off with angry looks so I smiled a welcome in the Polynesian way and took her bundles as she plumped on her ample rump. Then – horrors! – she beckoned and was joined by another woman of similar bulk and baggage.

Forced to the very edge of the deck cargo, I manoeuvred swiftly to ensure that I was alongside one of the slender vertical posts supporting the roof. Only then did I realise, on looking up, that the iron did not extend all the way to the edge of the deck but ended twelve inches short. There was no gutter so when it rained I would cop the lot. Decidedly tight-lipped by this time, I broke out my precautionary Kwells and thought longingly of the comfortable cabin in the *Sea Princess*. But perhaps it wouldn't rain.

The sound of much nose-blowing heralded sailing hour. A little girl near me burst into tears three times as she waved to her Daddy on the pier, but each time it was a false alarm. At one point she broke off suddenly, did her business in a white plastic pot, and the contents were briskly tossed overboard, passing over my head in a glittering arc shot with rainbows. At last the engine gave a cough or two, the sailors slithered over the passengers to haul in the warps, and the *Ekiaki* headed out to sea.

The meaning of her name I never did discover, but "sicky-yukky" was an appropriate alliteration. At the first tilt of the deck wet-eyed folk all around me folded against each other like a lot of slipped books. The wind came from astern so we moved in an envelope of oily diesel fumes through which the yellow fire of the swift sunset shimmered like real flames. My giant Polynesian neighbours thrust hankies over their faces, tucked sheets like table cloths around their shoulders, and flopped on the spot as if their bones had melted. As it fell completely dark I put on a jumper and with great difficulty wriggled into my daughter's pink sleeping bag patterned with elves and fairies. I could lie down if I jack-knifed my knees but this was eerie because they jutted over the ship's side. With much more wriggling I managed to extract my handkerchief from my pocket and roll it into a doughnut to pad the red-raw point of my hip bone. Before long, both women rolled against me, pushing me to the edge. Then there was a sudden convulsive eruption. Desperate fingers clawed my legs. A great weight pinned me to the rail and for an endless interval I felt every contraction of the woman's stomach as she was seasick over the side. When the spasms at last subsided and the pressure on my legs slackened, I closed my eyes and with gritted teeth forced myself to think of beautiful things. When at last I allowed myself a furtive glance at my watch it was just eight o'clock.

It is characteristic of Polynesians that they are never so happy as when they are in a heap. They like to rub shoulders, quite literally, and to be in human touch in a way that makes an Englishman's hackles crawl. Closely packed in a crowd, leaning against each other, seems to give physical comfort and psychological support. Nobody but myself and a dour Swede, crammed against the hot funnel, seemed the least bothered by the crowding. I was concerned about other things, too, such as the lack of lifeboat and lifejackets. There was a small crumb of comfort in knowing that one's bed was a raft of timber. I was also curious as to why the people who were history's greatest navigators were also such bad sailors.

The peopling of the Pacific was the greatest feat of maritime colonisation in history. At approximately the time of Christ, the essentially Neolithic Polynesian culture that had developed over a millenium in the islands of Tonga and nearby Samoa (the relationship between the two in antiquity is hard to read) launched out into the blue. The triangle of ocean they covered makes the Atlantic look small and is in fact a good bit larger than Africa. The tiny islands they found were not on the rim of the ocean but in the middle of it. In *Polynesian Seafaring** Edward Dodd marks the clear distinction between the

*Dodd, New York, 1972

coastwise character of all Western man's voyaging, up to Captain Cook's time when our technology was at last able to find longitude, and the "blue water psychology" of the Polynesian. If the European sailor went out of sight of land, maybe for days at a time, it was only to take a known short cut. All his senses, like radar, were tied to the land. But the Polynesian sailor adapted himself to the maritime environment. The open ocean was not for him a region of terror but of security. He was at home there. His vessel was small, but as any yachtsman knows, bulk is no guarantee of safety at sea and a well-found cockleshell can ride a storm that sinks great ships. Freeboard was low and canoes might swamp, but there were many people to bail and many paddles to provide auxiliary power. In the island way, people used canoes as we use motor cars. The lagoon was their forest, and a man spent half his life afloat upon it, hunting and gleaning. The first Europeans in the South Seas were constantly amazed by the sheer numbers of canoes, Cook commonly recording that his ships were surrounded by as many as five hundred.

How did they find their way when they had no way of figuring and no written language? The European system of navigation is techno-logical: we measure, calculate and tabulate, combining observations with trigonometry and time to get a "fix". The Polynesians used the patterns of the moving stars. As Dodd describes it:

> These tracks when you know them give you a multitude of related bearings to tell you where you are. These are not latitudes and longitudes that go at right angles east and west, north and south. These are great arcs of light like bars of a celestial cage that, as you move about within it, show you from many related directions and many graded heights just where you are. From the sky patterns above, if you know them well enough, you know your place beneath.

As the stars constantly vary their paths, the navigator aimed not at the star itself but at the certain "pit" from which his pattern of stars emerged and the "pit" into which they fell. Individual stars merely indicated the constant spot on the horizon. For this reason the navigator's "day" began at sunset and he travelled by night when his senses were most alert. At sea the sunlit hours were of little use.

Lying along the rail of the *Ekiaki* and staring down at the black waves it was easy to imagine the raw uncertainties of Polynesian voyaging and the lulling fatalism that would engulf the senses of those with no active part to play in the reading of the stars. It began to dawn on me with only a faint sense of alarm that waves were getting closer. The ship was rolling more heavily to port than to starboard. We were developing a list, perhaps because the timber on the deck was becoming waterlogged. But there was no point in worrying about it. If we turned turtle it would give me something to write home about. An unlucky wave slapped against the starboard bow and spray thundered on the thin tin roof. I closed my eyes and tensed: if the ship rolled my way now I would cop the lot. It did and I did. A curtain of cold seawater dropped from the roof, soaking me to the skin. A young mother near my head was comprehensively seasick into the nest of blankets in which she lay with her baby. For about the tenth time one of the women retched over my legs. Around two in the morning there was a commotion when the mate came through the crowd with a torch, kicking people awake and telling them to move to the starboard side to correct the list. Half a dozen people staggered a few inches on their hands and knees and subsided. The mate seemed satisfied.

I must have dozed. Around 4 am I opened my eyes and realised the water was moving past the ship in the opposite direction. We were steaming backwards. The wind had risen. Blankets and sleeping mats whipped like flags. Had we run aground? A searchlight lit up a long streak of pale green water churned to a froth by the wind, and at the end of the tunnel of light I saw a tiny dinghy packed with people. More passengers!

Dawn came as the mucky sort of light that creeps through northern cities on cold mornings. It brought thick horizontal rain of the kind that makes moorland sheep turn their backs and stare at their front feet. For hours we dodged in the lee of a small *motu*, a tiny island, while the dinghy made endless trips across two or three miles of bouncing water to a distant village. I ate my biscuits but was dying of thirst, and sat with my mouth open to get what trickles I could from the edge of the roof.

I was bound for the island of Lifuka on which Pangai was the principal village. Every time the ship paused at some island I asked whether this was Pangai. The people around me conferred, deciding whether it was Pangai, and always assured me it was "next stop."

At last, in mid-afternoon, the ship limped through dead-flat water dimpled by raindrops to a strip of white sand overhung by dripping palms. The sky was grey, the sea was grey, the place looked forlorn but evidently it was Pangai at last. There was a wharf but it had no deck. A man wandered down the sand, stripped to his shorts, and swam out to meet us. He fixed a light rope to his middle, swam powerfully to the outermost pile, swarmed ten feet to its summit, and hauled over a heavier warp which he made fast. We had arrived, and now all we had to do was get ashore. I was tempted to dive over the side. In the drumming rain I could hardly have been wetter or more miserable.

The problem was resolved by a lugger that happened to be in from another island. It came alongside and there was a struggle to get aboard. I was last over the side but the lugger was so crowded that there was no space. All I could do was launch myself blindly into the throng. There was a blood-curdling scream and a ball of muscle wriggled from under my feet. I had stepped on a pig. I saved myself by snatching at the rucksack of the Swedish traveller in front of me. He grabbed a Tongan girl who nearly dropped her baby, and she snatched at the shoulder of a man who kept his balance by throwing both arms around the middle of an old lady. The Swede shot me a filthy look. All the Tongans roared with laughter. The lugger backed away and came alongside a low stone jetty. Last aboard was first off. I jumped on to clean sodden grass and was fifty paces under the palms before I stopped to look back. There were splashes alongside the *Ekiaki* where they were throwing drums of fuel over the side and swimming them ashore.

Seletute's guest house was a neat, flat-roofed bungalow on green lawn in a fenced garden five minutes' walk along the puddled road. It had wooden front steps, louvred glass windows and a plastic Virgin Mary enshrined in a grotto of cemented rocks and seashells by the front gate. Seletute herself, (the name is a transliteration of Gertrude, as Salote is of Charlotte) was a stout, amiable little soul with long black hair piled up in a bun, a long black dress and bare feet. "Welcome to Pangai, welcome to my little house," she beamed. Hot cup of tea. Cold shower. Dry clothes. And, most miraculous of all, a four-poster bed. It was made of thin black-lacquered alloy and the canopy was silvered with a cloud-like lining of evening gown material. But who cared. For $8 a day including three meals, this was paradise.

Dusk was early because of the rain and I sat in the creeping darkness of the glassed-in verandah until Seletute's son brought in an oil lamp. Arnie and Anita from some far-flung corner of Alaska were sore because their booked and confirmed reservations on the day's plane failed to materialise, but they produced a couple of large bottles of beer and we all cheered up a bit. There was Mike, a young Australian on his way to a scholarship in fine arts at Harvard; Gianluca, a young Italian businessman in very tight jeans; the inevitable Berliners. This silent pair, when they left next day, refused to pay Seletute's full rate on the grounds that they had not eaten lunch, although she had put it on the table for them. "After all," Seletute complained hotly, in terms that seemed oddly out of place in a remote little South Sea backwater, "a deal is a deal, right?"

Dinner was mullet, diced meat and vegetables, and corned beef, all out of tins, and boiled taro leaves tasting of spinach. As we tourists slumbered comfortably in the house that Seletute's husband had built with $5,000 earned during a year as a seaman in New Zealand, the landlady and her children slept in a low thatched hut outside. Now her husband was away at sea again, saving more money. "We are going to construct the first motel unit in all the Ha'apai Islands", she told me proudly, dishing up the morning's breakfast of pan-fried bread and Nescafé.

The office of South Pacific Island Airways was a little shed on the highway of muddy puddles and occupied by Fina Wuata and his wife Fehi (Fay). "Sorry, the flight's full up and already two on standby". But I was confirmed, dammit. "What they told you in Nuku'alofa is no concern of mine." When was the next flight? "Maybe Saturday." Three days away. Couldn't he call up head office by radio? "Wish I could, but I haven't got a bloody radio – the aircraft is supposed to be bringing one in when it comes."

I walked out into the pouring rain and splashed along the road to the shore. The *Ekiaki* lay soggily in the grey dimpled water. Nobody could be seen moving, though there must have been nearly a hundred people camped under the sagging tarpaulins screening her decks. No, I couldn't face that again. But why was it, stranded in a comfortable house on a palm-clad South Sea isle, that I felt so discouraged? I had no schedule to keep. The delay had no significance. But the breezy and placid tempo of my voyaging which had begun in the *Hawk* had been sabotaged by this brief contact with other travellers worried sick about their flights. Without realising it I had caught the germ and clicked naturally into the rat-race that was my accustomed environment. It was one thing to recognise the fact, but it took a real effort to laugh at it.

Lifuka, the biggest of about 120 islands in Ha'apai, is six miles long and has 3,000 people living in five villages. It is connected by a quarter-mile causeway recently built by the New Zealand army to another island of similar size and narrow crescent shape. Every village had its own large church, sign of status. In rain the houses constructed of thatch, boards and roofing iron in varying proportions had the appearance of meanest hovels. Crowded together outside some industrial city they would have been condemned as unfit for decent habitation. But here, when the sun finally blazed in a blue sky and the womenfolk got busy spreading their washing to dry on flowering shrubs, there was no sense of impoverishment. Quite the opposite, in fact. Though ramshackle, the houses were much loved. They were ventilated by fresh ocean breezes and widely spaced in vistas of green turf. Vegetable gardens bursting with produce were fenced against pigs and poultry; here and there a lone palm, a shady breadfruit tree, a frangipani with its heavenly scent. Menfolk were busy in their plantations, making copra and cultivating yams, taro, and other staples. When schools came out the gently steaming grass was flooded with children in bright uniforms, like hordes of butterflies. On the shoreline were clustered some low thatched huts where children from outer islands lived during term-time in the care of an adult who shared the duty on a rotating basis with others from the village. It was the end of term. Pretty wooden whaleboats sailed in, bringing in heaps of coconut husks for cooking fuel during the next term, and setting off again with the village children and heaps of shopping.

The two trade stores were on opposite sides of the road and a hundred yards apart. Their stocks of hardware, tinned food, bottled beer, shampoo, baby baths and Minties seemed identical. Inside they were gloomy and dusty, with long wide counters and half-filled shelves climbing up to the murky twilight under the eaves. For a time I sat on a bench on the verandah of one of them, beneath an advertisement for New Zealand apples. I was reminded of the hitch-hiking jaunts I had made through the backblocks of that country as a youth, when I would sit at a deserted crossroads for long detached moments, measuring time by the occasional distant murmur of an approaching vehicle, the gleeful anticipation of its arrival, the brief thunder and dust storm of its passing, then the long retreat until total silence and a sense of abandonment returned me to limbo. Here, too, time jerked along in a series of independent events. A woman came along the road carrying a black umbrella and went into the Burns Philip store. Five high school girls appeared at the end of the road, their pale blue smocks catching the eye, and sauntered past me giggling into the backs of their hands. A dog with its tail held high crossed the road and disappeared into a hut where half a dozen youths played snooker. The woman came out of the store, some tins of fish under her arm, and walked slowly out of sight. A coconut fell from a palm with a thud. There was an angry shout and the dog raced out of the snooker hut with a surprised look and its tail between its legs; then, sniffing, it disappeared into some bushes. A Toyota pick-up truck lurched through the puddles and stopped outside. A stout Tongan in a faded shirt, trousers held up with a necktie, and bare feet, clicked in his throat and tipped his straw hat at me as he entered the store. From somewhere came the sound of a sewing machine. The man came out of the store with a bottle of beer in a paper bag and drove away, grinding in first gear. Some little boys floated sticks in a puddle and nothing came by to scatter their battlefleet until long after they had run off, for no apparent reason, like birds taking wing. A white man pedalling in stately fashion approached on a bicycle.

On this little island the pace of life was so tentative that I wondered what the effects would be of two events occuring at once. Was it even possible for two things to happen at the same time?

Bored with sitting, I followed one of the muddy tracks crossing the island and came out on windward side. To my surprise, the breeze was strong enough to make walking difficult. Head down, I found myself on soft sand and continued walking without looking up until I realised I was not descending a beach to the water's edge but going up hill. I was walking up the slope of a mound of graves. As the islands were so near sea level one could not dig down far before striking water, so the dead were buried high up. The coffins were covered in sand patted down like sand castles and decorated with coloured shells, Christmas-tinsel streamers on sticks, and orderly picket fences of nose-down beer bottles. For safety's sake I muttered an apology to the spirits and wished them Good Afternoon.

The shoreline a few yards away was desolate and deserted. The reef made a shallow ledge extending out for half a mile and against its far edge the storm waves piled in a misty line. The outer fringe of palms writhed furiously. When a wet squall lashed over the green water I ran for the shelter of a pandanus grove, keeping clear of palms that might bomb me with a nut or two. Among the spiky cactus-like trees all was quiet, mossy and festooned with damp cobwebs. I smoked my pipe and listened to the solitude, wondering how it would be to wash up in such a place in story-book style from a shipwreck. This glade was mossy enough to provide a comfortable mattress but the ground was water-logged and the wood pulpy, not the stuff you could rub together like a good Boy Scout to make a spark. I found a fallen coconut and tried to get through its thick burlap husk with my bare fingers but I may as well have been trying to open a can of beans without an opener. Shells on the beach were no help because they were blunt from being rolled against each other. There was neither fruit nor berry in sight. The sand was pock-marked with little holes and the tracks of crabs. I dug down with my fingers only to find the crabs inhabiting large shells into which they retreated at the least excuse. The water of the lagoon was made opaque by the waves, so gleaning or spearing was out of the question. To be shipwrecked here would be a tough and joyless experience, I decided. After all, even Robinson Crusoe had the guns, powder, sails, timber, seeds and tools salvaged from his ship to sustain his twenty-eight years of solitude.

The Polynesians had also brought tools and food plants on their great voyages, for the islands offered little in the way of life support. In fact their skill in transporting and transplanting banana, breadfruit and tubers such as yam, taro and the South American sweet potato was every bit as essential to survival as their renowned navigation. Virtually every domestic plant as well as animals such as pigs, dogs and fowls, were brought with them from the Indo-Malay region. Even the coconut palm, the giraffe of vegetables and supermarket of desert islands, was introduced. By instinct the Polynesians are a horticultural people, a nation of gardeners. Out of necessity they are seamen and travellers. Which perhaps explained why so many succumbed so easily to seasickness.

Little realising that the chiefs at Lifuka were plotting to kill him, and that they did not spring a surprise attack only because they could not agree whether to do it in daylight or darkness, Captain Cook spent three weeks here and called Ha'apai the Friendly Islands, a name made much of in subsequent tourist brochures.

In 1805, at the age of fourteen, an English youth called William Mariner had a very different experience. He had sailed from Gravesend in a 500-ton privateer called *Port au Prince*. In a year and a half the vessel had harpooned a few whales, raised money by holding merchants of South American towns to ransom, sacked churches, aimed for Tahiti but missed it, and arrived in a seriously disabled condition at Lifuka. As 300 natives captured the ship, Will Mariner tried to blow it up but failed.

> On coming on deck the first object that struck his sight was enough to thrill the stoutest heart: there sat upon the companion a short squab naked figure of about fifty years of age, with a seaman's jacket, soaked with blood, thrown over one shoulder, on the other rested his iron-wood club, spattered with blood and brains – and what increased the frightfulness of his appearance was a constant blinking with one of his eyes and a horrible convulsive motion on one side of his mouth. On another part of the deck lay 22 bodies perfectly naked, and arranged side by side in even order. They were so dreadfully bruised and battered about the head that only two or three could be recognised . . .

Taken ashore certain he would be killed and roasted, the young man was instead fêted and found himself a right-hand man of the high chief who invaded Vava'u and in a series of bloody wars brought most of Tonga under his rule. The two-volume account of his four years in Tonga is a harrowing tale of real life in the "Friendly" Islands – of defeated chiefs executed by drowning, of gladiatorial contests in which the aim was to tear open an opponent's bowels with sharks' teeth sewn on to gauntlets; of enemy warriors having their heads cut off with blunted oyster shells, and many other pretty episodes.

As warriors of the Lord, the Tongans are today no less fervent but their fancied friendliness is tempered by a royal reserve. Perhaps it is innate shyness, or a sense of inferiority; perhaps the narrowness of their isolated existence does not prepare them for the spontaneous gesture of hospitality that a visitor from outside craves. My impressions were confirmed when again I saw the white man pedalling his bike along the road. At first, though he wanted to stop, he could not do so because he would have had to put his polished leather sandals and socks into a puddle. He stopped along the road a bit and I splashed after him.

"G'day, feel like a cold beer?" he asked cheerily.

Father Rod Milne, from New Zealand, was a quietly spoken, fresh-faced Marist priest of around forty who helped in the school and the church. The Tongan people ran their own affairs, he explained carefully, but his support in both establishments contributed the benefits of a wider experience of the world. He lived in one small room in the church hall, and we sat in deck chairs to watch the edge of the rain-cloud clearing out of the west and the sun sinking into the gap. Soon a rosy light flared in our faces, etching the palms along the shoreline in stark relief.

Loneliness was clearly troubling him. Though he had visited Tongan homes on official visits, in two years he had never been invited spontaneously. When he left Tonga he thought there would hardly be a single person with whom he would exchange letters, though he still corresponded often with old friends in Western Samoa, where he had worked previously. "In fact," he admitted, "I feel quite shut out here: people are warm enough on the surface and give you a happy greeting when you meet them on the beach, but it is hard to go deeper. I think you would have to live here all your life."

The odd contradictions between religious ethics and sexual promiscuity which have appalled generations of South Sea missionaries and delighted every sailor since Captain Cook were much in evidence here, he maintained. Tongans told jokes dirtier than any other race he knew, but were so puritanical that they refused to collect horse manure for their gardens. As everybody lived together in small crowded houses they knew exactly who was sleeping with whom but never mentioned names or even talked about it, not out of any sense of shame or secrecy but because procreation was regarded as a fundamental physical activity and it wasn't all that interesting as a subject of conversation. On the other hand the proprieties were observed. Teenagers were never seen kissing or cuddling, neither in moonlight nor daylight. Although he was a priest it was impossible for him to take a mixed class of boys and girls to the school vegetable garden in the bush, because it wouldn't look good, so a woman teacher had to go along as a chaperone.

A Tongan girl who made herself available to a White man on a temporary posting, such as a doctor, teacher or technician, would see the transaction as a ticket – at least to as far as Nuku'alofa and preferably out of Tonga. "There is just nothing here," Father Milne said. "You can subsist but it is nearly impossible to make money. The cyclone tattered our bananas to bits and turned the coconut palms inside out but even if you grow something to sell there is no shipping. The *Ekiaki* is one of the bigger ships on the run and comes only once in five or six weeks, usually without warning. One man slaved to grow 500 water melons and got them down to the pier but at the last minute the ship decided not to come in because there were no bananas to load, so he lost the lot."

The orb of the sun was just touching the far horizon, silhouetting the distant cone of Kao which I had seen a week earlier from the cruise ship's rail, and it promised a lovely evening. The low light enriched the colours of the flowers. The setting of the village was that of a seaside botanical garden. Yet it was virtually everybody's dream to escape. Wasn't it strange, I asked the priest, that this should be? How did he account for it?

"I had often wondered about it," he told me thoughtfully. "But not long ago when I was working in Western Samoa a pretty and bright teenage girl shot herself. She left two letters, one for her parents, one to the Sisters thanking for their love and apologising for all the trouble she was causing, but she couldn't face things any more. I buried the girl next day. She was laid out in the centre of an open-sided hut, with two schoolgirls sitting at her head to fan away the flies. All the boys and girls from school sat around, cross-legged. And as I said Mass do you know what I was thinking about?

"I was looking at the dead girl who had not been able to face her problems. I was looking at the beautiful children all around her, brimming with health and vitality, I was looking at the blue sea sparkling under the blue sky, and the palm trees bending in the warm wind. And I heard the little noises of animals around the house. It was a picture of perfect paradise. It gave me a terrible jolt, suddenly to realise that people face the same pressures everywhere, the *real* pressures that can become too much. Whether you're in a great city or a suburban desert or a tropical paradise, the pressures of being alive are always there, always weighing on you."

The Australian art student, Mike, was in a lather because he had missed the plane, and, as a consequence, all his important connections. Finau had told him to wait outside Seletute's with his suitcase but forgot to pick him up. When Mike saw the Twin Otter fly in overhead he sprinted to the Police Station where the constable was reading a

Biggles book but was no help because his jeep had run out of petrol. Mike ran to the store, bought a beer bottle of petrol, tipped it into the jeep's tank, stirred up the policeman, and they were halfway to the airport when the engine broke down. Mike finished his journey on the back of a tractor and arrived just as the plane took off after waiting twenty minutes for him.

"Never mind, you can go the day after tomorrow," Finau told him brightly.

"Is there a seat?"

"No, I don't think so."

There was some consolation, we thought, because Seletute's daughter Loleta invited us three castaways – Mike, Gianluca and me – to a dance. Shy, reserved, and as beautiful as a princess, the girl whom I had observed washing up in a tin bowl at the outside tap was now wearing a discreetly polka-dotted cocktail dress that would not have disgraced any soirée in Europe, elegant red high-heeled evening shoes that set off her slender legs, and a posy of frangipani pinned to her bosom.

It was to be a fund-raising evening for the local church and Seletute told us there would be a supper, traditional dancing, and we would see people pinning and sticking paper notes and coins to the clothes of village maidens as they danced. We went in a little Datsun pick-up truck, twenty-one of us. It lurched through the puddles with its top-heavy load like a covered wagon in *Rawhide*, and at about the same pace. The stars were brilliant, the wind was warm, and the young Tongans in their best rig giggled and sang like teenagers.

The dance hall was a rustic shack of bare planks with a knotted and splintered floor. The window shutters, hinged along the top edge, were propped open and scores of people scrimmaged around them to peep in. It was clear that Loleta had accomplished something of a coup in bringing three *palagi* to the dance. Hardly had we paid our 50 *sene* and sat down on the narrow bench around the perimeter of the room than a bevy of pretty girls made for us and tapped our knees. The floor was crowded and shadowy, lit by only three pressure lamps hanging in the rafters. The seven-piece orchestra slouched languidly on hard-backed chairs on a low stage, playing guitars, a banjo and a tea chest. The first number as we were paraded around the floor was

> *Go…nna take*
> *A senn…timenn…tal journey…*

The dance style was formal and distant, or standard no-touch frugging. As number after number followed in rapid succession I noticed that many people were furtively copying my actions. And I can't dance for bananas. I also became aware of something different about the dancers but it took a time to put my finger on it. They were all wearing shoes. Those without shoes were the ones struggling to look in through the shutters. There was no traditional dancing. In vain I looked for some kind of refreshment, even a truck selling beer. Not once, inside or outside the hall, did I see a couple kiss or embrace.

Around 11.30 we scrambled back into the truck and rocked along under the full moon. Halfway home the truck backed into somebody's garden, an engine was manhandled aboard and put between our toes, then a projector in its case and a rolled up white bed-sheet. We were conveying the local cinema home to its cupboard.

After the various difficulties I had observed with the airline office I took extra care when my own departure date neared. Last thing, I checked with Finau. "All set for tomorrow?" I asked.

"Sure thing, mate. Ten-thirty, right here!"

Next morning Mike and I were at his office by 9.30. It was closed and there was no sign of life. At 10.30 there was still no activity. I checked the store. Where the hell was Finau? The storekeeper thought he might have moved his office and be working from home. Where did he live? Everybody knew, but nobody could explain. Then Mike spotted his white pick-up and we raced over the grass to intercept it. Finau was loading a pair of bathroom scales into the back as we ran up. "Where you guys been?" he growled.

The sky had been clouding over all morning and now the heavens opened. We rode to the airport on the back of the truck, as soaked to the skin as I had been on *Ekiaki*'s open deck. For once the bookings were not fouled up. After a turbulent flight when I was constantly hosed by a trickle of water, we made a slithery landing on a flooded runway, the nearest thing to water-skiing with wings. The roads to Nuku'alofa were awash with orange water. A jet had just come in from Auckland and the crowded little bus swayed sickeningly through pot-holes big enough to have been classified in England as village ponds. Exhaust fumes leaking up through the floor made three little children pink in the face and they dozed, looking dizzy. When I suggested to their father that they might be affected by carbon monoxide he realised it at once and we slid all the windows open. At that moment a big truck raced past at high speed and something resembling the Ganges in full spate sprayed into the bus. In the South Sea Islands you don't have to be in a boat to get wet or seasick. A plane or a bus will also do the trick.

No schooners now lay at anchor in Nuku'alofa harbour recruiting passengers and freight. No luggers were available for charter. No horny fisted mates haunted the waterfront bars looking for trade; there were no waterfront bars except the International Dateline Hotel which was no more romantic than a waiting room at a provincial airport. Neither passenger steamers nor banana boats were scheduled. I could wait six weeks for a freighter to return from New Zealand. It *might* be sailing north to the Samoan Islands. On the other hand it might not. Romantic whimsy took a back seat in a BAC 1–11 jet of Fiji's airline, Air Pacific, "Your island in the sky" on the No Smoking side of the aisle. It was the only way to travel.

11

THE CHIEF'S ALIA

A DREAM
IN THE NAVIGATORS

Even as the jet dropped low over a grey sea and splashed down in runway puddles steaming like hot pools, there was something different about Western Samoa. The men on the fire truck were already stripping down to shorts and dashing on to the wet grass to continue their interrupted football game as we taxied in. Then, as I crossed the tarmac feeling damp heat rising like a lawn spray, a young man sprinted out of the control tower to re-join the game. His T-shirt bore a picture of a girl in lacy knickers and the caption "Get 'Em Down Safely With Air Traffic Control". It dawned on me that, cordial and dignified though it was, Tonga had been somewhat deficient in the provision of chuckles.

The capital of this tiny independent state just south of the Equator, the largest community of pure-bred Polynesians living within their own authentic culture, is Apia (pronounced *a-pier*), a twenty-mile drive from the airport. Crammed in a narrow seat behind a loud Kiwi hardware merchant and his wife, who had won their trip in a raffle, and in front of a pair of discontented elderly Americans ("my Gard, if our hotel isn't air conditioned I shall die ...") it was hard for me not to feel mocked by the earlier travellers whom I was lamentably failing to emulate. Thus Robert Louis Stevenson had written of his own arrival at a Pacific atoll:

> The tide being out, we waded for some quarter of a mile in tepid shallows, and stepped ashore at last into a fragrant stagnancy of sun and heat ...

But if you are unable to charter a schooner in which to roam the islands for seven months, as he did, and if there is no choice but to gain first impressions from a ramshackle bus, a twilight arrival does feed the romantic imagination a rich shot of vitamins.

Upolu, the main island, 45 miles by 12, is slightly smaller than nearby Savai'i. Both islands are dormant volcanos, the latter having oozed some lava into the sea as recently as 1908, and their barrier reefs are fragmented so that in many places the black-sand beaches are open to the ocean. As the high cloud-chilled interiors are steep and densely bushed, the 160,000 people live in classic villages beneath the palms along the shoreline. Ordinary life is exposed to view in a way that Westerners could conceive only by imagining a crowded campground in the Garden of Eden. The Samoan house or *fale* (far-lay) has no walls. It is a beehive dome of thatch, an elipsoid shape of matchless beauty, supported on numerous stout posts. The floor is a raised platform of coral fragments, raked smooth. When it rains, louvre screens of plaited fronds are lowered like a Robinson Crusoe version of the venetian blind. Even the newer houses retain the style, with floor to ceiling windows all round. It would be like living in a band-stand, I thought, as the bus clattered along the shore of the glassy lagoon. As darkness fell, pressure lamps and kerosene lanterns flared under the rafters and each of the strange see-through abodes became a stage of serene and candid domesticity. As there were neither street lights nor other vehicles, each pool of light seemed to float in the moist earthy darkness like Chinese lanterns suspended in a garden. In every house bedding and sleeping mats were heaped on a massive double bed. Chests of drawers looked strange with no wall at the back of them. Nearer town the lights became more glaring, for here there was electricity, and a refrigerator standing all alone in a coral-floored hut washed with Neon light made a strange spectacle. The glow of a hurricane lantern or the stub of a candle would reveal the communal water tap, where people gossiped as they filled their tin cans, or soaped themselves down with cotton *lavalavas* clinging wetly to their brown bodies then rinsed the suds away with scoops of cold water. How impossible it would be for us, with our notions of so-called civilisation and style, to exist in our northern city suburbs with open spaces for walls and the camouflage of the night our only privacy. Yet here it seemed the most natural thing in the world, a picture of harmony and a vivid example of what they call *fa'a Samoa* – the Samoan Way. The serenity of the little stages lit in the darkness reminded me of a piece I had read by the poet Rupert Brooke who came here just before he died in the First World War, and wrote of Samoa:

In the South Seas the Creator seems to have laid himself out to show what He *can* do . . .

Imagine an island with the most perfect climate in the world, tropical yet almost always cooled by a breeze from the sea. No malaria or other fevers. No dangerous snakes or insects. Fish for the catching, and fruits for the plucking. And an earth and sky and sea of immortal loveliness. What more could civilisation give? Umbrellas? Rope? Gladstone bags . . . ?

Any one of the vast leaves of the banana is more waterproof than the most expensive woven stuff. And from the first tree you can tear off a long strip of fibre that holds better than any rope. And thirty seconds' work on a great palm leaf produces a basket bag which will carry incredible weights all day, and can be thrown away in the evening. A world of conveniences. And the things which civilisation has left behind or missed by the way are there, too, among the Polynesians: beauty and courtesy and mirth.

Perhaps the next best thing to wading ashore from a trading ketch is stepping out of a cosy hotel that has the atmosphere of a South Seas boarding house, crossing the road, and letting the eye roam along the curving shoreline of a charming, cranky, patched-up capital. To my left, across the curve of the bay and partly concealed by large trees shading the busy waterfront road that is the main street, were the two-storey, wooden, balconied government offices built by the German colonial administration at the turn of the century. Scattered among them were various churches: I was to find that a Sunday morning stroll along Beach Road was like flicking the dials of some heavenly wireless as different harmonies floated out through the hooked-back shutters and mingled in the sea breezes. Beyond, clustered round a totem of English civic dependability in the shape of a clock tower standing in the centre of a traffic island, were the two principal trade stores, the lively market and bus station, and the magnificent policemen uniformed in sky-blue tunics and *lavalavas*, brown leather sandals and white London-bobby helmets. Many an English village is bigger by far than Apia. And the whole place had an air of faded obsolescence, as if somebody had decided that it was hardly worth nailing the buildings to the ground or giving them a lick of paint because the inevitable hurricane was bound to blow them away. Behind the faded red roofs the green hills swept up, like the curving face of a wave, into a white crest of cloud.

The bay made a sharper curve to my right, so its outline was like that of a fish-hook, and its barb was the commercial wharf where the fancy new container ship recently given to Western Samoa by West Germany was discharging anonymous boxes. A river ran swiftly beneath a bridge at my feet and the strip of beach below became a picturesque scene at sunset. Young men cantered horses into the sea then slid from their backs and made them swim. Fishermen with circular nets of fine monofilament gathered ready to cast, tip-toed through the shallows with hardly a ripple; the nets flowered from their hands in a perfect airborne disc then splatted on the glassy surface and the lead-weighted edges sank quickly to trap the tiny fish below. Children swam with home-made goggles and fired pebbles from sling-shots. Further out, a couple of cruising yachts flying sun-faded ensigns lay at anchor.

In 1889 this small harbour protected only by a breakwater of coral reef and largely open to the north was the scene of an extraordinary tragedy. Throughout the middle part of last century when the Pacific Islands belonged to anyone who cared to raise a flag, many of them – Samoa, Hawaii and Fiji included – begged Queen Victoria to take them under her wing but Britain was reluctant and America was involved in her Civil War. But Samoa through the 1880s was claimed by three different powers – Britain, Germany and the US. While the Samoans engaged in long-running battles, the consuls declared Apia a tripartite municipality under European law, like Shanghai, and each of them secretly intrigued with contending chiefs in hope of winning control. With the situation teetering on the brink of out-right war, a hurricane swept out of the north. Seven warships were at anchor in Apia, but they were so intent on watching each other that none dared to leave. Only the British ship HMS *Calliope*, in an epic of seamanship, managed to claw her way clear and survive. The sailors of the German and American ships cheered as she inched by, making barely one mile an hour, but they themselves were doomed. Four ships sank and two were beached. Although the warring Samoans formed human chains to pick sailors out of the surf, 146 men died. The tragedy defused the argument and after prolonged discussions Germany annexed what is now Western Samoa, America took the islands of eastern Samoa where it had already established a naval coaling station in the harbour of Pago Pago (see next chapter), and Britain was conceded a free hand in Tonga and elsewhere. Germany administered ably and happily until New Zealand took over during the First World War and ruled until the country gained full independence in 1962.

It was a few months after the hurricane that the wind blew in a schooner called *Equator* and from it landed a strange figure: the weedy, pale, literary Scot who settled for the sake of his health and became beloved by the natives as *Tusitala* (Teller of Tales). In the South Seas, Robert Louis Stevenson, author of *Treasure Island, Dr Jekyll and Mr Hyde*, and other classics, found "a way of keeping alive". So wracked was he by pulmonary illness that he called himself "the flimsy man", but in Samoa,

> Day after day, the air had the same indescribable liveliness and sweetness, soft and nimble, and cool as the cheek of health . . . I had come to my own climate.

On 300 acres up the hill three miles beyond town, exactly between the warring factions, he cleared a garden and built a grand house. When he provided a feast for the high chiefs put behind German barbed wire, and secured their release, he became not just their friend but virtually a god. After only four years in Samoa he died suddenly, at the age of 44, and more than 300 natives toiled with axes and knives to clear a track to the summit of Mt Vaea, 1,200 feet above the town, then his frail remains were passed along it, from hand to hand, to their resting place.

Today Vailima, his house, is the official residence of the Chief of State, and the grounds and Mt Vaea are a national park. The loud songs of a church youth club barbecue picnic filtered up through the dense bush as I puffed my way up the steep track, and, dripping like a squeezed orange, arrived at a plain white cement tomb on which is inscribed the famous epitaph that includes the (misquoted) lines,

> *Home is the sailor, home from the sea,*
> *And the hunter home from the hill.*

Apia is so shabbily and engagingly picturesque that it is not hard to sprawl in the shade of a tree on Beach Road, the Samoans courteously and warmly making room for you, and imagine the scene at the turn of the century. Traders in wrinkled white ducks with native girls on their arms gossiping under the verandahs. R.L.S. himself riding down from Vailima on Jack, a retired tramcar horse from Auckland, to catch up on the latest developments of the political imbroglio with which he regaled the readers of *The Times* in London – a skeletal figure with long hair, a pinched face, wide-apart protruding eyes, and a tailored oriental sash around his middle.

The sun-baked and sea-washed little town had few resident Europeans now that the country was independent, except "experts" brought in on temporary assignments. But it was full of oddities. "No Porking" was chalked on a street sign, under a picture of a pig. When I talked with The Hon. Tupuola Efi, the young Prime Minister, in his balconied office, he first fetched me a bottle of cold beer from the fridge then folded his massive bare feet under his *lavalava* and joked about the rugby game he had just finished playing. As we talked, a little mouse ran out of the skirting of the old building, wiggled its whiskers, and retreated. And next day, when he greeted the Chief of State at the opening of the national assembly, or parliament, he was as usual in bare feet.

There were seven newspapers in the town but they appeared irregularly, on different days. One gave no less than ten inches on the front page to the news that the projector bulb in the Tivoli Theatre had burned out. The story detailed the arrangements being made to fly in a replacement (by airmail, it turned out, not special delivery), and listed the films which would *not* be seen. Another paper blazed ROAD TOLL! in big letters on its front page, and the story beneath comprised no more than seven words: "There are no road accidents this week." The agony column of *The Sun* had a question from a twenty-year-old boy, signed "Cheeky", who said he was getting little sexual satisfaction from his girl friends because he preferred making love in a public place where there was a chance of being caught and thrown into jail. The newspaper counselled him to take his fetish to Tokyo.

Of sailing schooners, trading ketches, or even motor ships that had dropped anchor in Apia Harbour in days gone by and in which I had confidently expected to find a berth, there was not even an echo. The bones of some kind of inter-island trader were gathering moss under the trees. There were a few glassfibre runabouts by the market building that jutted over the water. Otherwise, the harbour was empty without even a canoe in sight. How could a proud little country that made such a virtue of its Polynesian values have set its face so firmly against the sea? There was nothing for it but to go by bus, but here I found Polynesian character in plenty.

The buses were little more than a crudely built wooden shed on a truck chassis. This one, called The Bluebird, stood out in the blinding sun near the market radiating visible heat waves. A couple of young people lying on the narrow wooden benches stirred as I climbed up. What time did the bus go? Two-thirty, they said sleepily. With half an hour in hand, I took a seat on the shady side. By half past two the bus had filled and we were looking out for the driver. At half past three the passengers were still talking quietly, smoking, chuckling. "What time does the bus go?" I asked the man next to me. He consulted with others in Samoan, then told me, "Two-thirty, she go." Oh, good.

At four there was still no driver. Beside me, the man was hand-rolling his fifth cigarette. He picked the straggling ends of tobacco from each end of it with practised fingers. "Maybe this is the next bus, I dunno," he said.

"What time does the next bus go?" I asked.

"Three o'clock, supposed to."

I went and had a cold beer. When I looked out at half past five The Bluebird was still there. There were other buses but by then it was too late. Next day I hired a motor scooter. The shop had four little Hondas but none would start so I read a book under a tree while the other three were stripped of various parts to make the fourth one serviceable. After a couple of hours I was off, on a bald front tyre. From the see-through houses came shouts of "Goodbye! Goodbye!" as I cruised the beautiful coast road. People lying fully clothed in the sea waved languidly. Women bathing together in a large freshwater pond in the middle of a village made remarks which no doubt would have made my hair curl had I understood them. Young men walking along the white dotted centreline, carrying bundles of coconuts slung from poles on their shoulders, lifted their wicked bush knives in salute and stepped aside to give me room to pass with an inch to spare. When I stopped to photograph surf rolling into a black-sand beach the engine would not start. As if by magic a dozen children materialised, formed a circle, and chirped as I tried to flog the engine into life in a monsoon of sweat. Then, the most unlikely vision of all: a South Seas cop rolled up on a mighty Honda. Even his beefy army boots could not do the trick but he did have an inspiration. Crouched like a stork atop the tiny red machine, I swerved down the road powered by a dozen children screaming like a whole tribe of Suzukis and Yamahas.

My introduction was to Pastor Masalosalo Sopoaga who lived in a village called Solosolo a short way along the coast. Masalosalo of Solosolo: it took a bit of practising in front of the mirror. The Pastor's house was easily the largest in Solosolo but he was not expected home for fifteen minutes. An hour and a half later I inquired again of the boys playing volley ball outside, and was told Masalosalo would be back in fifteen minutes. So I rounded up some children for another push-start and put-putted along the coast to the Methodist Theological College where the signposted path led me across green lawns and a cricket ground, and down a ravine, to a beach of boulders. Here, a stream flowing from a fissure in the rock had been dammed to make a freshwater swimming pool above the high-water mark. It was a moment of perfect tropical delight.

A gentle breeze riffled off the lagoon, rustling the palms. Little sea-waves splashed against the stone wall enclosing the fresh water that reached out from the black basalt cliff like a tongue of brilliant turquoise, for the pool had a bottom of clean white sand. So sensuous was the place that my skin prickled and it seemed a shame to have to don a swimsuit, but I did.

The chill of the water took my breath away as I dog-paddled beneath the low roof of the cavern. It was black overhead, the rock knobbled and sharp in places, but the sand beneath was so brilliant that I seemed to be swimming up a river of liquid light. As the roof closed in I felt a little frightened but I only had to stop swimming and the current would propel me into the sunlight. The stream gave a little kink, blocking the daylight behind me. How far could I swim in this enchanting, mysterious place? Would I find a jabbering Ben Gunn round the corner, wild-eyed and strange? Then I became aware of a strange soapy taste in the water. Were those bubbles floating past me? I heard a giggle, and my hackles rose, but I continued paddling. Then, around the corner, in the dimness I beheld two Samoan maidens sitting on a rock ledge shampooing their beautiful black hair. It was a moment out of a fairy tale and in my surprise I sniffed water up my nose and choked. Treading water, I was whirled the length of the cavern and spat out into the diamond bright sunshine. But romantic illusions can go only so far, and I did not swim back into the cavern. My two beautiful *wahine* who presented such a perfect picture of Polynesian delight had been screwing up their eyes against the smoke of the Marlboro cigarette that each held in her mouth.

The Pastor had still not come home, so I turned in the reluctant Honda and tried to rent a car but failed: there was no waiting list, it was first come, first served, and all half-dozen cars were out. It was then I discovered that just nothing gets done in Apia after four o'clock, so I went back to Aggie's and absorbed some cold beer.

Born in Apia, the daughter of an English pharmacist just before the turn of the century, Mrs Aggie Grey is probably the only South Seas landlady to have been featured on a national postage stamp. She is a famous character, not least because the media portray her as the original Bloody Mary of James Michener's story *South Pacific*. On one occasion the redoubtable Mrs Grey grew so angry at being questioned by reporters who presumed her to be the true-life version of a Tonkinese Madam running a sailors' flop-house on an exotic isle, that she refused to disembark from the ship which had brought her to Sydney and went straight home again. Indeed, James Michener took the trouble to write and confirm that when he wrote *South Pacific* he had never been to Apia.

When her Samoan husband became bankrupt during the Second World War, Aggie started a hamburger joint for the US military men who came over from Pago Pago. Over the years her establishment has grown into a 200–bed tourist hotel, with wings of bedrooms scattered among tropical gardens behind the façade of the original colonial-style wooden hotel overlooking the harbour. Its wide and airy verandah, so breezy that the flower vases are bedded in heavy cement weights, is the dining room. There is no menu: you eat what you are given, which isn't difficult. And you are told where to sit, which ensures that every meal is also a conversation, perhaps the first and only one that round-the-world package tourists get. Here you might well encounter that elusive figure featured prominently in many a guidebook, "the real-life Somerset Maugham character." It is much more likely that you will sit with a cruising yachtsman in for a nosh-up, an earnest official from the WHO headquarters in Manila, or a UNESCO expert in philately. Most evenings Aggie appears in a golden ball gown and bare feet, her shoulders decked with flowers, to dance with guests to the strumming of guitars and not a microphone or loudspeaker in sight. Beer is served by the bottle, but you can have a glass if you ask for one.

A lucky break at morning papaya-and-coffee put me at a table with two Americans talking about returning their rental car, so it was that I had a battered and bald-tyred little Datsun to my name and at last made contact with Masalosalo of Solosolo. When I drew up at his see-through Manse I thought I had missed him yet again, but at the sound of my sandals on the cement steps a mountain of flesh erupted from within a child's playpen. The Pastor had been lying next to a restless infant, comforting her and cooling her with a pandanus fan, to help her drop off to sleep. Now he hitched up his *lavalava*, swung his legs over the rail, and warmly welcomed me to his home. A man of forty-one with a massive girth and an expression that was half worried, half quizzical, he had studied in Auckland, Chicago and Jerusalem and had recently given up his position as principal of the Congregational Theological College to gain pastoral experience.

Sitting in cool armchairs of polished wooden slats while yesterday's volleyball game continued noisily in the dazzling sunshine, we talked for hours about *fa'a Samoa* and the changes which this uniquely Polynesian social order would have to make.

The basis of Samoan life was the organisation of people into family groups. Each family elected from its most highly born and respected senior members, a leader called the *matai*. All the *matai* of a village met in a council, called the *fono*, which in turn elected from within its own aristocracy the various levels of chiefs. Its strength was that leaders were chosen by consensus on the basis of achievement and ability, but in these cash-consumer times its weakness lay in the question of ability to do what?

"To appreciate the *fa'a Samoa*, you have to think of it in terms of your own family," Masalosalo told me as he fanned himself gently. "Who would be the chosen figurehead of your family? Grand-dad? Uncle George? A cousin of your own age? And if he were selected by other members of the family, would you ungrudgingly do his bidding?

Tonga is an overcrowded group of lush but tiny islands where subsistence is a full-time and desperate struggle. Gleaning on the reef at low tide (right) produces shellfish and octopus. Passengers (below) crowd aboard the little ship *Ekiaki*, in Nuku'alofa.

Loaded down with flowers, Premier Tom Davis dances with school children welcoming him to Pukapuka, one of the widely scattered Cook Islands; elected leader of this tiny country, he is a former doctor, research scientist and space surgeon.

In the Cook Islands graves are customarily tended with loving care and strewn with flowers that form grottoes of pink and white.

A Gauguin painting in real life, this woman on Nassau Atoll in the Cook Islands idles away the long, limp middle hours of the South Seas day by reclining on a mat and watching nothing going by.

Landing supplies on Nassau Atoll, in the Cook Islands, the whaleboat rides the surf into a tiny niche in the reef, then it's "all out" before the next wave smothers around the bow.

Fishing in traditional Polynesian style with a barricade of palm leaves in the shallows of Suvarov Island, which is normally uninhabited except by passing yachtsmen.

If you lived in a traditional rustic way it would not be too hard. He would give orders for the day's work on the farm. In our case, we work in the plantations, or fish, or build houses. He apportions plots of family land when somebody needs a house. To build it, everybody chips in and lends a hand. He makes sure that nobody is in need. Everybody shares whatever is available. If you earn cash some of it goes to the *matai* himself, and to certain causes he decides are important, such as sending bright young people abroad to school or buying a new tractor. And if you buy things with your hard-earned cash they are "borrowed" willy nilly, be it the Toyota that is your pride and joy, or a new bra that somebody needs for a party. If you need it, take it. The family is one. On the other hand there is no such thing as insurance, mortgages, rates and superannuation. When it is you who is in need, everybody else rallies round.

"It is an excellent system", he went on, "that ensures the survival of so many of the values of family society which in the West are diminishing rapidly. But it goes to pieces when the wise old men, knowledgeable in the ways of the seasons and the waves, are no longer recognised as the most appropriate family leaders. The young and educated generation are now achievers. They speak English, have jobs, travel, and have shown that they can make money. But they are largely unversed, or at least inexperienced, in the traditional ways of life.

"So what it comes down to, were it to be assessed in your terms, is that your *matai* is either an old man knowing nothing of the modern world who leads a Stone Age life in a thatched hut, and alienates by his reactionism the up and coming generation, or he is an impatient and materialistic young man with Western values but a desire for status who is not necessarily respected by his equally educated and worldly contemporaries and is certainly not greatly admired by the family Elders."

In Western Samoa there was a further complication because only *matai* may vote. This has led to the creation of hundreds more *matai* for political purposes and the whole system is in danger of breaking down. Instead of one senior man holding six or seven titles, a single title might be shared between two or more individuals, most of them young men. Those without titles are left frustrated and recalcitrant. There is a practical problem, too. Traditionally, the posts at each end of the *fono* were reserved as positions of honour for the highest chiefs to lean against. Now, there are more chiefs than posts and no chief desires to sit behind or to one side of chiefs of equal status.

"And how many children did you find to push your Honda yesterday?" the pastor inquired. "Twenty? Thirty? And look at the youngsters out there playing volleyball. Did you wonder why none of them are at school? It's because the *matai* are playing cards all day and taking no interest. I have managed to persuade some chiefs to form their own council, because something must be done or the village will die, but this also has the effect of dividing the chiefs and their sons into two camps and I fear I might be creating just the kind of village rivalry problem that 200 years ago would have been settled by a battle on the beach."

Among the first Western goods to hit the dockside in abundance in Apia was pea soup in tins, and the word *pisupo* entered the language for all canned foods. Later it came to refer only to corned beef, a great favourite, which New Zealand meat companies canned with added quantities of fat which they called the Pacific Islands recipe. Today, Western Samoa has a *pisupo* economy for it is based entirely on the insatiable desire for Western goods, though they are often inferior. Western-style beds give you insomnia but the fresh-smelling pandanus sleeping mats are cool and comfortable. Western toilets give you constipation and tin roofs give you a head-ache besides being hotter in summer, cooler in winter, and going rusty the year round. Western lino floors go tacky under foot, windows are prone to break and need cleaning; if it isn't raining they have to be kept open and if it is raining who wants to watch the rain? Western plastic bags go stretchy and break in the heat, yet plaited leaf baskets are bigged and stronger. But in every case it is the Western-made umbrella rather than the equally efficient banana leaf that the people want. The only problem is that while Samoan goods are better, and free for the stooping and plucking, Western goods have to be paid for in hard cash.

Western Samoa is typical of the tiny South Seas nations (except Fiji, with its sugar), so it is interesting to speculate on whence that cash could be derived. When New Zealand took the country from the Germans, it encouraged copra production but prices were hit by the depression. Cocoa was planted to take its place, but the plants had a life of only thirty years and when they started to die off in the 1950s, villages put their plantations into bananas; the love letter I had received from a sexy Dorothy in 1958 was just one banana in one million cases exported every year to New Zealand alone. The banana trees were hit by a succession of botanical diseases, not to mention cyclones, and the market was lost to Ecuador. The result is that Western Samoa now exports less copra than it did in 1920, less cocoa than in 1930, and almost no bananas.

Survival is not in question in Samoa. A large part of the land is not developed at all, the soil is rich, there will always be food and shelter. But a subsistence living from the land and sea will not fulfil the aspirations of Samoa's middle class for Western-style bungalows, cars, kitchen and electronic gadgets, and the opportunity to travel. The taste for Western goods is a relatively new phenomenon which started less than a decade ago when United Nations and foreign aid funded various development projects that brought money into the country. Far from making the country more commercially agile, the development projects – factories, tar-sealed roads in the suburbs, running water to houses, electricity, new hospitals – merely made life more attractive in Apia and sucked in people from rural areas. Yet it was on these whom the country depended for growing food to feed itself and crops for export.

Tupuola Efi, the Prime Minister, told me how deeply troubled he was about the desire for Western goods, especially tinned food. They lived in the Garden of Eden yet a quarter of their expensive imports were "essential" foods. Special quotas were imposed on all imports, as well as taxes. Import duty on a new car, if you could get an allocation, was 135 per cent. There was enormous pressure for electricity in the villages despite the fact that the general wage was only $2.80 a day and a single unit of electricity cost eighteen *sene* (cents).

Two factors had contributed to the economic fantasy that his people lived, Tupuola told me. One was the great amount of money remitted back to Western Samoa from relatives working and living in New Zealand, American Samoa, and other countries. "Many people simply depend on what they are sent from abroad, so there is no need for them to work and they become complacent," he said. "The *fa'a Samoa* unquestionably allows a lot of people to coast and take advantage of others."

The second problem was over-education. Samoans had always placed a high value on learning, and a teacher told me that not only was the standard high, but discipline, tone and attitude were streets ahead of schools in New Zealand. As in Tonga, education was seen as a passport out of the place and Western Samoans did well. Few graduates came home, and those who did expected highly paid government jobs. "We're turning out pen-pushers in droves," Tupuola said. "We've got PhD's in social sciences and psychology coming out of our ears but what good is that to a happy little island in the South Pacific? What we need is agriculturalists and welders and carpenters – skilled people who can *do* things. No thank you, no more thinkers in Samoa, we've got more than enough already."

It was this philosophy which explained, in part, the reason why one of the three diplomatic missions in Western Samoa is that of Red China (the others being New Zealand and Australia). The Prime Minister had just returned from a formal visit to China and his mind was filled with images that had excited him. "I'm not kidding myself that we Samoans can work as hard as the Chinese," he said with a worldly grin, "but I do believe a garden island like this has a lot to learn from being exposed to the Chinese and their mud and bamboo technology. For example, what's the point in talking with some high-powered New Zealand or Australian economic specialist about the commercial and energy-saving advantages of using a horse and cart in our plantations instead of a tractor? But the Chinese are geared to think in precisely those terms and they have a lot to teach us."

Tupuola had swigged from his beer bottle and tilted his swivel chair so his broad shoulders pressed against the wall. His soft voice was hard to distinguish over the hum of the air conditioner. "After all, the spirit of common enterprise has existed among Polynesians always, so communism at its simplest and most basic level is not for us an extreme to be dreaded but only a slight shift from the way we have lived for hundreds of years," he went on. "We Samoans work communally for the village and for the church, and to add another dimension and work communally for the country would not be so difficult and is not necessarily an option to be despised. The whole village thing is geared first to everybody doing their bit and second to leaving nobody in the lurch: this is surely the essence of all community welfare."

So was Western Samoa to become a tiny red satellite in mid-Pacific? The Prime Minister laughed and shrugged, conversationally smoothing ruffled feathers. "Not a bit," he said. "You must remember our motto, and that our people hold it very dear to their hearts: *Fa'avae i le atua Samoa* – Samoa is founded on God."

When I saw Masalosalo again I asked him about the stresses brought about by education. "It's quite true that in the small island environment, education is in many senses inappropriate. In the first place, at school a child is taught to be an individual, to be himself, to make up his own mind, and this strikes at the very heart of traditional concepts of family unity and strength. Secondly, parents often have little education so children gain an inflated idea of their own intelligence. Thirdly, they despise their thatched hut because they have read in social studies text books that it marks them as savages. Finally, it makes young people dissatisfied. A young man who grows taro and sells it in the market can get a dollar apiece, which is a good price, but he is conditioned by his education to work as a clerk in a government office for three or four dollars a day." And there was one other factor. "You know, home *is* sweet home, in Samoa. The sun always shines. Nobody is hungry enough to work – I mean really work." The Pastor grinned and spread his hands. "In this country, we even grow our own carpets."

Luamanuvae Pa'i greeted me courteously and hospitably when I arrived out of the blue with a letter of introduction and a ten-pound tin of *pisupo*. He was a mountain of a man, not light brown as most Polynesians are but burned black by sun and wind. He was not only the high chief of his village at the eastern end of the island, but a fisherman. "You are most welcome in my house," he said in a deeply rumbling voice, giving me a small bow of solemn majesty as he shook my hand. In fact he had two houses, one a flat-roofed Western-style bungalow with many louvred windows, which he had built for his elderly mother, and the other an attractive *fale* where his wife was resting, her mattress spread on the floor of crunchy coral. She had a dose of dengue, a pernicious kind of flu which the beachcombers used to call breakbone fever. When I said that I was interested in fishing, he said a word softly and from the far side of the fenced-in compound a small boy came running. He took my finger and led me across the dusty road to the beach of white sand and pointed. Out on the lagoon, its surface swirling with the lustrous reflections of a pink and golden sunset, a dozen young men were fishing with a long net. They laid it in a half circle from canoes then a couple of them ran splashing through the shallows, chasing fish towards it. The ends were drawn in and scores of little silver fish glittering pinkly in the sunset jumped like fleas. As the boys untangled the fish from the mesh they held them in their teeth by the tails. I noticed that some of the older boys, handsomely muscled and athletic, were heavily tattooed with elaborate traditional patterns about their loins, buttocks and thighs.

The last rays of the setting sun touched a little fleet of canoes, paddled in through a gap in the reef, by men and boys with goggles and fishing spears in hand, after a day's diving. By the time I had waded with them back to the fringe of beach, where palms leaned out like passengers trying to get air in a crowded bus, it was already dark. An immense billowing mattress with enormous pillows, and above it a mosquito net hanging like a Turkish tent from the rafters, had been laid out in the *fale*. "We have made your bed," Pa'i told me gravely. Then he took me by the elbow and led me to the post on his right hand. "Now you must sit, for we will have our dinner."

The chief was a first counsellor of the Mormon Church and was also giving dinner to four young students of Christ, two girls and two young men. They came carrying Bibles, grave of countenance, the boys wearing *lavalavas*, white shirts and broad ties, the girls in simple cotton frocks. The coral cracked under my knees and every unaccustomed muscle complained as I joined them, kneeling, for fifteen minutes of singing and prayers. Dinner was frequently interrupted by people who called, and the chief had a plastic leather-look briefcase behind him in which he kept his cheque-book. He told me that all the nineteen *matai* of the 200 people in the village had agreed that everyone should work. He ran a tight ship, so to speak. At five o'clock he blew a conch shell – "Then all the strong people go up the hill to the plantation. If they do not work I fine them, say two or three *tala* (dollars). If they do not pay, well, then I speak to them very much." Every month they had a village meeting and he reported on profit and loss. Profit was invested in equipment or machinery, or soaked up by the people's needs. And when there was a loss? "Well then we must work very hard," he rumbled without a flicker of a smile.

The small children fell asleep when they were tired and were hauled into line and covered with a counterpane. Pa'i climbed into his single bed and shouted for one of his sons to switch off the generator. I unfurled my mosquito net and crawled on to my enormous mattress.

Despite the lullaby of the surf on the reef and the wind rattling the palm fronds I did not sleep. The wandering moon blazed brightly into my eyes. A cloud passed over and handfuls of rain splattered freshly on my bare chest. The wind it brought bent my mosquito net into hard curves, like the topsail of a galleon. Dogs strolled in and out by the open walls, crunching on the coral and scratching themselves. Pa'i snored contentedly and the children coughed and stirred.

When sleep eventually did come it seemed I was allowed only a couple of minutes before I was rudely woken by Pa'i drumming loudly on an empty fuel drum with a paddle. It was still pitch dark and the stars were eclipsed by a misty low cloud. The chief was invisible in the darkness but for the faint outline of his yellow Hawaiian skirt. "The weather is good for fishing", he assured me and thrust into my hand a mug of hot water containing a single lemon leaf. I sipped it while the village woke around me. Cocks crowed loudly and dogs barked. I heard the impatient toot of the town bus awakening some sleepy market-goer and soon it rattled by in a cloud of dust. Lamps flared in the surrounding houses and I saw bedrolls being lifted into the rafters. Only the small children slept on, undisturbed.

In one easy lift Pa'i hoisted a big outboard motor to his shoulder and we crossed the road to the beach. I rinsed my face in the warm water of the lagoon as we waded out to the *alia*, a catamaran con-structed of aluminium on the lines of traditional local fishing canoes. Each hull was open, like a dinghy, so you could sit in it, but there was also a bridge-deck on which there was a small cuddy, like a lean-to with windows. Of 200 such fishing canoes designed and built in Western Samoa and made available to villages at heavily subsidised cost, 116 had been repossessed by the government because the people could not – or could not be bothered to – meet the modest repayments.

The rising sun was lighting the sky overhead but we remained for a long time in the cool shadow of a low cloud, first pulling in a fish or two in the reef passage, then skimming along the glassy green backs of the rollers as they gathered to full height moments before crashing head over heels on to the reef.

The sun found a narrow slot in the cloud and flared through in a blaze of watery orange that speckled the rolling ranges of the open Pacific with dewy gold. In the humid light the white breasts of the circling terns and boobies became a lurid pink. At once, having got under the birds, Pa'i and his two helpers hooked six fish in quick succession. Then I looked up, the birds had gone, but black specks circling in another patch of sky two miles away signalled another shoal and we went after them. Bloody water swirled ankle-deep in the bottom of the boat and occasionally a bonito lying in it quivered thunderously as its nerves congealed. I felt cold and a little seasick, but satisfied to be part of this easy subsistence on the ready bounty of the sea.

Perhaps it was in such a dawn, a little over three centuries ago, that the French explorer Louis de Bougainville had sailed this way and, far from the visible land, had encountered in their frail canoes, a group of fishermen like Luamanuvae Pa'i. How thunderstruck the fishermen would be when the light resolved nearby the towering, creaking majesty of a European sailing ship. Small wonder the Polynesians called the questing explorers who hailed them, Gods of the Sail. And the white men, admiring the nerve and seamanship of the fishermen so far from land, gave to the distant islands the name Navigators' Archipelago.

Now the navigator's canoe was driven by a twenty-five horsepower Johnson outboard engine. The skin of the canoe was clammy aluminium. The fishing lines and ropes on board were nylon or polyurethane. Pa'i wore a digital watch that twinkled like a Christmas bauble on his massive forearm. Yet last night we had dined on fish snatched from the sea, breadfruit plucked from the tree and toasted a light golden brown, mutton flaps in coconut cream, and orange cordial. I had slept in a thatched house and woken at cock-crow to freshen my face in the warm lagoon and embark on a food-hunting adventure that was certain of modest, if not abundant, success. A brisk encounter with a good shoal of bonito could land fish worth $250 without much trouble, and that paid for a lot of mutton flaps, a lot of orange cordial, and – even at $2.50 a gallon – quite a lot of petrol.

The Western Samoans, I thought, had perfected the gentlest art of living. They were a stylish people, living up to their own standards and culture yet unremittingly Christian in their outlook. Briefly, I had experienced in Pa'i's household the simple, lagoonside way of life that has been the envy of Western man for two centuries. How contented he must feel, I thought, and how rich to live in such harmony with Nature in a benign, perfect climate.

Over there! Pa'i swung round to head in the direction of my out-thrust arm. The lines blurred as fish after fish was hauled into the boat to be stunned senseless with a stick of timber. Then the birds disap-peared as mysteriously as they had assembled. We lurched over the unrhythmical swells until another squadron drew us away. Suddenly I became aware that all the goosebumps on my arms and legs had gone, that there was not a cloud in the sky and the sea was a fantastic blue. It was ten minutes before seven.

As we breasted a particularly large lump of water Pa'i gestured with a lift of his thick arm towards the faintest blur low in the east. It was neither grey nor creamy like a cloud but was a faintly darker shade of blue, a jagged triangular formation jutting out of the sea. "Over there is paradise", the chief said simply. "That is Tutuila – American Samoa. Over there, Uncle Sam gives you a government job. Over there, plenty of money for everything. You don't have to get up early in the morning to go fishing or dig in your plantation. Uncle Sam gives you everything you need. It's paradise."

12

QUEEN SALAMASSINA

UNCLE SAM'S PARADISE ISLE

The ferry to American Samoa made the 50-mile trip on alternate nights. On the day I bought my $8 ticket an Apia newspaper carried a news item about one of the nine-seat aircraft that shuttle frequently between the two Samoas for the benefit of bureaucrats and tourists. The plane had filled with smoke on take-off and returned quickly to Faleoleo. Passengers and pilot changed to another plane which, on lift-off, had risen at an ever-steepening angle – "Like a rocket," one passenger described it. A stall and inevitable disaster was averted when the pilot realised the controls were still locked. But my smugness at having chosen to voyage by sea did not linger long.

The steel-built ferry *Queen Salamassina* had the kind of dimensions you would expect of an island queen; she was nearly as broad as she was long. In every other respect the blue and white vessel had the queenliness of a sea-going garage. Watching her swing into Apia Harbour I was reminded of the crude plastic toys my son floated in the bath. There was nothing graceful about her blunt bows, flat stern with a ramp for loading half a dozen cars, few windows in the passenger saloon, and a permanently fixed deck awning that had the look of a suburban car-port. The ship had been built to operate from the end of the island, near Luamanuvae Pa'i's village and so reduce the length of the crossing by a third, but the ugly little ship was too large to fit through the very narrow opening in the reef. A national programme to blow more access channels in the reefs around the coast had been abandoned when the dynamite was used instead for the depth-charging of fish.

The high wire gates to the wharf were opened a crack and passengers were permitted through one at a time, so getting aboard was an uncomfortable scrimmage in the moonlight. The saloon was already crammed with recumbent bodies staking out their sleeping space, but no way would I be trapped in a stuffy cabin all night. On the upper deck, beneath the corrugated plastic sun awning, were a number of coffin-like wooden boxes in which lifejackets were stowed. One was still free so I unrolled my pink sleeping bag and stretched out on it, like a body on a slab. Between the boxes there was just space enough for a man to lie, as long as his shoulders were not too broad, and these spaces, too, filled up. Beside me was a Seventh Day Adventist pastor from Savai'i, a neat man easily taken for a bank manager with his tailored *lavalava*, crisp white shirt, bald head, serious round face and black Samsonite briefcase. Soon every horizontal space was filled, the large women simply folding their legs beneath them and becoming immovable pyramids of flesh, as if fixed to the deck by suction pads. The ship sailed at ten o'clock, backing and filling across the harbour to avoid the anchored yachts and manoeuvring strangely, as if her rudder could move only one way.

At first it was balmy. There was a brilliant full moon and as the lights of Apia disappeared astern, the whole sky became a hazy golden purple. The breeze was slight, and I nestled comfortably in the sleeping bag with both feet up on the ship's rail and my hands behind my head, more than content to be adventuring at sea on the broad bosom of the Pacific. My romantic pleasures seemed fated, however. Soon the moon was blotted out by brisk dense clouds. The waves began to peak sharply, and slap against the hull. Flurries of spray became airborne. The ship lurched with the grace of a cardboard box and I had difficulty anchoring myself on the slippery glossy paint. I tried to close my mind, dreaming through gritted teeth, but it was impossible. A seaman unrolled a tarpaulin and lashed it down but it barely reached the rail and when the lashings broke, it thundered endlessly. The pastor and I wrestled with the whipping ends and finally abandoned it. Then it rained, a cold penetrating rain straight out of the southern winter. I rolled myself in the sleeping bag but there was no shelter. It was like sleeping in a flag. I envied the pastor, stretched out in the shelter of my box, until he arched his back with a shouted remark that might just have been a curse and sprang to his feet. A rogue wave had punched through the open railings and three inches of water raced like a tidal wave over the entire deck. We sat side by side on my box, the sleeping bag over our shoulders, while rain and spray flew around us. The crossing was always like this, he told me.

Half an hour before dawn, with all seventy of us on the upper deck huddled in a human heap for warmth and shelter, many sick and everyone soaked, a brigand with a bare torso and a headband came around dispensing US immigration forms. Through a gap in the tarpaulins on the lee side of the deck I spotted clusters of brilliant red lights. No landfall of waving palms was ever greeted with such relief as those runway lights of Pago Pago International Airport. The day did not so much break as soak through. The nearby land was just a dark wall, like a mossy rock veiled by a waterfall, climbing up into the clouds. I was reminded of an almost identical landfall I had made once in Greenland, but that ship had central heating and a coffee shop.

Tutuila is a high thin island eighteen miles long. With many bays and headlands it is like a green leaf that has been gnawed around the edges by some giant caterpillar. In the centre it is almost bitten in two by the grand harbour of Pago Pago (pronounced *pango-go pango-go*). Enclosed by nearly vertical rock walls festooned with tangled tropical vines, the harbour is in fact a drowned volcanic crater but it has the air of a hothouse. It is a mile wide and three miles long, but near the entrance it makes a right-angle turn so the inner part is totally sheltered. As soon as you turn the corner and leave the unruly Pacific astern, the tongue of rain-dimpled water becomes perfectly still and dark, as if you had mysteriously arrived at a secret lake in some jungled mountain range. The garish, brighter-than-life buildings scattered along the foreshore look unreal, as if made from matchboxes and cigarette cartons in a kindergarten. Stumpy, brightly coloured buses look like nursery toys. The score or more of oriental fishing boats clustered around the two tuna-canning factories, listing at odd angles as they are unloaded, seem to have been made from folded newspapers and turned soggy in the bath.

A little warmth stole into my bones as the ship slowed and the breeze died away. A stout cop in full American fig – sun-glasses, dark uniform, badges, night-stick, revolver, cap, cigar – growled "Have a nice day" as I squelched over the ship's stern-ramp and was admitted to Uncle Sam's paradise in the South Seas.

To an eye conditioned to the relative material impoverishment of islands like Tonga and Western Samoa, the density of vehicles, and the state of them, was striking. Not only gleaming, gas-guzzling limmo's but macho pick-ups with four-wheel-drive, stiffened springs, and Indianchief emblems. Many were so comprehensively corroded by the salt spray which spurts over the island's coastline roads that their rusty body panels were held on with wire and parcel string. A cruising minibus stopped for me, and for twenty-five cents took me a couple of miles to an hotel. A few months earlier a four-engined Orion aircraft of the US Navy had dropped half a dozen display parachutists, turned inside the fiord, then ripped its tail fin on the cable of an overhead railway spanning the harbour. The cable car, empty at the time, slid down the wire and crashed into a tuna-cannery. The aircraft, with seven men on board, twisted in the air and crashed headlong into a wing of the hotel. Now, in the drumming rain, it seemed that the ruins were still smoking. A notice by the swimming pool listed fifteen rules for proper behaviour, while the little beach outside my room was governed by ten rules. The shaggy carpet in the room reeked darkly of compost. The bed smelled as if a mountain man had been hibernating in it. The air conditioner noisily blasted in a breeze of rotting cabbages. As I opened the bathroom door a large brown toad hopped out, so I prodded it outdoors, into a puddle. Despite the Do Not Disturb notice hung on the door I was disturbed no less than three times during the four or five hours that I tried to sleep: a maid, an air conditioning maintenance man, an electrician who wanted to check the lightbulbs. But this, I discovered, was par for this sloppy, seedy, melancholy spot where nobody cared much of a damn about anything.

It is only fair to declare that my spirits were in any case fairly mildewed by the solid dementing rain. The moist tradewinds slide up the 2,000 foot crags of the sea-mountains rimming the harbour, chill suddenly, and their belly-cargo drops in a ceaseless cataract. Somerset Maugham must have struck similar weather, when he changed ships here in 1916 and found the setting for his famous short story *Rain*:

> Meanwhile the rain fell with a cruel persistence. You felt that the heavens must at last be empty of water, but still it poured down, straight and heavy, with a maddening irritation, on the iron roof. Everything was damp and clammy. There was mildew on the walls and on the boots that stood on the floor. Through the sleepless nights the mosquitoes droned their angry chant ...

The boarding house where Somerset Maugham stayed a night or two while awaiting a steamer for Apia was also inhabited by a refugee prostitute from Hawaii called Sadie Thompson. In his story, through which the roof-thunder and damp spray of the rain seeps as relentlessly as traffic noise in a city, a fanatical missionary sets out to reform the girl but is himself seduced and cuts his throat. Today, knifed bodies are quite often found floating in Pago Pago Harbour, but they tend to be oriental fishermen rather than Presbyterian missionaries. Sadie Thompson's boarding house – "It was a frame house of two storeys, with broad verandahs on both floors and a roof of corrugated iron ..." – remains, but it too has lost the edge of romance for it is a Valupac Supermarket.

At the village of Vaitogi, on the coast out beyond the airport, I found Mary Pritchard who remembered the original Sadie Thompson.

An indomitable old girl, half Samoan by birth and wholly Samoan by heart, Mary was only twelve years old at the time and says she hardly knew what a prostitute was. "But I do remember, and I remember being very surprised by it at the time," she told me sweetly, "that Sadie wore a bracelet around her ankle. In fact, I have always wondered how Sadie actually practised in that place because when I was a little older I worked there briefly as a waitress and found that the four or five bedrooms adjoined each other but there was no corridor, so you had to go through one room to reach the next."

I had ridden out to Vaitogi in a little bus that had transfer stickers of Donald Duck all over the windscreen and brake lights on the inside, so passengers would know when to hold tight. Then I paddled through the semi-flooded grass to reach the old lady's house, a traditional *fale* but one with walls and windows between the posts. Surrounded by gardens and flowering shrubs, it stood right on the shore. Inside, the beams and walls were hung with beautiful *tapa* mats and a mass of pot plants. The strange clunking knock-knock of the *tapa*-mallet does not echo through the villages of American Samoa as it does in Tonga, Mary explained, because the people have forgotten how to do it. She had herself taught American, Swedish and Japanese women who were interested in traditional crafts. Before long, she predicted, they would be commissioned to return to teach the Samoans how to do it. Meanwhile, Mary was trying to keep cultural talents alive by organising a summer school for children. "The problem is that young people do not think of themselves as Polynesians but as Americans, and what American kid could be bothered to beat their dress material out of tree bark?"

As we talked the sun came out. Mary escorted me to the water's edge and told me the legend of the village. An old woman living with her grandson had been denied their shares of food so they walked together into the sea. When the villagers searched for them they found only a turtle and a shark which were the spirits of the couple, and ever since they had been able to call the turtle and shark by singing a song called *Fonuea Fonuea*. Had Mary herself ever seen it? I asked.

"Oh yes," she said at once. "I have often seen sharks, of course, and turtles. But one day when I was here alone and humming the tune of the song I saw a strange rust-coloured shark, not very big, and with it a large turtle. Twenty years later, after I had been away for a long while, exactly the same thing happened and I remember thinking they hadn't grown a bit. Funnily enough, my sister was away for twenty-six years and she had exactly the same before and after experience."

Like a small boy out of school I capered along the beautiful shore-line. A giant surf crashed into the black lava and I watched a big

Samoan, a *lavalava* flapping round his legs and a US Marine steel helmet on his head, fishing with a long rod; it was the only time I ever saw an American Samoan involved in a subsistence activity, but from the flashy look of his tackle I thought he was more likely to be fishing for fun than out of necessity. There were few pigs and hens to startle drivers in these garden suburbs, as in Western Samoa. Nearly all houses were American in character, but village meeting houses were traditional. The *matai* system remained strong here, Mary had told me, and was not diluted for political purposes as it had been in Western Samoa because it was forbidden to split titles, but the new generation of *matai* were educated whizz-kids out of touch with traditional customs and values, and many returned from their new homes in Hawaii or California just long enough to get the status of a title.

At Leota, a girl of no more than twelve cavorted in the shallows and when she caught sight of me undid the buttons of her wet shirt. Splashing and giggling and displaying her little breasts, she emanated sexuality. I was ashamed of my thoughts because she was so young, and I walked stolidly on, but it was just this kind of sprite that had enchanted the early travellers in the South Seas. In this case, her teasing was no doubt a promiscuous prank but – not counting the Fijian girl whose *mumu* had fallen to her waist as she came flying down a steep pavement on a skateboard – it was the only bare nipple or blatant invitation I encountered in half a year's wandering through the islands.

To celebrate the return of the sunshine I had a vastly expensive dinner at the hotel. A vamping dance group performed a South Seas floor show that might have gone down well in Birmingham (Alabama or England, it makes no difference). It featured a Tongan who looked like a Chinese chef and played an electric guitar in his teeth. The audience of American tourists, most of them on two-day stopovers, went wild.

In my room I switched off the noisy air conditioner and slid back the patio doors. The sound that floated out of the thick ferny darkness was just about the last thing I expected: many young voices chorussing the harmonies of a lilting Polynesian song. I chased another toad off the carpet, locked up again, and followed my ears to the source of the music. Next door was a large modern auditorium where 35 teenagers were rehearsing for a concert tour of Fiji and Tonga. Every evening for a week I spent my evenings sitting quietly in the background, listening. The kids worked hard, from six until midnight. One song was so rousing that I asked for a translation and was given a copy of the programme notes which put the new Polynesia quaintly into perspective:

Oka, Oka, La'u Honey
A love song of the Broadway Musical Comedy style comparing the loved one
to the desirability of desirable cuisine (food). In this case, the lover is
compared to the Hellaby corned beef, Fijian biscuit, and a dish of mixed
vegetables including tomatoes and peas . . . It also urges marriage temptation
and out of wedlock pregnancies can be possible.

The melancholy irony of this smug little island is that American
Samoa epitomises the state of comfortable dependence on cash and
Western goods to which so many aspire. "There is paradise," Luamanuvae Pa'i had said, gazing with envy at the distant peak of the island
of his dreams. And if you assessed paradise as an accountant, he was
right. American Samoa had only one-sixth of the population of
Western Samoa but it received three times more aid. It was not only
water that fell in cataracts from the heavens, but dollars. In American
Samoa a bountiful Nature had been replaced, measure for measure,
by benevolent government. Arcadia thrived but the traditional image
had been adjusted: here it was not fruit that grew abundantly
wherever you looked, but government cheques.

As long ago as 1872, America recognised the strategic value of an
excellent harbour like Pago Pago in the middle of the Pacific and
concluded an exclusive agreement with local chiefs to operate a coaling station, essential to steamships on long-haul transpacific routes. In
1900 the entire island, and a handful of smaller ones nearby, were
ceded to the United States who agreed to establish good government
and to protect the rights of the Samoan people. Until 1951 naval
officers had supreme authority and ran the place like a ship, not
sparing too much effort on such things as education and social services.
When the Department of Interior took over, well-meaning do-gooders
initiated a blitz of money. The Samoan people became so dependent
on US aid that twice they voted against the idea of electing their own
governor in case they cut themselves adrift from the bounty of Uncle
Sam.

Today the various administration buildings with their low eaves
and enclosed verandahs still give the place the air of a Naval station,
but it is in sore need of a Commanding Officer's inspection. The outer
villages are beautiful but Pago Pago is the seediest place in the South
Seas, a skid row in paradise.

Garbage litters the streets. The waitress in the take-away food bar
wears a white nylon trouser suit and red pinafore in approved apple-
pie American fashion but the tables are cluttered with dirty glasses and
plates which attract flies, and are seldom wiped down. The island is
almost entirely urbanised, with good sealed roads, but apart from the

200 inches of water a year that descend from the heavens it has no rivers. The result is that most villages have such a serious water-supply problem that infectious hepatitis occurs ten times more frequently than in the US, a rate which would have any ordinary American community declaring itself a disaster area. Vast sums are invested in the infra-structure that might well be appropriate in a dynamic industrial community but are entirely irrelevant in a South Sea island only twice as large as Manhattan and populated by 30,000 people. An unnecessarily ambitious international airport; push-button telephones; two television channels; a complex TV education system which has lamentably failed; an aerial railway. None does anything to help people help themselves.

The market in Pago Pago is virtually bare of produce. Although it is true that much of the island is too steep for cultivation, it is also undeniable that barely half the land capable of cultivation is actually used to grow fresh food. Even bananas and taro, the island staples, have to be imported from Western Samoa. The island produces nothing except canned tuna. The raw material is landed by fishing boats from Korea and Taiwan, the labour provided by Western Samoans on temporary permits. The island has no fishing boat to call its own and there is hardly a dinghy or a canoe to be seen drawn up on the beaches.

So what do American Samoans do? As Pa'i told me with perfect accuracy, they work for Uncle Sam. Any person with skill and ambition soon leaves the island for Hawaii or California. The majority of high school graduates, girls as well as boys, join the US military forces, especially the Marines in which the warrior-brave Samoans flourish. The stay-at-homes drift into secure Administration posts which make no demands and deliver a fat pay cheque at the end of every week. White Americans hold them in poor esteem. "Conscientiousness in this place simply does not rate," one disenchanted American adviser told me. "Work is just a place to come to for a bit of a sit-down and a gossip with your friends on the telephone. Samoa is so pleasant: you don't have to worry about keeping warm, or fighting off savage beasts. Ambition and drive and hard work aren't necessary. Even money is not *needed*, but it is more convenient to spend a day sprawling behind a desk and to buy deep-frozen French fries from Idaho at the supermarket on your way home in your new pick-up truck than to slave in a plantation digging with a pointed stick."

The result is a visible seediness in the people, too. They are shockingly obese, especially children and young people. It came as no surprise to read in a medical report that women aged between thirty and fifty in American Saoma are no less than twenty-two pounds heavier *on average* than their cousins in Western Samoa. No doubt a similar ratio exists among men, but they seem to wear it better, gaining a stoutness that adds to their naturally regal demeanour.

Workers are possessed by a maddening and in-built kind of sloth. It is a poor journalistic trick, perhaps, to base one's criticism of a country on the fact that in seven successive breakfasts at its "luxury" hotel, I did not once get a fried egg with its yolk unbroken or finish a meal without being irritated by the sloppy, disinterested attitude of the staff. What if the whole country were run on the same basis? Largely, it is. For example, power outages are frequent because, I was told, the local engineers seldom bother to put lubricating oil in the generators. It was exactly the same disease, but on a larger scale, that I had observed among the Kanaks of New Caledonia and the islanders of the Lau Group. Here it did not seem to be cultural confusion that was to blame ("Who's finger on the starter button?") but sheer indolence and boredom. Having sentenced themselves to a cash-dependent economy the American Samoans seem to have discovered that life has nothing to offer them but the unremitting tedium of attendance at whatever white collar job they happen to obtain. It is small wonder that alcohol consumption per head is not far short of a gallon of beer per head per week and a gallon of spirits per year – one of the highest rates in the world.

While watching a Saturday morning baseball game on the *malae*, or village green (it's a special kind of home run if you can hit a ball through the glass doors of the Legislative Assembly across the road), I fell into conversation with Al Lolotai, an American Samoan who had been a professional footballer in Hawaii for years and returned home to be Director of Recreation. When he told me what his job was I just about choked, for I could not bring myself to believe that the people of a beautiful South Seas island needed to be taught how to amuse themselves.

"It's true, I'm afraid, the picture of the placid Polynesian living by his sunny lagoon disappeared from here a long time ago," Al assured me. "We've gotten ourselves an American lifestyle but we've caught American suburban neuroses, too. People are going off their rockers due to hypertension. Our kids won't go to school unless they can ride. Nobody is bothering to teach traditional skills. The parents are so busy attending offices that there is nobody to teach the kids how to swim and death by drowning has become a real problem: I am trying to get funds for a municipal swimming pool so we can teach swimming in an organised way ... Yes, just like they do in Iowa. It's a Goddam shame, I know it."

It is a grim outlook if the smug and sleek fat cats of American Samoa are truly the models of the South Sea Islander of the future, but the conclusion seems inescapable. Western countries try to fortify island economies by providing work opportunities in small factories such as the beer and cigarette factories in Apia or the new saddlery plant in Nuku'alofa. But the benefits are short-lived because they do nothing for primary production and serve only to attract more people away from subsistence activities. Western Samoans want to live in American Samoa. American Samoans want to live like proper Americans in the contiguous forty-eight states. Many Americans and Europeans dream of a lagoon-side existence on a tropical island. The whirlpool of dissatisfaction is tragic.

Not everybody goes along with the American Dream they are living, though it is hard for an individual to know how to resist it. Falelua Lafi is a bright young American Samoan who studied for five years in Western Samoa to gain a degree in divinity, and was now a director of the Congregational Church youth programme. What he saw of his contemporaries in American Samoa appalled him. "Here, all you have to do is show your face at work and you know the money will come at the end of the week," he said. "But in Western Samoa young people know what development is, they know what it means to save and to struggle. Here, security kills initiative, development and individuality. Our kids are jelly-fish, with no opinions and no ambition. When the young people of today are the chiefs of tomorrow, I think American Samoa will be nothing but a small and unhappy little American welfare town in the South Pacific."

Welfare payments have not yet struck American Samoa but it is bound to happen. When I met Asuemo Fuimaono, a dynamic person-ality with a fierce turn of phrase who had been the colony's delegate to Washington and was now Secretary of Samoan Affairs, he raged at his inability to block the introduction of a Federal aid programme to provide meals for the elderly. "This is just the kind of thing that poisons our culture as Samoans," he stormed, hunching forward in his chair like an angry wrestler. "You can't blame people for taking it. They put Grandma's name on the list then give the stuff to their children and it's all junk food, look at how fat the kids are! But our people are soft, they just sit and collect. I'd like to see Uncle Sam helping people to help themselves. For a start we need a technical education system that produces skilled men, and we need incentives to make them stay here. One reason there is no industry is that there are no labourers: when the canneries opened I was personnel manager for eight years and had to go to Australia and New Zealand to find skilled men."

The two fish factories, owned by Star Kist and Van Camp, are side by side on the foreshore a mile across the harbour from the town, three miles round by road. In hot weather the oily smell of steamed tunafish hangs like a foul smog over the harbour. Between them, they can 1,000 tons of fish a week and are supplied by 200 Taiwanese and Korean long-liners which quarter the whole Pacific for ten months at a time. Less than four per cent is caught in American Samoan waters because – like so many South Seas Islands – it has no rivers delivering nutrients to the sea, there is no mixing of cold and warm currents to churn up nutrients from the sea-bed, and the shelves on which the islands stand fall away within four or five miles to great depths. The beautiful blue of the open Pacific springs from its clarity, and this clarity results from the absence of plankton and other organisms on which fish can feed. In short, much of the Pacific is an ecological desert. Less fish are caught in the entire Pacific Ocean than in the small, land-girt, shallow and muddy North Sea.

Stiff as boards with bloodied flanks and bulging eyes, the frozen tuna are unloaded from the small ships into large bins, defrosted in saline solution, cleaned, loaded into trolleys, steam-cooked, then placed on conveyor belts and dismembered into shreds ready for canning by scores of women in white nylon over-suits. The vast factory with its concrete floor, clattering production lines, revolting smell and scraps of tuna meat sticky underfoot, were a special kind of Hell. And virtually all the labour force, a thousand people in each factory, had come across the water from Western Samoa, the Garden of Eden, and sacrificed their placid way of life to drudge for eight hours a day. Why?

"Oh for the money, and anyway, I like it," one smiling woman told me, her long hair pinned up under a white paper hat. She was a quality controller and spent her day opening and checking cans. In Apia the basic wage was barely $3 a whole day. Here, she earned that much an hour. But why did she need money? "For my family in Apia. We like to eat all good things, like corned beef and tinned fish. I send money to my mother and my brothers and sisters, so they can buy good things for their children. One day I want to visit my sister in New Zealand. She sends money to our family in Apia, too." These industrial workers were perfectly happy, for they were fulfilling their dream which was to obtain what they regard as the luxuries of life. Like tinned fish.

I met Governor Peter Coleman on a fishing trip. It had been found in Hawaii that fish will congregate around any object floating in the ocean. Long ago, Polynesians had anchored mats on long ropes to attract fish and now this idea was being developed by American marine scientists who, with their wonderful flair for a phrase, had coined the term Fish Aggregating Devices. One of the small development schemes that had been accomplished in American Samoa was the laying of a number of FADs around the coast. They had proved so successful that shooting incidents had occurred when fishing boats got their trolling lines tangled.

With an insulated bin of ice cubes and cans of American beer, the governor was taking Dr Tom Davis, premier of the Cook Islands, to show him the FAD seven miles off Pago Pago and he invited me to go along for the ride. Besides a number of officials, and a fisheries man who drove the little launch, there was also a fully uniformed cop, complete with revolver and shiny black boots, who was there to guard the governor, the premier, the beer, or all three.

The fish aggregating device was three fuel drums filled with foam and welded together, with a flashing light and radar reflector to mark its position. They were moored to the bottom with a mile of rope from which bundles of burlap bags trailed in the current. It certainly worked, for there was a strike on the instant the governor's lure passed within a few yards of it, and he wrestled in a magnificent *mahi-mahi*, the rainbow-coloured fighting fish known in some oceans as dolphin or dorado. Gaffed aboard after a brisk tussle it beat the deck in a thunder of rainbows, its glossy flanks turning a neon-bright green streaked with turquoise, silver and blue. The colours flared for three minutes then faded to a dull grey as the magnificent specimen died. It was the only time I was ever saddened by the death of a fish.

It happens that once in a while a cargo ship heads out of Pago Pago and turns east for the widely scattered and tiny atolls of the northern Cook Islands. For once in my life I was in the right place at just the right time. When I looked out of my hotel next morning the *Mataora*, a trim white ship with pale blue rails and a yellow funnel, was chugging up the harbour. Her lines were recognisable as a coaster of about 500 tons built for Baltic and North Sea waters. In Pago Pago the ship was also embarking Dr Tom Davis, premier of the Cook Islands, and his small party. Not only would we sail to some of the most alluring and isolated islands of the South Seas, atolls that were the antithesis of the handout paradise that was American Samoa, but the voyage would be something of a State Visit.

13

MATAORA

A VOYAGE TO
MOST DETACHED PARTS

The wide ocean was so stuffy with congealing heat that one wanted to open a window to let in some air. The sun stood directly overhead, not so much a chandelier as a flamethrower, its scorching light crinkling the eyes as if it were a strong wind. The sea was a mat of gently undulating blue all the way to a sharp horizon in every direction, with hardly a cloud to cast a shadow. The swells were ruffled by a plodding little breeze from dead aft, a breeze that matched exactly the measured tramp of the little *Mataora* as she marched, seemingly on the spot, trailing a short white feather of foam. Funnel gases pop-pop-popped from the squat funnel then swirled around the deck so all of us felt a little sick and dizzy. The only movement of air was generated by the ship's limping roll. When I lit my pipe, the smoke blew first to one side, as one gunwale was dipped under, then it blew back again as the ship lurched lugubriously the other way.

The *Mataora* was a dainty, neat ship with low freeboard midships, the superstructure aft, and half a dozen small cabins in the tuck of the stern – the tapered part of the hull directly above the screw where the noise, vibration and stuffiness verged on the unbearable. The mess-room had a table with raised edges to stop plates sliding off, with room for six, and a tiled floor. Along the side deck were two w.c. compartments with cold showers and basins that drained on the floor; one of the lavatories had a seat. Rolling along in our own cloud of b.o. we were so close to the equator that the captain, a roguish islander called Paranapa Ben Marsters, reckoned I would see it if I took the binoculars to the masthead. The rolling meant that the effect of the wooden awning on the stern deck around the funnel was reduced to a narrow band of shade in the centre. And here we sat, gazing and sweating and coughing, our course north-east for the island of Pukapuka.

The Cook Islands lie in two groups widely scattered over the blank space on the chart between Samoa and Tahiti. Eight islands are of the high volcanic variety and lie within 150 miles of the main island of Rarotonga, itself a circular volcanic island with a keyhole of a harbour in its narrow fringing reef and lagoon. The northern islands are atolls, specks of dry land on the very fringes of existence. The islands are so remote from each other that their discoverers, notably Captain Cook after whom they were named, Captain Bligh, the *Bounty* mutineers, and missionaries, took about 120 years to track them all down. Cook described them as "the most detached parts of the earth" and with some reason. Pukapuka is 715 miles to the north-west of Rarotonga and Penrhyn is distant 737 miles north-by-east. The total land area of ninety-five square miles is about the same as Malta, a fraction the size of Singapore, but the fifteen pieces are scattered over an area of 900,000 square miles and are inhabited by 18,000 people. This is rather less than the number of workers at Heathrow Airport, London, or the population of a New York skyscraper during office hours.

The Cooks were settled by Polynesian voyagers and Rarotonga may have been the base where the fleet of canoes assembled for the great migration to New Zealand in the fourteenth century. As the history of the islands was passed down by word of mouth and frequently dressed up as legend, and the tradition was stymied by the missionary influence a century ago, the true facts have become difficult to authenticate. The islands were declared a British protectorate in 1888, largely to prevent the French from increasing their sphere of influence, and New Zealand took over responsibility for them in 1901. Self government in free and independent association with New Zealand was granted in 1965, and there are more Cook Islanders living there than in their home islands.

Politically the Cook Islands achieved notoriety in 1978 when, for the first time in the history of Britain and the Commonwealth, a judge sacked a government. The judge of the New Zealand Supreme Court found "unlawful conduct of monumental dimensions" and a government which he described as "a perversion of democracy." Albert Henry, a former bus conductor and labourer who had been knighted for his long service as premier, was turned out of office and deprived of his title for rigging elections by using government money to fly supporters in from New Zealand to vote for him. An hour after pronouncing his verdict the judge swore in as premier the leader of the opposition, Dr Tom Davis (since knighted), a remarkable man who was now sprawling in a slatted deck chair that had most of its slats missing, and dozing in the shade of a baseball cap with gold leaves on the peak presented to him by a visiting US warship.

He was a tall, heavy, kingly figure of a man with a nose like the prow of a voyaging canoe, a mane of dark curly hair touched at the sides with grey, visible scars of a serious operation for cancer of the throat, and an accent more at home in the clinical laboratories of Boston than on the surf-washed shores of the South Sea islands he governed. Born in Rarotonga the son of a Welsh sea-rover and an island girl, he had been the first Cook Islander to qualify fully in medicine. After establishing a medical service to be proud of, he had sailed away in his cruising yacht to take up a Harvard Fellowship: it was some voyage, for it was the first west-to-east crossing of the southern ocean by yacht and he did it in the middle of winter with his wife and children, once being reported lost in a hurricane.

In America he had become a specialist in environmental medicine, worked in Alaska, designed footwear for the US military, led the team that sent the first rhesus monkey into space and became a senior medical monitor on the Mercury space programme.

It was while he worked in Boston as a consultant research scientist in clinical medicine that he began to receive letters and tapes from family and friends in the far-away Cook Islands and learned that all was not well. The silver-tongued Albert Henry was bringing fear and depression to the islands. Communities that voted for his candidate received the new generators and water tanks they needed but others were forgotten. Civil servants who did not vote for him were fired. He paid himself and his ministers, many of whom were members of his family, large salaries. In 1971 Davis returned home the way he had left, under sail. He stepped ashore from his yacht to a tumultuous welcome and established an opposition party. After a long struggle that split the island people as bitterly as a religious war, Dr Tom Davis had finally triumphed. Now, with his new wife Pa Ariki and two members of the government, he was making an official tour of the islands he had last seen as a youth.

A slim, erect, noble figure of a woman with haughtily arched eyebrows and big brown eyes behind large tortoise-shell sun-glasses, Pa was a Polynesian aristocrat in her own right, one of three *Ariki* (ruling chiefs) of Rarotonga. She claimed to trace her ancestry back a thousand years to the chief who arrived at Rarotonga from Samoa at the same time as another contender came from Tahiti. They apportioned the island between them by pushing off the beach in their canoes and sailing around the coast in opposite directions until they met. When the Duke and Duchess of Kent were visiting Rarotonga, and Sir Albert Henry broadcast a message telling all men to go to the

Victory Theatre to learn how to bow, and the women to go to the Empire Theatre for curtseying lessons, Pa Ariki refused to let her people go. "The Takitimu people bow or curtsey to nobody." she stated.

With his eyes screwed up behind his thick muscular forearm, Nihi Vini lay on his back on the red steel deck. The Minister of Outer Island Affairs, he was a tough man with a beaming smile, a bulging belly and a prodigious appetite. Teariki Piri, green about the gills despite the Kwell I had given him from my supply, was a slim, younger fellow with a shy expression and a droopy moustache; he had been a physical education teacher until he won a seat in the Legislative Assembly. The premier's head lolled over the paperback I had lent him. Pa dozed beneath a big pandanus hat, half waking as the box on which she was sitting started to slide when the ship made a heavier than usual roll.

This was what I had come for. The long aching days. The tedium of the times between. The spring-cleaning of the mind that sweeps away the cobwebs of the last port of call and makes you fresh and eager for the treat of the promised landfall. But if I could be so revived by just two nights and a day of sumptuous wall-to-wall monotony, how must the nineteenth century whaling men have felt, making a lush and flower-scented landfall after twelve months at sea without a break?

A low ribbon of reef and sand encircling a lagoon, an atoll is the very soul of Pacific romance. From a high-altitude jet it looks a writhing contrail that, in falling soggily on the sea has somehow lost its elasticated tension. From lower down, as the frigate bird sees it, the barrier of the encircling reef is a causeway of boiling white foam and thickets of green, only yards wide, between the blue of the rolling deep and the green of littler sharper waves flickering over the lagoon: a green lake in a blue ocean, walled in by white sand, white surf, and a strip of tossing palms. But land that to a seabird or an aviator is a jewel of astonishing beauty is to the mariner a death trap. All they see of it is the strip of palms, seeming to grow straight out of the sea. The rest is obstructed from view, behind the hunching shoulders of the swells rising to smash on the reef. On board a sailing vessel with the wind astern, to sight the breakers at night is already too late. Later, in Tahiti, I spoke with an indomitable old girl called Dorothy Walker-Levy who had traded around the islands for pearl shell for twenty years with her husband. On her first voyage, it being hot and stuffy in her bed, she had slept on the floor and been troubled by a strange pounding noise that seemed to carry through the deck boards. Her husband told her to go to sleep but the skipper recognised the sound at once and threw the schooner about to sail the other way. The sound was the thunder of waves crashing on to the reef of an atoll, just ahead in the darkness.

The reefs of Pukapuka are notorious. At various times since Commodore Byron sailed by in HMS *Dolphin* in 1765 it has been known as Danger Island. Captain Ben was on the bridge early and hunched over the radar. When I joined him at dawn we were close enough for the bar of white sand fringing the palms to be seen peeping over the curve of the Earth. Glassy swells cracked against the encircling reef and spilled over into the quiet lagoon beyond. I had a bowl of cornflakes as the *Mataora* hove-to on the lee side. A boat like a large wooden dinghy came out through a gap in the reef. Palm fronds decorated its gunw'le. The men in it, stiff in brightly coloured Hawaiian-style shirts, dark trousers and beautiful hats woven for the occasion, produced a typewritten programme of events for the Premier and his party.

About 700 people lived on Pukapuka and it seemed that every living one of them was gathered on the beach as the outboard motor was cut and the laden surfboat drifted into the sand. Only the chairman of the island council and a handful of his followers, supporters of the toppled Albert Henry, had not shown their faces. An elderly man waded out but instead of taking our bow to haul us in, as I expected, delivered a thrilling and elaborate challenge of welcome. With that traditional formality complete, many hands grabbed the gunw'les and the boat slid briskly up the white sand so Pa Ariki could step ashore without getting her feet wet.

At every kiss another *lei* of flowers was looped over heads. My shoulders were crushed by their weight. Children in grass skirts and crowns of flowers did a lively dance of welcome. Then a five-minute stroll along a wide pathway of crushed coral, under palms dense enough to cast a twilight of shade, to the centre of the island. Here was a clearing and a large open-sided roof that drained into massive cement water tanks, the Piccadilly of Pukapuka. The official party sat in glaring sunlight on the brilliant white coral while speeches were made and children danced, Tom Davis and Pa Ariki swinging their hips with the best of them. During his term of office the dethroned premier had organised a competition for the design of a national flag but had ignored the choice of the judges in favour of a circle of fifteen gold stars on a background of pale blue; this was thought to have nothing to do with the fact that his own party colours were also pale blue and gold. One of the first acts of the new premier was to resurrect the winning design, a circle of white stars on a dark blue ground, and its ceremonial hoisting was symbolic of the new order.

Then we were led into the welcome shade of the village roof where –

beneath a Roll of Honour listing two names of islanders killed in the First World War, and faded photographs of the British Royal Family since George V – long tables groaned with food. Heaps of coconut, crab, lobster, steamed fish, roast pork, and all the starchy things that Polynesians find so delectable, like yam, taro, sweet potato, and arrowroot puddings. Women behind us swatted vigorously with palm fronds to keep the flies away. Apart from the magnificent crabs, the liveliest taste – moist and sharp, like consommé – was that of what looked like slivers of slimy fried onion. I ate a lot of it, scooping it up in my fingers: it proved to be eggs squeezed from the big black sea slugs that littered the lagoon like sunken driftwood.

I drained my last coconut and sat back, sated, as the Premier made a speech of thanks. I felt totally wilted by the heat: although it was shady, the weight of it on the roof was almost tangible as if the sky were seeping army blankets. I glanced at my watch, expecting the time to be early afternoon. It was not yet ten-thirty.

The thick *leis* were damp and sticky on my shoulders and the sickly smell was getting up my nose so I hung them on a post and strolled round the island. The place seemed deserted. Like nocturnal animals the people had withdrawn into dark nooks and crannies of their houses, waiting for the torpor of the middle of the day to pass. A few gave me a wave, and we talked a little of New Zealand where everyone had friends and family, but they were just being polite to a visitor. Their minds were asleep and they spoke as if, at any moment, they would keel over in the dirt and doze off. But atoll life is like that. From the moment the boat slid into the glassy water near shore it had seemed that all my plugs had been pulled. It was peaceful, yes, but disconnected too. We had made a landfall but there was no traffic, no tarmac, no telegraph poles, no shops. Not even a street light. But it was not only the furniture of ordinary life that was lacking. There was an uncanny feeling of disorientation, of aimlessness. I sensed that all the tomorrows of Pukapuka would be just the same as today, suspended like a specimen in a glass jar of sea and sky.

In the hot sun I walked completely around the island, hard going where the white sand was thick and soft and scattered with coral razors. I hoped to spot some activity, a fishing party, a boat trip to a *motu* across the lagoon, anything. Nothing moved except the hermit crabs, and the surfboat ferrying roofing iron ashore from the ship's hold. Melting, I returned to the sheltered, shady centre of the island and Pa called to me from the verandah of the doctor's house. Her feminine instinct divined the source of all my anxieties and troubles, and she led me by the hand into a dim kitchen where there was that most remarkable of all treasures in the South Seas, a fridge filled with cold beer.

The Premier came in for a beer and sprawled with a sigh into a deckchair. He appeared to be feeling the strain of non-events as much as I, yet he was a native. Every tick of time seemed to gasp, like a car being started with a flat battery. But slowly the knots of shade lengthened as the sun began its slippery slide. There were more speeches round the flagpole, quieter and more earnest. I was presented with a pandanus hat and a sleeping mat, traditional gifts. The sun flattened as it touched the horizon, firing a golden glow horizontally through the grey trunks of the palms. I heaved a sigh of relief that there would just be time to see our way out through the coral heads. But it was not to be. We were escorted to the feast table once more, to carry on from where we had left off.

Under a prickle of stars we climbed into the surfboat. A hymn was chanted in shrill voices by women up to their knees in water. By the light of a single hurricane lantern held over the bow, we crawled across the lagoon to the reef passage and were whirled through it by the current to where the *Mataora* rocked heavily in the swell.

What a transformation! The little ship was loaded with deck passengers. Gone was our peaceful eyrie on the stern deck under the awning, and the long hatch cover forward. The upper deck was packed with families. A tarpaulin had been slung like a ridge tent the full length of the hatch to give shelter to the people camping beneath it with bundles of coconuts to sustain them on the voyage. The limited bathroom and lavatory facilities were in a state of siege, though not once in seven days of sharing with eighty seasick Polynesians did I find them in a dirty or unpleasant state. At slow speed the little ship trolled away into the darkness and the only light to wave to astern was the soft glow of the hurricane lamp as the surfboat found its way back into the lagoon.

The other islands were the same but not the same. At Nassau, named by an American whaler after his ship, the surfboat was driven by paddles because the landing place was a mere niche in the reef, scarcely fifteen feet wide. We hurtled in on the face of a large wave, arrowed neatly through the gap, and as the wave died the paddlers leapt out to hold the boat against the backwash. I took Pa's shoes and the Premier rolled up his trousers and we waded ashore to the challenge, the drinking nuts, the dances, a warm kiss or strong handshake from each of the entire population of ninety-three. Again the flag and the slug eggs. Again the longest day, and the sunset chorus of speeches and hymns. It was charming. It was enchanting. It was good to feel the breeze in my face again as the ship set course for the next black moon of land rising on the dawn horizon.

Palmerston was outwardly an identical pretty, clean, somnolent footprint on the ocean. But here the fermenting jealousies that I had noticed in a political sense at Pukapuka, and suspected but not identified at Nassau, were manifested in a sad way that brought to mind Father Rod Milne's remarks in Ha'apai ("People face the same pressures everywhere, the *real* pressures that can become too much").

In the middle of the last century a young Lancashireman called William Marsters ran away from home, signed on a whaler in Liverpool as a cabin boy, joined in the Californian gold rush and fetched up in the South Seas. At Penrhyn Island he took three wives and sailed to what was then the deserted island of Palmerston which had been discovered and named by Captain Cook and inhabited at intervals by piratical Europeans who slaughtered each other on the beach. Here he founded a dynasty.

Old Bill Marsters, a patriarchal white-bearded figure in a palm-thatched hat, fathered about twenty children and ruled with an iron hand. He divided the 300-acre island, the large encircling reef with its islets, and the lagoon, into three parts, one for each family, and he imposed strict rules about inter-marriage. For a long time the island was noted for its quaint mid-Victorian Lancastrian English which persisted until recent times. Now hundreds of Marsters were scattered through the Cook Islands, including our own skipper, and sixty-two remained on Palmerston. The three families were headed by Ned, Bob and John. At eighty-three, the only surviving grandson of the founder, Ned was a wrinkled, bow-legged, bright-eyed figure with snowy hair, a gummy smile and a crooked stick on which he propped up his equally crooked frame. His day-to-day affairs were handled by his son Bill, a man of some power on the island who was not only next in line to head the branch of the family but was also the preacher and government representative. This meant that he had use of the government surfboat, for example. He was a grave, stolid individual, friendly but even on short acquaintance seemed as unyielding as a missionary. This, it seemed, was part of the trouble.

On our conducted tour of the little village we saw the lovely church built of huge timbers from the five-masted British windjammer *Thistle*, wrecked in 1900. The mahogany pulpit was reached by a companion-way, complete with brass rail and its original paint, from the French three-masted barque *La Tour d'Auvergne* that crashed into the reef in 1913. A hen coop was made from the wheelhouse of the British motor yacht *Gilda Day* wrecked in 1972. During the terrible 1941 hurricane when people had tied themselves to trees to survive, the church had been carried intact 200 yards on a single wave, and afterwards dismantled and rebuilt, board by board. We also saw the community deep-freeze, razed by fire. It had only just been repaired by the crew of a New Zealand warship, following the last sabotage attempt when its wires had been cut. Now it was a smoking ruin. The freezer was on Bill's land and the other families were jealous because it gave him a certain right of ownership. Whatever they did for the island was likely to have the same result, Dr Davis told me, and I noticed that he was careful to devote exactly the same length of time to his visit at the house of each family head.

The speeches on this island were made not in Maori but in English and I was startled to discover what the Premier had been telling his people. "You must get away from here," he commanded, speaking as a headmaster does on graduation day. "You must work hard and make copra and save money so you can leave this place to see the outside world. Then you will come back refreshed and ready to work again, and happy to be home. For I want you to remember this ... I want you to realise that anything you do for yourselves is not just a selfish act, it is a strike for your country ..."

Was this a prime minister speaking, or a family doctor, I wondered, as the thin Boston accent lifted above the distant thunder of the rollers on the reef. When I asked him later if it wasn't a curious recipe for economic revival he defended himself stoutly. "We're not really talking about a national economy but about twenty families living out here in oceanic space. You can see with your own eyes that the place is littered with coconuts. They can't be bothered to pick them up to make copra because they have sunk into a state of mental numbness. This can be a very destructive force in such remote islands. And people do have to get out of the place to broaden their horizons, if only to come back realising how lucky they are."

All my life I had dreamed of the coral atolls of the South Seas so it was a shock to hear a medical man and scientist of world repute describing them as palm-barred prisons. And to appreciate the terminal boredom of those numbing afternoons when I had sat under the trees with the islanders, staring at the glittering sea. If I lived there how might I spend my days? I could fish, or go by boat to the other *motu* scattered along the reef, or plait myself a hat, or dig in the sticky black mud of the taro swamp, or gather coconuts to make copra to buy my way out. Otherwise there was nothing. Nothing.

That evening after dinner I stood on the wing of the ship's bridge staring at the dark sea,

> *Close to the sky-eyes of the night,*
> *Dancing with the souls of dead warriors*

when Nihi Vini stood beside me. We had been born in the same year, he on Penrhyn Island, so I explained my surprise at the premier's policy and asked him what life had been like for a growing and educated boy on a far-flung atoll. "I suppose you think it's very beautiful, all that sunshine and the warm sea, as all White people do," he said. "But there is nothing to do except climb coconut palms or go fishing. All the time I was a kid I had only one thought, to escape. And my friends thought the same. We thought of nothing else, talked of nothing else.

"In fact, quite a lot of us did escape. I mean literally, we ran away. Kids stockpiled food secretly then stole a canoe and sailed away in the middle of the night. After all, we'd been filled with stories about our forefathers. We could handle canoes at sea as easily as you and your friends in the suburbs handled bicycles on the pavement. We weren't scared of the ocean and we knew a little about the stars. When I was fifteen years old, four groups of my contemporaries went away. One canoe, with three boys and two girls, landed on Rakahanga about a hundred miles away, and thought it was Hawaii, 1,500 miles to the north. One group reached Samoa and eventually returned. Another group was never heard of again, though their canoe was found on a beach in Western Samoa. Many years later, when I went there myself, I recognised some of their names which had been changed slightly and I went to see them. We recognised each other but never spoke of what they had done, nor of our old lives on Penrhyn."

While digesting this incredible laconic account I thought back to what I was doing in Auckland at fifteen: haunting the wharves, gazing at the liners and freighters that might convey me to the land of Hornby trains, Raleigh bicycles and Fleet Street. "What about you, why didn't you go?" I asked.

"Well it was all fixed," he told me. "Four of us made a most secret pact. We hoarded coconuts, dried fish, clams and other supplies, and selected the canoe we'd take. We made a solemn vow that if we starved we'd each offer our bodies for food and select the victim by pulling straws. A week before we were to go my father said he was taking us all to Rarotonga for a trip. Once we got there I found cars and trucks and mountains and Roy Rogers and a whole new group of people so I never thought of it again. Oh yes, when you are young and ambitious in islands like these, you have to resort to desperate measures."

While courageous young natives seek desperately to escape, others dream of the simple pleasures of self-sufficiency in isolation, and one in a million actually tries it.

When Tom Neale had himself cast away on the uninhabited atoll of Suvarov, between Nassau and Palmerston, he was dumped on the beach with a Gladstone bag of clothes, six pairs of rubber shoes, and some odds and ends that included seeds, tools, the driveshaft of a

Model T Ford to use as a crowbar, volcanic stones to make an oven, bamboo poles, spare wicks for his lantern, a cat, and a bicycle pump. A bicycle pump? How else would you spray your breadfruit trees with the soapy water in which you boiled up your bedclothes once a week?

A New Zealander who had roamed the South Seas for thirty years running trade stores and ships' engines, Tom Neale lived alone on the island for three periods totalling sixteen years. Named after the Russian vessel which discovered it in 1814, and more commonly known as Suwarrow, or as "Tom's Place", the atoll is a bulgy sort of square in outline. Anchorage, the largest of about ten little islands scattered along its fifty-mile perimeter, is about five acres in extent. It had been inhabited at intervals during the early part of this century, and by coast-watchers during the Second World War whose little hut and water tanks Tom took over. When storms loomed, he buried his tools, sealed matches and a pair of rubber shoes five feet down in the sand, for in 1942 a hurricane had washed seas clean over the island and the people had survived only by lashing themselves to the branches of the biggest tree. In his book *An Island to Oneself* Tom Neale does not come across as a crank or a mystic. He was a tidy self-contained man who welcomed visiting yachts, becoming cranky only when their crews picked the coconuts in the lowest palms.

In less than an hour he would spear a dozen fish in the lagoon, to cure in lime juice. He caught a mullet-like fish with a feather-baited hook and baked them whole in leaves in his oven. "Every fish in the lagoon seemed to queue up for my table," he wrote. Besides, there were crayfish winkled out of their hiding holes on the reef by night. Wild poultry which he domesticated for eggs and fresh meat. Ten-egg omelettes made with pink-yolked tern eggs when thousands of seabirds nested on the island's sandy spit. Massive burrowing coconut crabs with pincers as big as a human hand ("They would have eaten me, had I died"). Breadfruit and papaya. Coconuts for lemonade, cream, fruit, biscuits, chook-feed. Bananas, pumpkin, shallots, tomatoes, rock melon, cucumbers and sweet potatoes in his garden, once he had learned to fence out the hermit crabs. He lived entirely off the island except for tea, coffee, and an occasional pinch of curry powder, though he spun out his tea leaves by using them five or six times. His table cloth every night was a square of polished lino, his plate a leaf. And he wrote in his book of the joy of his day,

I would get up in the morning, put on my *pareu*, brew my coffee and suddenly reflect that by rights I should be in a pair of long trousers, jangling a bunch of keys ready to open the store. I had escaped! That was the overwhelming sensation, that was what made these early days so unbelievably wonderful and precious: I had cheated authority, fate, life itself, and all by a miracle.

When the *Mataora* turned her slim bow south towards Tom's Place everyone was excited but it was a bad trip. The south wind was brisk and cold. Seas poured along the side decks, splashing over giant turtles being taken to market, and licked under the tarpaulin tent. On the upper deck everyone rolled up in their mats and lay like sausage rolls. In the late afternoon of the second full day of it, we turned along the sheltered lee side of the bulwark of reef and the passengers came out of their mats like hermit crabs out of their shells. In smooth enamel-bright water we ran along a string of islets tufted with palms. Hundreds of birds wheeled and screamed over Tom's omelette factory and Captain Ben turned in through the entrance and coasted up the west side of Anchorage, a hundred yards off.

Two yachts lay at anchor further out. A dinghy was pulled up on the sand. Four sun-tanned people with faded clothes and ragged hats stared at us; another was sitting on a rock along the beach. The little ship crowded with tousled grinning heads must have presented a strange sight but nobody on shore waved. For twenty minutes we drifted, staring at the island, then Ben put the wheel over, punched the engine into slow ahead, and began to head out. The entire ship was deathly silent as the island glided by. As if, having glimpsed paradise, the heavenly gates were closing.

Dr Davis and Pa were in the wheelhouse so I made pistols of my fingers and told them it was a hijack, we were going back. Pa laughed. "You're too late, the mutiny's on, we're going to anchor for the night."

"Well I do think it's important to evaluate the copra potential with a view to settlement," the Premier admitted with a twinkle. Indeed, Ben was keeping the wheel hard over. The ship made a full circle and as the anchor chain thundered through the hawsehole in a cloud of rust there was a series of explosive splashes as the first bunch of deck passengers hit the water and struck out for shore.

For twenty-four hours Tom Neale's private paradise of peace became a magnificent Polynesian barbecue. Three years earlier, Tom had closed up his shack and gone to Rarotonga for medical treatment where he died of cancer at the age of seventy-six. So he was not on the beach to greet the invasion but his presence was felt everywhere. The first problem, however, was to get ashore. I didn't fancy swimming, now that it was dark. Lance, the bulky engineer, had launched his little dinghy but it swamped halfway in and sank like a stone. But in Pukapuka the Premier had picked up a canoe for the Rarotonga museum and this was launched with the ship's derrick to get us ashore.

It may be the wide open spaces of the South Pacific but the 200 people of Apataki Atoll, in the Tuamotu Archipelago of French Polynesia, are concentrated on a mere scrap of dry land, scarcely higher than the level of the ocean and little larger than a city park.

The inter-island schooner *Temehani* unloads boxes of biscuits and canned goods for the Chinese shopkeepers of Huahine, in the Society Islands.

One of the last bastions of the "beach European" in the South Seas is the island of Moorea, seen across the Sea of the Moon from Papeete (top left). Among a variety of white entrepreneurs and escapees who have obtained a footing on this beautiful isle are English artist Jean Shelsher (far left, lower) riding down from her pole house in the hills, and Californian Donald "Muk" McCallum (near left, lower), one of the Bali Ha'i boys. Reggie Smith (right, with his native wife Céline and their daughter) washed in unintentionally in 1922 and has never left. Yorkshireman Marty Pease arrived as a water-ski instructor, clapped eyes on the beautiful Luana (above, and front cover) whom he married, and now bakes chocolate cakes for a living.

Yachtsmen sail the oceans to find romantic South Seas anchorages like this, Robinson's Cove, Moorea.

"Try one of these," said George. The lively young galley boy had a fire going and half a dozen parrot fish cooking in hot, steaming leaves. He handed me one and I walked along the beach, picking at the flaky white flesh, to another fire where the yachties were baking their own fish. They were Americans, one girl heavily pregnant, fine and fit young people with long sun-bleached hair. But their eyes were dull and glassy and they spent long periods gazing at nothing. "Hello, where are you guys from?" I asked conversationally.

"The yachts," they said. A sour lot, probably on drugs, so I left them to it. Nihi told me later he was certain that *motu* around the lagoon were being used to grow marijuana by yachties who anchored here for long periods, but it was impossible to check out, let alone take any preventive measures.

Soon after sun-up when I paddled ashore again, I was reminded of Beachcomber Island ("Another shitty day in paradise") where I had been half demented by boredom. Here was the antithesis, a South Seas subsistence carnival in full swing. Heaps of red and blue coconut crabs teased out of their burrows during the night lay everywhere around George's fire, their dangerous pincers bound with pieces of palm frond. Others were being boiled up in large tin cans of sea water on the fire, and George broke off a massive claw which he handed to me. Girls sat cross-legged among clouds of white feathers plucking the sea-birds they had batted out of the sky with long poles. Stakes of hard *miki-miki* wood with sharpened ends had been driven into the sand to husk the young coconuts that lay around like heaps of green cannon balls. Somebody hacked open the top of one for me, as you would open a soft-boiled egg. George tipped his head at the girls and said confidentially, "You want a bit of Polynesian rabbit, John, I can fix it for you?" He was grinning but not joking. He might as well have been offering another piece of fish, so matter of fact was he. I declined in the same casual vein. "Let me know if you change your mind, eh, the Pukapuka rabbits are pretty good."

I washed my fingers in the lagoon and spotted Nihi Vini, up to his knees with a long, three-pronged rusty spear poised over his shoulder. He was at the end of the island, where the open sea washed over the reef. In the clear water, ribbons of multi-coloured fish rippled nose-to-tail just beneath the surface. It was a sensational sight. Nihi flung the spear, jumped after it, and brought up a fat parrot fish about fifteen inches long. It was coloured like a psychedelic birthday cake, turquoise and inky blue, streaked with red as Nihi ripped its gills to kill it and passed it to Teariki who threaded it on a piece of vine. For an hour I followed them along the reef, then Nihi gave me the spear. You could sneak to within twenty feet of a fish before it darted away so I tiptoed carefully as close as I dared, lined up my shot, allowing for deflection, and threw with all my might. Bull's-eye. Survival, it seemed, was that easy.

On the lagoon beach a crowd was organising a fish drive. They had cut many palm fronds to make a green fringe some 300 feet long and supported every thirty feet or so by a man. We walked out into the lagoon until the warm water was up to our armpits then circled back. The rabbits lay in the shallows fully clothed, singing shrilly, though whether it was an ancient chant or a Pukapuka pop song was hard to tell. Then all of us began to walk towards the beach, doubling the palm fronds over and over as the perimeter closed in. Dancing like electric impulses on a massive screen of coloured light, the fish mustered worriedly in a pack, darted suddenly in all directions to be confronted by the advancing green barrier, then returned to the centre. Faster and faster we advanced, splashing and shouting. To and fro, weaving frantically, the fish flashed. Then we ran, kicking and splashing, splashing and shouting. The fish were a frenzied mass, beating the sea to a froth. Everybody fell on them, stunning fish with rocks, hitting fish with poles, flicking fish up to dry sand. Peppermint-coloured fish flew in all directions. We got about 150 in the space of a few minutes, and the women strolled out of the shade with baskets woven from palm fronds in which to take them out to the ship's freezer for sale in Rarotonga.

Three times the aqua-ballet with its frenzied kill was repeated, each time further along the beach. We waded a channel and reached the sandy spit, and fished again. But suddenly the glare and the sun hit me. Lying in the water was no help, for the bottom was pure white and even with sun-glasses my head was spinning. The insides of my elbows and knees were getting crusty and stiff. The salt under my shirt rubbed like sandpaper. I thought I might have as much as twenty minutes in hand but then I would certainly swoon.

I set off alone, not realising what a long way we had come, and the channel where the current ran swiftly was now quite deep. I had just reached the deepest part when dark shadows in the water resolved themselves into a nest of reef sharks, small dangerous ones three or four feet long. One detached itself from the rest and circled me very rapidly, about twenty feet away, so fast that I could not turn my head quickly enough to keep it in sight. Then it circled again, closer. Frightened, I flicked my waterproof camera off my neck, swung it on its strap, and brought it down with a thwack. The shark made off and when it returned I was already in the shallows.

I showered under Tom Neale's water tank and felt better in the shade. His little wooden shack was shabby and on the verge of collapse, but was being carefully maintained. The rusting roof had been re-paired and the gutters cleaned out. The path was swept and the encroaching creepers cut back. Coconuts had been cut to feed the hens. As I stepped over the threshold a bush rat scurried out. Inside, an old alarm clock was stopped at five to three. There was a rusty flashlight and a deckchair. The paperbacks in a mouldy heap on the sagging bed included *Slipped Discs* and *The Return of the King*. The workshop outside was stocked with wood-saws, wire, a wheelbarrow and lots of tools. Pinned to the wall of the shack and framed in a length of rope was a notice in Tom Neale's hand:

TO WHOM IT MAY CONCERN
I am obliged to leave here to go to Rarotonga for medical attention and will probably be away at least a month. I earnestly hope that any visitors will respect my property. The gate to the fowl run will be tied open for the fowls to be able to fend for themselves. Any eggs they may lay, people are welcome to them. I may state that I am virtually forced to leave everything here, you name it, it's here.

Tom Neale, March 11 1977

Below this notice and carefully wrapped in a polythene bag which also contained pens and pencils, was a ledger. On its first page was a picture of a lean sun-tanned man in a floppy hat and a *pareu*. Beneath it was written in blue felt pen: *The above is Tom Neale, the man who enacted all our dreams and will live in all our hearts for his individuality.*

Sensing a prickle of alarm, I sat on Tom's verandah and started to read, for what the ledger contained were the names of all the cruising yachts that had visited and the comments of their crews. I knew that in his first three years on Suvarov, from 1952 to 1954, Tom had been visited by six yachts. Now I made a quick count of the entries in the log: fifty boats in 1978 and sixty-eight in 1979 including a cruise ship. The foreword of the book proclaimed loftily in scrawled ballpoint:

Please consider that the enjoyment of this place is more possible because of the work and consideration of those who came before you and before me. For instance, there is good water in the tanks because when they became rusty and foul they were cleaned; when holes occurred they were patched. There are eggs to be found and roosters for the pot because your unknown friends were not greedy. Of course there are those cretans [*sic*] among even us who have not yet learned where greed and abuse leads to. But let's leave these guys to Karma and treat this place the way it treats us . . .

The book, it appeared, had been established by a certain Pam and Toot of the ketch *Noanoa*. Not content with casting their spell of righteous blackmail over Tom's Place (... among *even* us ...) they had compiled a long list of Work To Be Done. And somebody else had added: *Let Suvarov be a living memorial to getting away from it all.*

Tom Neale would be squirming in his grave, I thought. I was strangely tempted to throw the book into the sea and thus preserve for other adventurers the freshness of the place. The magic of an uninhabited island is that you feel you can get away from the uplift of bossy moralists, even if you agree with the sentiments. Not on Suvarov. On the day I get to Heaven I will find Pam and Toot sitting at the gate reminding me to take my hat off and wipe my feet.

I stretched out under a tree by the beach. "You're sure?" George pressed. "Now is a good time for a rabbit, makes you sleep good ..." Had I desired it there would have been no chance, for even my elbows were sunburned.

Little waves lopped into the canoe as we paddled out to the ship in the late afternoon. The gunw'les carried a strange cargo of coconut crabs that gripped the wood in their pincers. On board they were suspended on string from the stern-deck awning where they swayed ghoulishly with the roll of the ship. At sunset the *Mataora* motored out of the beautiful lagoon leaving Tom's Place to the tender mercies of the glazed yachties. They did not wave. Almost at once we struck the same heavy south-westerly that had been so murderous the day before. Our chairs screeched agonisingly on the saloon's quarry tiles with every roll and we had to eat one-handed, hanging on with the other. Before turning in I looked out on the stern deck. The girls were silent now, rolled up in their mats and groaning sickly while the blue and red crabs swung crazily over their heads on cords.

14

POMARE BOULEVARD

THE NUCLEAR NEW CYTHERA

It was not merely the bright swampy heat of the morning that made steam come out of Don Silk's ears as the *Mataora* docked in Avarua on the island of Rarotonga. Our unscheduled picnic at Suvarov had had a cumulative effect, so his other ship was also delayed, and a freight of hundreds of cases of pineapples was in danger of going rotten in the sun at Atiu. Besides, the pounding we had suffered in the last two days at sea had flooded the ship's forepeak and inundated the electric windlass motor. So Captain Ben was in trouble for being late, in trouble for not reducing speed, and was wearing a long-suffering expression.

The last supper on board had been fried turkey tails, or parsons' noses. In these days of kit-set food packages I supposed somebody had to get the arse-end of the bird, and as the South Sea Islanders liked their meat rich and fatty they were welcome to it, but it was a warning that before long we would be drawing straws and eating each other so I was glad enough to look out my porthole at dawn and see the peaks of Rarotonga on the horizon. The island is about twenty miles round and fringed by a narrow lagoon. The reef touches the shore at Avarua, where the harbour is so small that when freighters come in, yachts must cast off to give them turning room. On the other side of the island the lagoon is just wide enough for the yacht club to race sailing dinghies. The town scarcely exists: in any city suburb a row of shops provides as much of a metropolitan focal point as Avarua. Only a handful of shabby, sun-faded government buildings around the Post Office, one bank (the only one in the country), a modern general store of the kind you would find on the prime corner site of a back-country cow town, a couple of ramshackle picture theatres and a half dozen boutique-style shops in wooden shacks. Accommodation in the hotels can be so tight that you must have a reservation before you are permitted to land. But in a sense the whole island is the town. The people inhabit pretty, well-equipped, wood-and-iron bungalows amid flowering shrubs on small plots around the coastal fringe, and cultivate citrus orchards and vegetable gardens on the inland slopes reaching up towards the basalt pinnacles in the centre.

There were no buses so I rented a motorbike and circled the island at slow speed which took an hour, then circled it again until I came to Don Silk's house and we drank cold beer in his sitting room overlooking the lumpy blue-grey sea. A neat wiry man with a sun-tanned bald head and a brisk manner, he seemed an unlikely figure of a man to be a South Seas ship-owner but the way he had accomplished it was even more unlikely. He was a truck-driver with adventure in his heart, running his own small transport business in New Zealand, when he decided the horizons of an isolated farming community were too small. He sold up, bought a little cruising ketch in partnership with his friend Bob Boyd, who was a cook and sign-writer and with his wife and little girl they sailed away to a new life in Vancouver. Along the way they put in at Rarotonga, arriving on a Friday night. On the Monday morning Don walked up the road to clear Customs for Tahiti but he never did leave. On the way back to his yacht he saw the wreck of a copra ketch holed on the reef and dragged up the beach. It would be a pity not to patch her up and sell her, Don decided, but first they would have to sail back to New Zealand to get their tools . . .

Within a year and a half the enterprising pair had relaunched the *Siren*, filled her hold with all the goods they could afford, and sailed to the distant atoll of Manihiki to open a store and trade for pearl shell. One thing led to another. Their boat was wrecked while entering Avarua at night, strewing the harbour with the thousands of tomatoes she was carrying. They had a bigger one built in Hong Kong and lost her on another reef while loading pineapples at Mangaia. Don found a bigger but older coaster in Denmark and sailed her back, across the Atlantic and the Pacific, with a cargo of beer and a crew of itinerant young New Zealanders. One ship could not do enough for so many scattered islands so they bought another coaster in Sweden, changed her name to *Mataora*, nearly lost her when the cargo shifted in a North Sea storm, and sailed her out to the Cook Islands. Suddenly the Silk & Boyd partnership that had started with a 28-foot yacht was a shipping line, one of the few to flourish in the South Seas.

But Don could not help me get to Tahiti, 650 miles to the east. Shipping links were virtually non-existent. The steady procession of cruising yachts arriving at Rarotonga and permitted to stay seven days came out of the east with the wind behind them: one might hitch-hike westwards towards the Samoas and Tonga but it was rare to find a yacht heading east at this latitude. Reluctantly I turned my Suzuki towards the airport.

Until 1961 a flying boat flew what was called the Coral Route through the islands. It was a two-day trip from Suva through Apia and Aitutaki (an atoll north of Rarotonga) to Papeete. Your ticket included a a printed sheet on which it was politely suggested that you keep your swimming costume in your hand baggage, because you could take a dip in the lagoon while the plane refuelled. And there was always the possibility, which happened twice at Aitutaki, that the plane would break down and you would have to camp for a week on a *motu*. Today, the tradition of the Coral Route is kept alive by an Air New Zealand DC-10 that makes a weekly trip from Nadi to Rarotonga and Papeete, but for all the coral you see you might as well voyage by submarine.

We roared off in the dark from a rustic airport where the transit and departure lounge was a lawn fenced with wire-netting and furnished with park benches under thatched shelters. We landed 100 minutes later in the dark and entered a marble-halled air terminal complete with Hertz and Avis desks, a baggage carousel, and a coffee shop large enough to entertain the entire population of Palmerston Atoll in one corner. There was a different smell in the air, too. Not only the fragrance of flowers and fruit and humus that hangs in the steam rising off the tarmac after a passing shower, but whiffs of *Madame Rochas* and fresh *croissants* and stale *Disques Bleus*. Was I still in the South Seas, or had the plane mysteriously diverted to Nice? Even three more days of turkey tails for dinner would have been cheerfully supportable if they had spared me such a jarring instant transition. How could I be in Tahiti, yet still have on my tongue the taste of a Rarotongan raspberry-ripple ice cream?

But my heart, stomach and mind caught up with me next morning. Fearing that breakfast at the Holiday Inn would be as mouldy as the shaggy carpet in my $35 room, I hailed a passing "truck" and rode into town for a coffee and bread roll at a quayside cafe where at least I could pretend that I had just stepped ashore eager for the long-awaited treat of the richest and most spectacular island in the South Seas. As it turned out, to arrive by *le truck* was the next best thing.

What the Tahitians call a "truck" is to the municipal bus what the sailing schooner is to the steamer. Fleets of them parade continuously along the island's single coast road, picking up passengers wherever they signal from the roadside. They have the cab and chassis of a light

truck to which is bolted a home-made wooden shack. You mount by
steps at the rear and, stooping under the low roof, scuttle to a space
on the wooden benches on either side. In that delightful and easy
Polynesian way other passengers willingly make room, help with
parcels, and pass an unprotesting baby from hand to hand when a
young mother with a hibiscus behind her ear comes aboard. It was the
seven o'clock rush-hour and the morning sun was already hot, making
a smoky blue funnel of the traffic jam. From each of the crowded
trucks, disco music pulsed loudly on stereo cassette players. As my own
truck edged along, a teenage boy riding shot-gun on the rear step
blatantly fingered himself with one hand while making eyes at a pretty
girl with a basket of orchids on her knee. He wore a yellow football
shirt, tight denim shorts, striped athletic socks and Adidas running
shoes. A shark's tooth dangled on a thin gold chain round his neck.
With hot eyes he stared unblinkingly at the girl, fresh and slender in
a pink cotton dress, who appeared not to notice him. A number of
passengers giggled as they caught each others' eyes across the cabin.
Then the boy let out a Tarzan whoop, jumped lightly from the slowly
moving truck, sprang athletically over the bonnet and roof of the
Renault 5 following behind, and with another happy shout disappeared up a leafy lane. The girl did not smile.

At the market the passengers climbed out and queued to pass their
fare (about sixty cents) to the driver. Already the truck was filling up
again, for the market had been in full cry before dawn. Fish, fruit and
coconuts were lifted on to the roof, along with a motor-mower, the first
of those I had seen in the South Seas, as shoppers piled in. Cluttered
Chinese stores veiled behind the dust floating in walls of brilliant
sunshine, lay on either side, dark caves of hardware, baby baths and
lavatory brushes. A *gendarme* whistled angrily at the truck and waved
it on as others turned into the street behind. On a balcony above me,
an old Chinese man so wrinkled and shrunken that he seemed to have
been hung to dry in the sun like a piece of fish, turned his French
newspaper to the light and peered myopically through the wire
spectacles. A ravishing Polynesian beauty with lustrous black hair and
radiant eyes hooted and glared from the wheel of her BMW as I
stepped across the street, forgetting that here the traffic drove on the
right.

I walked a block, crossed the tree-lined Pomare Boulevard, and
came to the Pacific Ocean. Here it does not have the muddy tang of
mangroves as in Suva, the green murkiness of Nuku'alofa, the dust of
Noumea's mineral smelters, or the dark jungly look of the harbour at
Port Vila. In Papeete the Pacific is bright and blue and deep and
positively sparkles its invitation to adventure. For Tahiti is the loveliest

island to look at, and the loveliest to look from, in all the Pacific ... the world. No other island I know is such a rich feast for the eye. It is a land on which the eye lingers with the appetite of a starving man seeing a mirage of steak and eggs. The green lushness makes your mouth water, its spectacular and mystical beauty takes the breath away, and the allure of its reputation makes the heart beat faster.

From jagged volcanic peaks 7,000 feet high, spiny ridges and desic-cated gorges – rugged lava-lands clothed in ragged jungle – drop steeply down to the narrow coastal fringe where the people live in a succession of villages. Where rivers cut down the steep ravines and meet the sea the reef is broken so the Pacific swells thunder right up to the black-sand beach in billows of white. In the noon-day heat a massive pillow of cloud streams downwind of the high peaks, like the steam of an express locomotive. When the wind pipes up, as it does in the middle of the morning, the island seen over the racing waves, trailing its plume of cloud, might itself be steaming full ahead.

When at last you catch up with it, and enter the embrace of Papeete Harbour, what gives the waterfront its magical sense of beckoning promise is the view. From the quays of Papeete you do not gaze out on a level and empty horizon, as at Apia or Rarotonga. Only twelve miles out on the dancing water lies another island which, though not as large as Tahiti, is even more fantastical. Through most of the hot day Moorea is merely a jaggedly dramatic silhouette, blurred by veils of distance and trailing its own flying capes of cloud. It is not so big that it dominates the horizon, but is framed in such perfect proportion that when the setting sun drops behind it, the entire island is back-lit like a cathedral in a stained-glass sky.

In a shady café on the sidewalk of the boulevard I found a quiet table and here I came, every morning for two weeks, for a breakfast of *café complêt*, a read of the morning paper, and a gaze at the harbour before I got down to work. The boulevard was in fact a succession of *quais* fronting the harbour. To my left, through the trees, sixty or seventy cruising yachts were moored along the grassy bank, their bows pointing towards the reef and their sterns made fast to coconut palms. Scores of children wearing masks and flippers swung on their ropes. High on every yard-arm the *tricoleur* flew as the traditional courtesy to the host port; an Australian yacht had hoisted the Dutch flag by mistake. These were the blue water dreamers who had sailed into the most romantic of South Sea harbours. *Sundowner* of Honolulu, *Baron Rouge* of Vancouver, *Kate Kelly* of Melbourne, *Oma Tako* of Cape Town, *Hard Rock* of New York, *Auroch* of Brittany, *Groais* of Newfound-land ... Boats home-made of rough cement and galvanised pipes, angular steel boats with baggy-wrinkle growing like moss in their rigging, sleek glassfibre racing yachts making fast passages around the world, and sturdy plodding cruisers that breathed images of Conrad, Masefield and Gerbault in every splice and shroud. All had awnings rigged for shade, wind funnels making the most of the breeze, washing hanging out to dry, and ensigns so faded and wind-whipped it was often hard to distinguish the Stars and Stripes from the Red Duster.

To the right of my sidewalk table was the commercial part of the waterfront. Here was the corner where the sleek fishing launches called *bonitiers* unloaded their catches of skipjack tuna and carried them on poles to the market; the big wharf where I had docked in the passenger liner taking me to England twenty-one years before; the *Quai Galliene* where the little boats left every morning for Moorea; the military base for French warships; and on reclaimed land opposite, connected to the mainland by causeway, an industrial zone with quays where little ships loaded for their irregular voyages to the distant archipelagos of French Polynesia.

Quinn's, the most famous watering hole in the South Seas, had long since disappeared. The Bounty Club, Punk's Disco, La Cave Night-club, and a succession of sleazy bars and pool rooms had taken over. In this part of town, filled with the shrill whine of power generators, like the engines of a ship, the girls with painted faces who tried to catch the eye were as sad and brassy as prostitutes in any port anywhere, and there was nothing of the free and easy Polynesian humour in the winks with which they solicited the sailors and soldiers who whiled away their idle hours in T-shirts, tight shorts and running shoes.

Papeete was peppy, glossy, noisy: a South Seas city in miniature. It even had traffic lights, an escalator, and municipal buildings with automatic glass doors. Of its famous endearing charm, however, I glimpsed only the sketchiest fragments. As when a stout Tahitian in an open car was caught at a red light just as rain came down like a cataract of marbles. I watched him leap out of the driving seat and run to the rear of his car, and expected to see him erect the soft-top. Not at all, this was still Tahiti. He whipped off his shirt and shorts, tossed them into the trunk, and with the rain bouncing off his bare belly and shoulders jumped behind the wheel just as the lights turned green.

At first, having spent so long in the oceanic outback of the other islands, I was dazzled by Papeete. I ate excellent food and drank wine in good restaurants. I bought a bottle of liquor at a supermarket and a bunch of limes at the market, and mixed rum punches which I drank from a Coke bottle while swinging my legs on a jetty, and watching the always glorious sunset over Moorea. I spent many a cool cocktail hour in the cockpits of the yachts, and was twice offered snorts of cocaine which had never happened to me anywhere else in the world. It was a couple of days before the tragedy of the place began to register.

The limes I had bought were imported. The *wahine* who had nearly run me down was driving a BMW. A BMW! The most expensive *pareus* in the hotel boutiques were not bought by rich tourists, I learned from a hotel owner, but by girls who worked as waitresses. A hoarding on the way to the airport advertised the latest Buick with auto-shift, air conditioning, electric windows, radio, power steering: where did the happy-go-lucky Tahitian of the romantic story books find $30,000 to buy such a car? I remembered Jacques Sapir's cynical remark on *Hawk* ("The kids in Tahiti can't swim without flippers") and saw it was true. When I rode around the island in a succession of "trucks", and joined a party of fisheries scientists for a plane-trip out to an atoll in the Tuomotus, the sound that assailed my ears was not the thrilling thunder of the surf on the reef but the scream of suburban motor-mowers.

Papeete was an astonishingly rich place but it could not have earned such spending power – and a standard of living reckoned to be one of the top fifteen in the world – on the strength of what it produced. For practically nothing was made here. Only drinking water in plastic bottles, thonged sandals, printed cotton *pareu*, excellent *Hinano* beer and good French bread. In fact, local activities accounted for less than fifteen per cent of Tahiti's income. No less than four fifths of its food was imported.

The answer to the mystery was that the taxpayers of Mother France lavished on these beautiful islands – where subsistence was probably easier and more comfortable than anywhere else in the world – sums of cash equivalent to thousands of dollars per head per year. And the Tahitians, having at first resisted and then fallen easy prey to the monsoon of francs, had allowed their French colonial masters to decide that Tahiti must die in order that they may live. It is the saddest, most ignoble story of the modern South Seas.

For two centuries the vision of Tahiti as an earthly paradise captivated the hearts and minds of writers, philosophers and travellers. The French captain Louis de Bougainville, who called at Tahiti in 1768, just before Captain Cook, was so enchanted by the water-speckled brown-skinned beauties who clambered naked over the side of his ship that he called the island *La Nouvelle Cythère* after the birthplace of Aphrodite, the classical goddess of love. Explorers, missionaries, scientists, adventurers and writers who followed confirmed that it was so, that casual sexual gratification without the complexities of loyalty and commitment was in these beautiful islands a way of life. And this was just part of the vision. In Tahiti fish and fruit were so abundant you hardly needed to stoop for them. What use was money in a benign environment where food, clothing and shelter were provided by bountiful Nature?

The consequence of contact between native island societies and technological man, hauntingly captured by the author Alan Moorehead in the phrase "the fatal impact", are well known. Venereal diseases came with the first discoverers. Missionaries shamed the people into clothes they did not need and imposed tyrannical regimes that deprived them of laughter and song. Epidemics of measles, influenza and other common Western ailments cut swathes through island populations and survivors seemed to lose the will to live. The French annexed Tahiti in 1843 when an English missionary used his influence to have two French competitors kicked off the island, a high-handed grab that dismayed the Tahitians and nearly caused a war between the two countries. But the French then administered with affection and a general disregard for any venture that might change the status quo. They trained no administrators, provided few facilities, imposed few regulations, with the result that until the early 1960s Tahiti and French Polynesia lingered still as islands out of time. At one stroke, in a matter of months, all that was changed. The French decided to make up for lost time. The fatal impact became the *coup de grâce*. The instrument they chose to inflict the damage was a two-edged one and in every sense the terminal weapon: they exploded nuclear bombs and the fall-out was francs by the hundreds of millions.

While other colonised countries all over the world were being stood on their own two feet, and Charles de Gaulle himself was stirring the pot and advocating independence as a desirable aim for all "subjected" people such as the Quebecoise, French colonialism locked on Tahiti. It came in two simultaneous waves.

One was the military invasion. Two atolls were occupied for testing nuclear devices in the atmosphere, and a third to act as a rear base. The army, Foreign Legion engineers and Atomic Energy Commission (CEA) all built headquarters and barracks in Tahiti. Within a year the island which then had a population of 60,000 was accommodating as many as 15,000 military men and technicians, most of them bachelors, none paying tax, all looking for a lovely *wahine* and with the money in their pockets to get one. The Tahitian *tane* (men) hit back. Military men were warned to walk facing the traffic so Tahitians on bikes or scooters could not sneak up behind and hit them on the head. To defuse the situation the military were allowed to wear civilian clothes with the result that tourists were mistaken for French soldiers and sailors and attacked. Then, although it had been illegal to operate a brothel in France since 1946, it was decided the law did not apply during military campaigns and that it would be a useful solution to the "outlet problem" to establish "relief stations" on charming little vessels anchored discreetly in creeks with hostesses supplied from the Orient. The idea fizzled out only when high school students protested vociferously, won the sympathy of the media, and pointed out that France had been party to a UN agreement prohibiting prostitution.

At the same time there was a massive influx of new settlers from metropolitan France and former colonies in Africa. New hotels sprang up to meet the needs of tourists arriving at the new jet airport. Overnight, the tiny and contented little country that for so long had been just off the map became a target for the worst kinds of colonial exploitation and shifty political two-timing. Local Polynesian leaders pressing for the modest degree of autonomy enjoyed by the Cook Islands were exiled or locked up on dubious grounds, and, during elections, refused permission to use broadcasting facilities, or prevented from using government inter-island vessels which were conveniently deployed on "urgent" administration business or drydocked for "repairs". It was also difficult to overcome the massive block effect of the transient military men and technicians who, besides the new settlers, were allowed to vote.

It is hard to be a guerilla in Tahiti. Everybody knows everybody else and there is nowhere to hide. When a bomb exploded in the Post Office and a French businessman was shot dead in his bed, the perpetrators were duly brought to book. Then the Territorial Assembly was occupied for many months until a shift of power in Paris resulted in a new constitution. In 1977 Tahiti was allowed limited internal autonomy; matters of justice, policing, finance, aviation, communication, foreign affairs, defence, secondary education, immigration, and broadcasting were kept in French hands. Tahitians did retain the full rights of French citizenship – with the corollary that they had no control over which Frenchmen could live in Tahiti – without being required to pay French taxes. Today Tahiti is a paradise in an unexpected sense for there is no income tax, no property tax, no sales tax, and education and medicine are virtually free. Local funds are raised mainly by steep import taxes, which means that the more Tahiti tries to make herself self-sufficient the less revenue she will raise.

Meanwhile, somebody had to do the digging. As the nuclear programme worked up steam, naval ships went round the islands recruiting labour. Within half a year about 5,000 Polynesians exchanged their tranquil existence as independent copra producers, farmers and fishermen for that of salaried construction workers on shift. Thousands more streamed into Papeete. Slums spread up the beautiful valleys, food prices spiralled, and the arrivals from France with exotic salaries and allowances cornered the leases in prime coastal land. Also, a new middle class of *demis* (half-castes) was created, together with the Chinese who had always been the merchants of Tahiti. This group opted heart and soul for the boom economy because at last they had the chance to shine, and with their Western work ethic were soon buying houses and cars and elbowing the native shanties even deeper into the valleys. But the material reward for persisting, for hanging in there, was spectacular. On the day he or she began formal study to be a primary school teacher, a young Tahitian earned $300 a week. About 1,200 local civil servants earned a minimum of $400 a week. If you were sent out from France the pay was fantastic. A *gendarme* earned about $900 a week, with a free house. A secondary school teacher earned two and a half times his salary in France, plus one year of his salary as an expatriation bonus, plus a cost of living allowance, and had the normal school vacations locally plus six months paid leave in France after three years' service. Tahiti is so rich – the new Arabia of the South Seas – that $400,000 was found to send a team to the South Pacific Games at Fiji, the bulk of it through lotteries and fund-raising drives, while the Cook Islands could raise only $10,000. In this light the marketing of Buicks suddenly made sense.

Despite the political changes, the policy of Tahiti for the French continued. All education was in French and the language was taught as in France, not as the foreign tongue it is for the bulk of the pupils. Predictably, young Tahitians dropped out of school and fell desperately behind in the education race. In the Territorial Assembly only three of the thirty elected representatives spoke good bureaucratic French, and there was not even a simultaneous translation facility on the simple scale of the English–Maori one operated in the Cook Islands. It was the French who chose radio and broadcasting programmes and the service filled no local need.

That extreme old-fashioned colonialism on a nineteenth-century scale should be alive and flourishing in a few far-away South Seas islands that a few people may dream about but even fewer know or care about may not be terribly surprising. What is surprising is the sheer scale of the enterprise in terms of geography. French Polynesia covers around two million square miles of ocean but its 130 principal islands add up to only 1,500 square miles of dry land: a ratio of about 1,300 to one. It includes five archipelagos of distinctively differing character. Three-quarters of the total population of 140,000, lives on Tahiti, mostly in Papeete. If Papeete were superimposed on Paris, the Mangareva Islands would be in Romania, the Marquesas between

Oslo and Stockholm, the Austral Islands in Sicily, the Society group that includes Tahiti would stretch to Cornwall and the Tuamotu Archipelago, a milky way of atolls and reefs, would fill most of central Europe between Berlin and Trieste.

The ample disregard that the colonial administration displays towards the just concerns of the local people, as well as those fairly expressed by neighbouring countries, is demonstrated in the disdainful way the authorities stonewall repeated requests for information about the possibly harmful effects of repeated nuclear explosions. So characteristically French are they in their arrogance that the whole situation would be comic if it were not nuclear fall-out that was the issue. Take just two examples.

Although the French claim to have made exhaustive studies of all flora and fauna before the tests started, and to have taken thousands of samples to guard against contamination, no figures have been made public. The authorities take refuge in reports they are obliged to make to the United Nations but which are not released locally. These figures, I learned, were based only on the effects of fallout on milk. But in French Polynesia milk is drunk only on Tahiti and there are no cows on the other islands. Measurements of fallout in rainwater, made by New Zealand scientists in Apia which lies directly down-wind of the tests, showed appreciably higher concentrations. Therefore the radioactive particles originating at Mururoa must jump obligingly over the top of all the French Islands, if only to prove right the French scientists who have stated from the outset that "not a single particle of radioactive fallout will ever reach an inhabited island".

There was suspicion, too, in medical monitoring. Many people believed cancer was occurring more frequently as a result of well over 100 nuclear explosions. The colony's doctors were provided by the French army. For a long time they simply refused to make figures available, and when a survey was finally released it applied only to Papeete's main hospital, ignoring those who might have been treated on other islands or who might have gone abroad for treatment, and it provided no comparative data for the pre-test period so there was no way to gauge a trend. If cancer was not increasing then the French authorities had adopted a mystifying way of assuaging doubts.

Yet France was not totally immune to pressure. Until 1975 the nuclear devices were placed in balloons tethered above the lagoon while ships stood off at a distance of fifty miles to watch the pillar of fire and mushroom cloud. So great was the feeling whipped up in South Pacific countries against the tests, resulting in boycotts of French goods, ships and aircraft, that it was decided to test the devices far beneath the bed of the lagoon. Now there were allegations that the atoll itself was cracking apart and leaking radiation as a result of repeated explosions. This the French blandly deny, and refuse to discuss.

The stickiness of the authorities towards any form of probing may be gauged by the fact that when I was permitted a half-hour briefing by the military information officer at the nuclear test headquarters in Papeete, more than five minutes was devoted to an exhaustive inquiry into the reason why my British press card had lapsed during my voyaging through the South Seas. The army colonel, the khaki creases of his uniform sharp enough to slice lemons, had a leg in plaster (a water-skiing accident, he said) and a handshake like the snap of handcuffs. We sat at a long baize table. One man took a shorthand note of everything that was said and a young naval lieutenant interpreted. I confirmed what I had learned about the military doctors ("Cancer is no more prevalent here than in any other society consuming pre-packaged food and smoking a lot"). I learned that offshore oil-drilling technology was used to position the devices 400 metres down in solid basalt, the same depth at which US scientists exploded nuclear devices of ten times the power in the Nevada Desert. I was told that a minimum of information was released because the media manipulated it indiscriminately. And that if I wanted to know more I should visit Paris.

As the lieutenant escorted me to the front door, and we shook hands in the sunshine, he said in an engagingly confidential way, "You know, I have been on Mururoa when a device exploded, along with about three thousand other men. We were playing *petanque* when the thing went off and the vibration was so negligible that it didn't rock a single *boule*."

When I mentioned this to M. Francis Sandford, the French Polynesian leader whose role may be compared to that of an elected local premier, he shrugged heavily in a very French way and said, "This is the question we are repeatedly asking but there is never a satisfactory answer: if it is so safe to explode bombs on the atoll of Mururoa, why don't they do it in France?"

Meanwhile, individual Tahitians were coining money and not too fussed about the secret, silent events taking place 700 miles to the south. The *demis* and *pieds noirs* (settlers from French Africa) and *metropolitans* were on the pig's back and praying the bomb might boom for ever. And at my café table on Pomare Boulevard, sitting in the sun from where I could gaze out over the lively little harbour towards enchanting Moorea, I read in the newspaper *Depêche de Tahiti* a comment by France's top man in Polynesia, M. Paul Cousseran: "One can be intellectually for the nuclear tests, or intellectually against them, but the fact is that this country lives off them. Polynesia does not produce what it consumes, it does not produce money for what it consumes, so someone must pay for it. Independence is not the problem in this country, it is dependence.''

When I took *le truck* to kilometre 21, riding with the wind in my hair and the stereo drumbeat of the latest pop song from Paris in my ears, Bengt Danielsson made the same point but added an interesting dimension. A tall pale-skinned man with a curious wispy beard hanging from his chin as if it were false and the elastic had snapped, he greeted me in the portentous manner of a north-European burgo-master and showed me to his library. This was the most traditional Polynesian building I had seen in Tahiti. On a wide lawn a few yards back from the lagoon, open to the breeze and cool beneath a thatched beehive roof, it was the most perfect setting for a study that a writer could imagine. Since he had arrived in Polynesia on the *Kon Tiki* raft after the Second World War, when the number of white settlers in Tahiti numbered 650, most of them men, he had witnessed at first hand Tahiti's entire sequence of anguish. His writing had so provoked the French that his status as honorary consul for Sweden was rescinded. Also, as the colonel had hinted to me with little subtlety, they believed Danielsson should not be taken seriously because he had an axe to grind: his own daughter had died of leukaemia. That was true, but the illness had apparently become evident while she was in Europe.

What we saw happening in Tahiti was a distillation – an exaggera-ted form – of the entire Polynesian dilemma, Danielsson thought. Until recent times the Polynesians lived in a comfortable manner with few worries. Measured by Western terms they did not have a very high standard of living, but they did have absolute security and few money worries. When cash was needed they could cut copra. They had their own ethos: they didn't want to work very hard, and you couldn't blame them for that, but there was no foreign competing group and they were happy to have the Chinese as small traders. Then the bomb business offered purchasing power. They exchanged their beautiful and more comfortable island life for poor shacks without gardens in the slums of Papeete, 60,000 of them. Why? Because bread alone was not enough. The desire for circus was equally compelling. The Poly-nesian culture of the old generation was largely dead and buried, but now the people found certain attractive new values in sport, hard liquor, money and a more loudly paraded religion. ''What draws people to Tahiti is not an economic problem,'' Bengt Danielsson explained, ''but a cultural one.''

Meanwhile I was searching for a ship. The brilliant sea lapping the boulevard beckoned its promise of the beautiful islands which natives were abandoning in droves. The tourist office on the main quay supplied in different languages excellent printed information sheets on every archipelago. They listed family homes and guest houses where you could stay for as little as $5 a night and told you how to get there. I was anxious to reach the Marquesas, said to be the last surviving outpost of South Seas romance, but the weekly aircraft was booked up for weeks ahead and my time was drawing in. For the best of reasons I could not afford to be stranded on some remote island or put myself out of touch for four to six weeks by taking a round-trip on a little cargo ship: at home in London my wife was due to have a baby. I telephoned the owners of different ships – in these islands they are still referred to as schooners, though the last sailing schooner has become a floating bar on the waterfront – but in typical South Seas fashion schedules were a matter of freight, fate and fancy. "My ship go, come back one day, maybe next month," one Chinese voice told me. Another said cheerlessly, "Sure. I sell you ticket, you wait for ship come back, no trouble."

However something of a schedule did exist within the Society Islands, so named by Captain Cook because they were so near to each other. Tahiti and Moorea were known as the Windward Isles of this group, while the Leeward Isles – *Les Îles Sous Le Vent*, as they were enchantingly known in French – could be reached by schooners that sailed every Monday night. The only problem was that every alternate week they carried drums of fuel and on those trips passengers were not allowed.

But I was in luck. That Monday the *Temehani* and the *Taporo III* were both taking passengers. For $10 I bought a deck passage *avec couchette* to islands whose names on the ticket had a dreamlike ring: Huahine, Raiatea and Bora Bora.

15

TEMEHANI

THE ISLANDS
UNDER THE WIND

As long as the traveller leaning his elbows on the scarred rail of the little ship making ready to sail made allowances, the scene on the *Quai des Caboteurs* was the stuff of romantic adventure. All the characters of the South Seas yarns were there, milling around the gangway. Instead of an infectious bubbling sense of fun that ought to have turned such an occasion into a carnival, there was a melancholy air of bomb-happy materialism.

The handsome Polynesian girl suckling a baby was sitting in a Datsun saloon. A sleek Chinese talked earnestly with the bare-foot, grey-haired Polynesian wearing work-shirt and shorts who proved to be our skipper, then sped away in a silver Chevrolet Stingray. Fat ladies having a jolly time farewelling some passengers had perched their ample bottoms on the bonnets of a pair of Peugeot 504s. Luggage being manhandled aboard from pick-up trucks was parcelled up in large cardboard boxes stamped Sony and National Panasonic. The coolie-cart selling frankfurters and fried eggplant with ketchup was a Volkswagen van.

The days of the *Temehani* were obviously numbered, but that could well have been the case for thirty years. Built of wood in Seattle during the war, to supply troops in the Aleutian Islands, she may have been old and battered but she was a stalwart little ship, low in profile and broad in beam. The bridge windows were starred by cracks where they had been hit, either by waves or by cargo being lifted from the forehatch, and the "eyebrows" that shaded them were dented and twisted. Abaft the wheelhouse was a squat funnel and the deck was covered by a wooden canopy. Beneath this, along the ship's centreline, were a number of bunks. There were no comforts of any kind: no food, no water, and if there was a lavatory I never found it. But one of the bunks did have a rubber mattress, and this was the one allocated to me. I spread out the contents of my sailbag, to stake my claim, and stood by as the ship filled up, twice fending off hijack attempts on my mattress.

At first glance the bridge of the ship seemed well equipped but closer inspection told a different story. The radar set, radio direction finder, and even the navigator's pencil sharpener were mummified beneath layers of shiny black paint. The compass was only half filled with liquid and its floating card appeared to be hard aground. But the ship pleased me more than the *Taporo III*, a modern steel freighter, loading just astern of us. The other ship might be faster and more efficient, but there were no broad and shaded decks to sleep on and she would roll like a corked bottle.

The farewell was businesslike and not in the least tearful. Around seven the engine was cranked up and the old ship cut through the reflections streaking the lagoon and curtsied smoothly to the open ocean. The deck was not crowded and families camped on their sleeping mats, the children settling down quietly. A young Japanese sitting cross-legged on his sleeping bag struggled to open a can of sardines with a sheath-knife large enough to deal with a killer shark. My neighbour was a gloomy young German breaking pieces from a French loaf held under one arm, and dipping them into a jar of peanut butter. "I hate the stuff but it was all I could find that was nourishing," he said. And as I opened my own tin of meat to smear on a bread roll he offered helpfully, "My God, if you knew what chemicals went into that stuff you'd throw it overboard."

His name was Bruno and he had given up a promising career with a Berlin chemicals firm to travel the world in little ships. This was the worst, he said, because his $8 ticket did not entitle him to a bunk and the deck was covered in wooden slats, uncomfortable for those less well upholstered than the average islander. After consuming his jar of peanut butter he ate all his fruit – "Otherwise, you might get rats running over your back in the night, and that's not nice." Then he had a bath in the handful of Air New Zealand cleansing sachets he had scooped into his pockets, and changed into baggy plum-coloured calico trousers. These were his latest invention, made to order in Bali, and he was planning to market them in Berlin. The trousers had nine different functions, but I could not remember them all. There was a thief proof elasticated pocket concealed in their folds. They could be converted to shorts or overalls, and used as a ditty bag. You could lace your feet inside the cuffs and use them as a sleeping bag. The aim of his travelling, he said, was to find the place where he could escape The Big Bang. I was surprised that his purple trousers did not also include a nuclear fallout shelter.

The old ship rocked and tossed with an easy lullaby motion. A fresh wind blew along the deck but it was not cold. Over the edge of the wooden leeboard of the comfortable bunk I could see the stars and, when the ship rolled to starboard, the wrinkled sea bathed in their faint glow.

The sudden silence as the engine stopped woke me just before six and I picked my way over sprawled bodies to the rail. There was nothing whatever to be seen, not even a reflected star. Then the ship changed course and half a mile ahead I saw a single street light. Then a chorus of cock-crows came out of the dark. The quay was utterly deserted as the ship grazed its timbers and a few moments later there was movement astern as the *Taporo III* materialised. After a time there was a series of lightning flashes, each one more prolonged, as a brilliant fluorescent light came on in a barn-like building across the road. Through its big window I saw tables with bright plastic cloths, and hard wooden chairs, on a bare cement floor. At the far end was a counter and a kitchen sink. Its front door was opened and pinned back by a large barefooted woman wearing a flowery frock and a crown of flowers. A dog wandered out, lifted its leg against the door, barked six times at both ships, and went back inside. Another cafe next door switched on its lights and opened its doors. Men wandered into the light cast on the road and stood and looked at us with their arms folded. Our skipper went down to the wharf and washed himself under the tap, hawking noisily into the sea. Tiny fish flickered out of the depths to inspect his offering.

In the time it took to consume a glass bowl of tepid dilute Nescafé and a yesterday's bread roll, Huahine came to life. Trucks came in with loads of vegetables and fruit laid out for sale under the trees. The moist grey light revealed motor-driven canoes and glassfibre boats approaching across the lagoon and long skeins of small fish threaded on green fibre were unloaded. The *Taporo III* had swung her fork-lift truck ashore and the whole place guffawed as it delicately lifted off the ground the back wheels of a Beetle just as the driver put in the clutch to drive away. Beneath the peaks of their baseball caps the stolid Polynesians flickered their eyebrows at each other as passengers came ashore from the other ship, most of them members of the rucksack brigade. It seemed that the natives rated white girls highly, no matter how slaggy their expressions after a sleepless and seasick night. It prompted the realisation that on Huahine an entire generation – between the ages of about eighteen and thirty-five – seemed not to exist. They had gone to Tahiti.

Lacking the other ship's modern cargo-handling machinery, the *Temehani* competed by carrying parcels for the Chinese merchants. Every space below decks was crammed with small-goods, which explained why I had not found the lavatory, and all of it was man-handled ashore. The contents of the cartons scrawled in black crayon with names like Le Fok, Lee Tsiam and King Wong provided an insight into life in the islands. There were cartons of Libby's tomato sauce, Pilsbury Plus cake mix (dark chocolate recipe) assorted (dispenser size) Kleenex tissue, Golden Circle pineapple pieces, Griffin's biscuits, Skippy creamy peanut butter, Planter's peanuts and cashews, Kellogg froot-flavored (*sic*) loops ... The quay became a sunlit Manhattan of stacked boxes, many of them stencilled KEEP CHILLED, among which stout Chinese men with slicked-back hair, white singlets and baggy black shorts waddled on clacking sandals to check off their bills of lading. I could not wander away because the captain did not know when the ship was sailing. "When we have unloaded," he told me. When would that be? "Pretty soon."

When the ship did sail, at eleven o'clock, Bruno and I were virtually the only passengers. The *Temehani* was more comfortable but a plodder and when we reached Raiatea in the middle of the afternoon the other ship had already left for Bora Bora. But if I had wanted to get there quickly I would have flown. The sun was brilliant, the wind fresh, and spray flew over the bow.

Though not as high and as spectacularly rugged as Tahiti and Moorea, the leeward islands of the Societies have an extraordinary lush and fertile beauty. Huahine, now that we had left it behind, proved to be two islands joined by a causeway that dried at low tide. Raiatea, about thirty miles round and 3,000 feet high, shared the same lagoon with a smaller island called Tahaa. Beyond, the steep pinnacle of Bora Bora jutted on the horizon like a giant beaching whale. Settled by voyagers who came probably from Samoa, these islands had for centuries been the cultural heart of Polynesia. It was from here that the great double canoes had set out for the furthest corners of the Polynesian triangle, spanning the boundless ocean at a time when Europeans remained convinced that the Earth was flat. On Raiatea were the remains of the most sacred religious sites in eastern Polynesia but to see them proved impossible, for I was the captive of a ship without a schedule.

At Uturoa only the cement-floored market hall, dim and un-crowded, offered a refuge from the heat. From one of a row of Chinese-run general stores that seemed to sell the same things I bought a litre of Tahiti's home-made orange juice and drank it down in one. Bruno was aghast: "Think of the chemicals!" A couple of young Americans, half-brothers called Pat and Buddy, let me have a cold shower in their $5 room above the pool den. They had been island-hopping for weeks, staying in guest houses, eating from the market, and living more cheaply than they could at home in California. But they were dissatisfied. Getting laid in the islands of free love, they said, was a great deal harder than in Los Angeles. Sex had its currency: an outward bound air ticket and permanent residential status at the gates of Disneyland.

The oracle of Uturoa was Charlie Brothersen, its mayor and barber. He was a trim, white-haired, bespectacled gent who spoke such perfect English it was hard to believe he was not some preparatory school headmaster on a holiday cruise. In fact he was born on the island, the son of a Dane and the grandson of a whaler who had been wrecked on a remote island and had reached Tahiti in a craft made from the ship's timbers. In the middle of the afternoon Charlie arrived on his sports bike and opened up his little shop which was decorated with flags and photographs of French and American war ships. He switched on the overhead fan, hung up his cap, and took up his customary station outside his door, propping his arm leisurely on a broom as if it were a shepherd's crook.

It was true, the bomb had disrupted everything and if it continued, the island people would be completely lost, he thought. Thousands had quit their ancestral lands to work in Papeete but he thought they were beginning to realise it was not much of a life. A few were drifting back but they had forgotten their old ways. The only people who knew how to make traditional fishing gadgets, for example, were some of the twenty-seven members of the local folk culture club, of which Charlie himself was president, and many of them were French school teachers. But everything was against the Tahitian, from education to job opportunities, and he didn't think the new generation would put up with French domination much longer.

As we gossiped in the shade I was struck by the great number of vehicles in the street. One family of Polynesians rolled up in a Range Rover to do their shopping. White sails cut across the lagoon, not fishing canoes but native children in a fleet of Optimist sailing dinghies: a race organised by the local *Club Nautique*. Did Raiatea have a communal well from which they drew buckets of money?

Charlie hitched his thumb at the gloomy interior of his little shop. "I'm a barber in this little place but I've put both my sons through medical school," he said. "A girl in a shop easily makes $400 a month, a man much more. People own their houses, there's no tax, so it doesn't take long to accumulate the deposit to put down on a car. A fisherman can sit in his boat just off the harbour and get five strings of fish worth

$7 apiece simply by throwing a net over. One of my sons is married to a head teacher and they're earning more than $2,000 a month each. Oh yes, this is called a paradise and it nearly is . . ."

Why nearly?

Charlie picked a white gardenia from a vase of flowers beneath his mirror, sniffed it appreciatively, and put it behind my ear. Then he smiled when he saw the sweet perfume of the flower register on my expression. "There you have the soul of Polynesia," he said. "Every morning on my way to work I pick one and put it behind my ear. It lasts all day and it doesn't cost me a cent. And that is the puzzle. Everything that is good about life in Tahiti is absolutely free of charge, so why do we need all that money?"

In the street I met the captain and asked him when the ship was sailing. He thought maybe six o'clock. At six Bruno and I went aboard and waited. And waited. At seven we tracked down a crew member playing pool. Maybe six o'clock in the morning. We had a plate of chop suey at a mobile diner near the quay and drank beer with Buddy and Pat, then slept in the deserted ship. At dawn nothing happened. I was having chop suey for breakfast when I spotted the captain and ran down the street to catch him. Perhaps eleven o'clock.

Wednesday was market day. *Bonitiers* trailing rooster-tails of spray creamed in from the ocean loaded with skipjack for sale. Little launches bringing bags of copra and passengers from Tahaa rock'n'rolled across the lagoon. Mynah birds clattered on the town's rusty red roofs as shoppers came in by road in Dodge and Cherokee pick-ups. At noon I retired to the shade of a tree with a litre of orange juice when the captain disturbed my doze. "You going Bora Bora? We're sailing now." At two the ship departed.

The captain sat in a chair out on deck, reading a comic book about the Green Berets zapping Viet Cong, and scarcely looked up. The mate lay dead asleep on the floor of the wheelhouse, his legs splayed for coolness. The helmsman listlessly headed the ship directly into a solid cliff of cloud. As its forward edge cut across the sun the captain looked up, casually folded over the page of his book and tossed it at the sleeping mate who grunted. A black stain on the sea, alive with flicking white arches of water as if big fish seethed on the surface, lay fifty yards ahead. The cloud above it was draped in flowing curves. The captain went into the wheelhouse and closed the door firmly after him. He knew something, that captain.

For a few instants the air around the ship seemed to sigh, as if the sky were filling its lungs. Then the squall struck. It was like being caught by a fire hose. I reeled along the deck, doubled up against the force of it. The sea hissed and smoked as if sprayed with red-hot rocks.

Rain flew horizontally, like a hail of spears, and there was no escape from it. After three or four minutes the twilight brightened. The sting in the rain eased. The veils of grey dispersed. And in the haze beyond, a vision lay revealed.

It was a 2,400-foot buttress of cracked and splintered rock cloaked thinly in green. Around it lay a level plain, its edges a succession of white-sand beaches. A lagoon of brilliant colour encircled the island. This was in turn surrounded by a rim of palm-tufted *motus*, also with white beaches, and these were protected by the barrier reef on which the Pacific rollers smashed in smothers of lace. Judging solely on its dramatic, stunning eye-appeal I could understand why James Michener had described Bora Bora as the most beautiful island in the world. But it was almost too astounding to be real, too perfectly suited in its proportions to portrayal on a picture postcard as a tourist paradise. If Walt Disney or the Club Méditerranée set out to create a fantasy island in the South Seas, they could hardly improve on the blueprint of Bora Bora.

It was a three-mile walk from the deserted jetty under the palms to the main village, Vaitape. Bruno elected to hitch-hike and lagged behind. A few minutes later he waved from the front seat of a pick-up driven by a wizened Chinese. When a red-bearded German driving an empty *truck* came along, I hitched hopefully and he slowed down just enough to snarl, "What do you think I am, a bloody taxi?" Beneath a canopy of palms and walled in by wild hibiscus, the level road paralleled the foreshore at a distance of about fifty yards. A dozen voyaging yachts rode at anchor in the lagoon, wind chutes adjusted to catch the breeze. A succession of Vespa scooters purred past me carrying beautiful young women wearing chic cocktail dresses and high-heeled shoes, their hair carefully groomed and tied up with flowers. Where could they be going, so many of them? The houses here and there were small wooden bungalows, well kept; from many of them blared loud music, mostly Country and Western. In a creek children were sailing boats of coconut husks with sails of potato chip packets. There were few gardens or signs of cultivation, few boats pulled up on the beach. Around many of the houses the ground was bare of grass and pock-marked with crab burrows. They scuttled away with a sinister rattle as you approached but after three or four minutes, if you remained perfectly still, they looked out furtively and emerged, a claw at a time. It was obvious that they liked to bake on the warm asphalt at night, for the road was dotted with rotting crab pancakes, flattened by car wheels.

As I crossed a culvert I heard a giggle and saw two girls, about fourteen years old and dressed to kill, sitting in the branches of a mangrove tree. They took no notice of me but made eyes at a pair of young French soldiers coming the other way in T-shirts and swimming trunks. It was at this moment, as I glanced over my shoulder to see how the soldiers had reacted – they were standing under the tree, looking up, and whistling – that I saw the squall.

The previous squall was a mere baby in comparison. Here came the father and mother: a wall of black lava advancing fast. I picked up speed, wondering where to shelter. In Chin Lee's store? No, I might get a bit further. In the Noa Noa bar? It looked expensive. The upper edge of the cloud was already ahead of me and I could feel the damp breath of the thing on the back of my neck. Then a sound like the wooshing rattle of a truck tipping gravel came along the road behind me, and just as the rain struck a gust of wind blew me violently down a path to the verandah of what proved to be the local hospital.

The roadway was grey with spray, smoking like surf. The giant mango tree peeled itself inside out and whole branches crashed down. Coconuts bombed down everywhere. Thunder cracked and rolled with such violence that I wondered if Bruno's Big Bang wasn't happening already. The storm was fiercely, furiously impressive and to me a little frightening, but what was even more impressive was the way people simply carried on as if nothing was happening. The dustbowl in which half a dozen children were playing marbles became a lake, but they shaded their eyes from the sting of the rain and carried on. A little boy in shorts was methodically throwing a ball through a hoop nailed to a post and when the rain was at its most merciless he put a bag of thick polythene over his head and continued shooting goals. Just over the hedge, on a grassy area that was the centre of Vaitape, fifty youths played a wild and unprincipled game of soccer, whooping with joy as long shots were braked in mid-air by the strength of the wind. Streaming water, a footballer grabbed a roll of bandages from a girl in the dispensary just inside the hospital door and sprinted away again.

Again it lasted only a few minutes and I paddled my way along the road to a little bungalow where a wooden notice on a post proclaimed *Chez Aimé*. A dignified Polynesian woman showed me a twin-bedded room that I could have for $7 a night including breakfast. The other bed was occupied by the traveller with the nine-function trousers.

As I left to rent a bicycle, a young Frenchman came limping in on a stick. His face was covered in gauze patches stuck down with plaster, purple grazes were inked with yellow antiseptic and his ankle was swathed in bandages. "You must be careful in this place," he said in a sorry tone. "The place is so beautiful ... The road is full of holes ... You go on your bike and look at the wonderful view and – Oops! *l'infirmerie!*"

When the French solo yachtsman Alain Gerbault sailed into Bora Bora in 1924, it was natives with garlands of flowers and fruit who paddled out in canoes to meet him, and with whom he whiled away the evening hours as they sat on his deck strumming guitars and singing. Today, when you sail your own little ship into this most beautiful lagoon, it is a burly French yachtsman called Alex who paddles out and shows you the place to anchor, within easy reach by dinghy of the *Club Nautique* he runs as a business with his wife and two little boys. Then the name of your vessel is chalked on a blackboard in the self-serve bar, and an account notebook is provided for you to enter the beer you take out of the fridge. My own chit-book was headed *Bicycle.*

When I cycled up at dusk, the air clean and fresh after the rain, the blackboard listed *Skookum* from San Francisco, *Nirvana* from Medford, *Similous* from Victoria, B.C., *Loumaran* from Ostende, *Ocean Mermaid* from Poole, *Miranda* from Melbourne, *Vanessa* from Mauritius . . . And the talk was all of the squall. Wind gauges had gone off the scale at nearly eighty miles an hour, hurricane strength. All the yachts had dragged and one, unattended, had been saved within three feet of a reef. Another had let go and faced the squall under power, the skipper protecting his eyes by wearing a diving mask. Alex had never seen anything like it in five years.

Alex du Prel had sailed out from America in his ketch and when he reached Bora Bora saw no cause to voyage further. He had the sun in his hair, beer in his belly, and a radio shack where he sat in the gloom for hours at a stretch talking with voyagers around the world. Once he had provided the rescue link for a yachtsman badly injured while chasing goats on an uninhabited island in the Marquesas; his wife had broadcast a Mayday which Alex happened to pick up. At Christmas Michelle happened to be searching the wavebands when she picked up a voice from the South Pole, where it was pitch dark and sixty degrees below. "Tell me what you are doing, Michelle," the faint voice had pleaded. And she had said, "Well, fellas, I'm blonde and I'm sitting under a palm tree by the lagoon wearing an itsy bikini and sunglasses and I'm drinking rum 'n' Coke . . ."

About 250 yachts called at Bora Bora every year. Between March and June the Panama gang arrived, most of them intent on circling the world and aiming to be well out of Fiji's cyclone season and heading for New Zealand before November. The California gang trickled in through most of the year, heading north of the Equator to avoid the cyclone season. The majority of ocean voyagers were couples. Shared boats hardly ever got this far and yachts with large crews had trouble leaving Tahiti. Most were either young people on a budget or early-retired folk of modest means. Hippies were weeded out by the Pacific. Nobody who was not serious about sailing got this far. But the character of voyaging was changing, Alex thought. Anchorages were getting crowded. It was no longer a novelty for even the most remote island to see a yacht, and the authorities no longer made concessions: like any other tourist you had to complete the proper formalities. Technically, for example, most of the Cook Islands were out of bounds because you had to clear at Rarotonga which was down-wind. The same was true of the Lau Group in Fiji, you had to sail through them to clear Customs at Suva, then beat a long way up-wind, so few people bothered. "Once it was a real adventure to sail the world by yacht but now it's ninety per cent a business of sailing from harbour to harbour and meeting the same old buddies whom you regale with exaggerated accounts of what happened in between," Alex said. For this reason he encouraged tourists to come to his yacht club, because yachties were happy to find landlubbers willing to listen eagerly to what they had done.

Tonight it was spaghetti and most yachties had rowed in for a social evening. As the beer flowed, so did the yarns. I heard of brushes with pirates in the Caribbean, with supertankers in Panama, and with gunboats off Colombia. One yacht had sailed up the Amazon and the skipper could not work out the cause of the funny clinking noise that worried him all night, until he realised at daylight that the piranha fish had cleaned his hull of barnacles. There were tales galore of whales that surfaced alongside and blew spray into the cockpit. Of surfing downwind in a screaming gale under bare poles listening to Beethoven's 9th Symphony on stereo headphones. Of the retired English bank manager somebody had encountered, who had sold up his suburban house after his wife died, bought a yacht, and with no experience set off around the world; at anchor in an atoll in the Tuamotus he had wondered aloud why his compass was a bit funny, comparisons were made with another yacht, and only then did the other yachties realise that the old man had thought he was anchored in a different atoll altogether, a hundred miles away.

But the strangest story (was it true? it might have been) was a second-hand account of a Canadian in a trimaran, which draws little water. He was on watch near the volcanic shores of the Marquesas in the middle of the night. It was dead calm and overcast, so there was not a glimmer of light. Suddenly his boat hit something. There was a horrible grating noise. He woke up his wife and son who put on life jackets. He sounded all round the vessel with a boat hook and could not touch bottom, yet the jarring continued. Thoroughly disoriented, he started his outboard engine and put the helm hard over, believing that he must be aground on a pinnacle and that he might be able to screw the boat off. But as he revved up, rocks started to land on his head. He had sailed unwittingly into a cave, or huge overhang, and was aground by the masthead.

A tradition in the cruising world is that when you sign a visitors' book you do not merely enter your names but take up a whole page, with photographs or drawings of the yacht and crew and a map of your route. Some are wonderfully artistic and for a couple of hours, half listening to the talk of near-misses with reefs and the irritations of Customs officials, I sat on the verandah drinking beer and thumbing through Alex's stack of log books.

Mr and Mrs Feet had signed-in their yacht *Feet First* and its dinghy *Feet Us*. The yacht *Seaforth* had a dinghy called *Back and Forth*. Skipper Dean Vincent III of the ketch *Eos* had attached his visiting card on which was printed: "Yachts delivered, white slaves traded, refugees smuggled, arms transported, ladies honoured, bribes arbitrated". And Celia Reed, who had sailed single-handed from New Zealand in her yacht *Manuiti II* demonstrated a frank sense of humour, to say the least, when she described herself in the logbook as "the only sailor with a man in every port". The crew of the yacht *Skana* had quoted from *Wind in the Willows*,

Believe me, my young friend, there is nothing – absolutely nothing – so much worth doing as simply messing about in boats.

But it was not all plain sailing and by no means all the reefs on which a vessel might founder were of the coral variety. One page was occupied by the record of the yacht *Reality*, of Bellingham, Washington. The photographs showed a good-looking couple with three beautiful children. In red biro they had described a Peyton Place drama under sail:

MILESTONES AND STUMBLING BLOCKS

Mid Nov:	Mike plays true confessions. Sharon flies home with children.
Thanksgiving:	Mike "reforms" and wants reconciliation. Sharon and children return.
Dec 21:	Mike plays more "true confessions". Sharon and children fly home. Sharon files for divorce.
Jan 4:	Mike leaves for Marquesas with two women.
Mid Feb:	Mike "reforms" again and wants reconciliation. Sharon flies to Tahiti for 3-week cruise.
March 11:	Arrive at beautiful Club Nautique. Mike and

Sharon plan for remarriage. Sharon flies home. Mike will sail home solo in penitence, so much for our world cruise!

To Alex and Michelle – Thanks for your part in the happy ending of our rocky voyage.

And in blue ballpoint at the bottom of the page Alex had added later:

Boat sunk 500 miles off coast of Oregon. Mike rescued by US Coast Guard.

The lagoon was awash in moonlight as I pedalled along the dark road, rather carefully for there was no lamp on my bicycle. The horrible scuttling of crabs made my skin crawl, and I thought it would not be much fun to lie hurt or unconscious at the roadside.

I had just got myself comfortable in my bed at *Chez Aimé*, having read for half an hour and turned out the light, when the night was cracked by a blood-tingling thunder of sound. Drums, right outside my window. I threw on some clothes and pushed through the bushes to a house set back from the road. A pair of pressure lamps hissed in the branches of a big tree, throwing a hard white glare over a bare-earth compound where forty young men and women in lines twitched and rolled their hips to the exotic, thrilling rhythm of a dozen drummers and guitarists sitting on a log.

It is hard to imagine a more vehement, energising, harrowingly lustful music than the naked drums of Bora Bora. Heard on a disc, or in the artificial atmosphere of a hotel, it is mere audio-picture-postcard. On a hot night with the smell of mud crabs in your nose and the tradewind rattling the palms in the moonlight it is a skin-pricking tattoo of passion, a haunting and urgent summons to some sensual embrace.

With scorn and sarcasm, an arch character in a grass skirt was drilling the dancers for the Bastille Day competitions. By day he was Frank Ellacott, an airline clerk. By night he was Coco, casting the spell of his big eyes and twitching hips on tourists in the island's six hotels. For three hours I sat there on a log, smoking my pipe, entranced by the music. Next day I met him on his Vespa. Two little adopted daughters, Titain and Titaua, stood up at the handlebars between his legs: their mother was his sister but she had been unable to cope with twins and though unmarried he had taken them over as babies. Every night for a month he would be coaching the dancers, he said, but he was concerned at the way the character of Tahitian dancing was changing to appease the tourists. The belly roll had never been traditional but had been imported, perhaps from Bali, and the skirt was never worn as low as possible but traditionally it covered the tummy button. "I'm so unhappy for Tahiti", he told me. "The kids want to dance like John Travolta, that's why they are so hard to teach. They only dance Tahitian style for the tourists and the money they get. Our dancing was always passionate but it had dignity. Now it is sexual titillation for withered old men in bermudas. They think our girls are like the hostesses of Bangkok, only cheaper and with flowers behind their ears. But it's very different from the Asiatic scene. Girls don't want money but fun. They might go with you if they like you, sure. But they don't like men who are here today and gone tomorrow. The tourist has no chance."

It was different during the Second World War, when 5,000 Americans were stationed on Bora Bora, and there were a great number of pale-skined Polynesians of my own vintage to prove it. But now the casual gaiety and warmth has evaporated. The islanders are slaves to the six hotels and the proliferation of crabs was a symptom of the decline of their spirit. The only way to get rid of the crabs was to poison or to burn them out with flamethrowers, and you could not even have a lawn around your house, let alone a vegetable garden, unless you made this effort. Nobody bothered because they had money. The girls who smiled automatically, as top secretaries do, when they were behind a reception desk of a hotel, were cool to the point of Parisian indifference when you opened a door for them in a store or the airline office. "All tourists are the same," Coco explained. "The girls know the average stay is 2.8 days. If you were one of the twenty-five Westerners living on the island they might raise an eyebrow in your direction after a few months. Meanwhile, you're just a number ..."

That was not quite true. What about the girls up the tree, teasing the soldiers? The dancer's puppy eyes brimmed with delight and he slapped his knee, the shell necklaces rattling on his neck. "I didn't say Bora Bora was dead," he laughed, "I just said it was dying."

It seemed an ironic twist of evolution that the Polynesian should work his heart out to obtain cars, television, junk food and alcohol, none of which they need, while Westerners flock to their beautiful islands and drift round the lagoon in glassfibre replica canoes wearing G-strings. If Captain Cook returned today he might remark in his journal that the sexual philanderings enjoyed by tourists paying $100 for a grass-roofed hut on the lagoonside were indeed a remarkable contrast to the elder Polynesians singing hymns in harmony in their church hall.

And I, too, became a victim of the changing attitudes. The island produced nothing except its beauty so there was no freight for the *Temehani*. I had booked to return in her to Papeete and when we docked the captain had said he would sail the next day. But he had sailed right away. I could wait a week for the *Taporo III* or fly back. After two more evenings of listening to the drums I took the ferry across the lagoon to the *motu* on which the US military had constructed the airstrip, and was back in Papeete within the hour.

On the quay I bumped into Pat and Buddy, the American wanderers whose shower I had borrowed at Uturoa. Buddy had his leg in plaster and looked pale. We had a beer and they told me a strange story.

On Huahine they had met a German artist, a long-time resident of Tahiti, and gone to a party. Walking home in the moonlight the artist said he knew a place nearby where a human skeleton showed in the sand, and they went to see it. Pat, the older bearded one, got the shivers and didn't want to go close. Buddy laughed at his fears, and touched a piece of leg-bone jutting from the sand. It broke in his fingers and he tossed it at his half-brother who swore at him and walked away.

Next day, the boys said, they were playing volley-ball on the beach and Buddy had cracked a bone in his leg in the very place where the skeleton had broken.

Perhaps the mystic spirits of the old Polynesian are not quite dead. Meanwhile, with time drawing in and the memory of my brief visit to Quinn's Waterfront bar as a teenager still bright in my mind, I asked these wanderers how one could best experience the famous *joie de vivre* of the real Tahiti. For Papeete without Quinn's was like Paris without the *Folies*. Somewhere there had to be the authentic action of the old pre-nuclear Tahiti. Their answer was confirmed by others I met in Papeete. A night club on the edge of town, near the military barracks, had taken over as the town dive but had recently closed. The only night music heard in Papeete now was blaring disco. To see authentic local partying when Polynesians let their hair down I should go to the One Chicken Inn. Saturday night at the One Chicken, everyone agreed, was really something. It was just a big thatched hut on the shore, with a dirt floor, only beer was sold. But you could hear Jack London and Bully Hayes and all those famous South Seas characters knocking at the bamboo door. All I had to do was get on a boat and sail across the Sea of the Moon.

16

MAIRE

ACROSS THE SEA OF THE MOON

The *Maire* was a shabby old tub built in Japan and showing it in the quaint oriental slant of her bow, but it happened to be Mother's Day and it seemed appropriate to sail in a vessel of that name. The alternative was a big-game fishing launch that would have been comfortable for six but was jammed with at least sixty, many of them making a slithering wedge of sun-roasting humanity on the open foredeck where there was not so much as a guard rail; such recklessness somehow seemed the more sinister when it was a Frenchman at the wheel rather than a happy-go-lucky Polynesian. In any case, there was hardly a brown face among them. All were tourists, or French residents going to their holiday houses on the whiter beaches of Moorea. The locals and all the cargo sailed in the motherly old *Maire* which had a large open upper deck with plenty of fresh air and places to sit. There was also a continuous shuttle of light planes between the two islands, but who would sit in a buzz-box, even for ten minutes, when you could sit in the wind and the sun, among boxes of fresh lettuces, listening to strummed guitars, even if the song was *Peace in the Valley?*

The Sea of the Moon was lumpy, reflecting the cloudless sky, and the 72-foot vessel rolled heavily and awkwardly over the unseried billows. But it was little more than an hour to the gap in the reef and the glimmering lagoon. The smooth water lapped a beach of blazing white, overhung by palms. Behind their leaning grey trunks, on the narrow fringe of land skirting the dramatically steep flanks of the cloud-catching peaks, were hotels and many houses. Neither quaint thatched huts nor even simple wooden bungalows inhabited by natives, but architect-designed holiday houses with floor-to-ceiling sliding smoked-glass doors, air conditioners, tiled patios with barbecue fireplaces, and lawns on which swing-ball sets were erected for the children.

Moorea is triangular in shape and the shore is about twenty-five miles long. Its northern coast is indented by two deep fiord-like bays separated by a massive bulwark of rock. At the head of each bay lie the fantastic spires of green-cloaked basalt, rising to 4,200 feet in the heart of the island, which account for its spectacular silhouette. One is Cook's Bay, at the head of which are the few scattered buildings of Paopao village, and the other is Opunohu Bay. This is famous among voyagers for its anchorage at Robinson's Cove where the soft white sand shelves so steeply that a deep-keeled vessel can tie up to a coconut palm (though technically it is illegal to make fast to a living tree).

A hint of the mysteries and surprises awaiting the unwary across the Sea of the Moon came in the form of a notice advertising Mini-mokes (small Jeep-like open cars) to rent for $10. On investigation it proved to be the rate *per hour*, with petrol, insurance and tax to be added. A Vespa for $20 a day seemed a better proposition. It had no brakes but who wanted to stop? If you missed your destination the first time you could just go round the island again, it was only an hour and a half.

At every South Seas landfall my arrival had been greeted by stern immigration officers. I never had trouble because I had an onward ticket and adequate funds, and I had no intention of staying, but many did, particularly the rucksack brigade intent on "living with some local family." The beachcomber idyll was a dead duck. Even if you had every intention of working, becoming a trader like Bob Paul on Tanna or a ship-owner like Don Silk of Rarotonga, it was exceptionally difficult (though not quite impossible) to get the necessary permissions. Often you could wangle an extended tourist visa, renewing it every six months if you kept your nose clean and didn't take either money or work out of the locals' pockets, but residential permits were as rare as three-masted sailing schooners. Tahiti is rather different because it is administered as a distant chunk of metropolitan France. Any French citizen can live here, and it is much less difficult for other Westerners – as long as they jig to the bureaucratic fiddle – to get extended permits of various kinds. As a consequence, any native of other South Sea countries who doubted the wisdom of his government's stand against foreign immigration should come to Moorea.

This beautiful island is committed to the indulgence of tourists and

French residents of Tahiti. It has a native population of 6,000 plus 3,000 tourists a month. Ten hotels and numerous weekend cottages occupy the best stretches of foreshore, and the natives live up the hill in the bush. Development land is worth about $60 a square metre. Only the southern shore of the island is undeveloped, where it faces the prevailing wind, and little native houses are tucked among the palm trees. But even here, when I rode my scooter down a short track to have a picnic lunch on a strip of beach, I was stopped by rusty barbed wire and a notice saying *Privée*. On the other side of the wire, further on, a big Citroen and a Mercedes were parked in the shade and a couple of *demi* families played in the water. In general, the only access to the lagoon was through a hotel. For me, a Westerner with a camera round his neck, this was no problem, but it could be tough on brown-skinned people who lived here.

The wholesale commercialisation of this South Seas island can put the traveller in a state of complex moral quandary, as I discovered. At anchor in Cook's Bay was a grey sloop called *Scheherezade* that a young Australian called Willi Bremer-Kemp, and a friend, had built with their own hands on the shore of Botany Bay. Here they had worked casually as handymen for a local hotel and made friends with the natives. When the roof of the One Chicken Inn blew off in a gale they helped to make a new one. Every morning, Willi said, he rolled over the side into the warm clear water. He scrubbed weed from a few square feet of the hull of his boat, then swam languidly ashore where the mangos were dripping off the trees. He picked one for his breakfast which he ate while sitting in the water – the right and proper way, as everyone knows, to eat a juicy mango.

Around the corner in Opunohu Bay was anchored a large motor-sailor called *Lancaster*, owned by a Sydney businessman who zoomed ashore in his rubber boat and chatted with me on the beach. He had a scathing opinion of "parasites" like Willi who, he claimed, stole fruit from native land. He threatened to sue me for libel if I mentioned his name, and to put his lawyer on my tail if I took a photograph of his boat. The friendly skipper of *Scheherezade* was not a bit surprised. It was typical, he said, of the new breed of South Seas voyager. Which was worse, to make friends with the local people and with their knowledge pick the odd mango that was going to fall off the tree anyway, or to demonstrate your goodwill and liberal values by paying $5 for something worth five cents?

That this dilemma should exist at all is an indication of the extent to which the South Seas way of life has been contaminated on Moorea. And this island proved to be unique in the South Seas for the extraordinary range of Westerners who by various means – whether fair or foul I wouldn't dare say, even if I knew – have secured for themselves the ecological niches abandoned by the natives in favour of the bracing competitive suicide of the cash economy. Individually, they are caring people whose record is no doubt above reproach. Collectively, they show that the romantic lagoonside idyll as it is perceived by dreaming Western eyes is still attainable on at least one beautiful isle.

Everyone knows where everyone lives on Moorea so there are no names on the letterboxes and it took a long while to locate the particular sandy track cutting through the copra plantations to Reggie Smith's little house in its lagoonside garden.

A grizzled, snowy-haired, fit-looking man of seventy-one, Reggie was neither a drop-out nor a dreamer. Born in a wool wagon in the New Zealand back country and left alone in the world at thirteen – "With naught but a horse, a bridle and a saddle," he said poetically – he had bummed various jobs and at the age of twenty signed on a fishing schooner. They were supposed to fish off the coast but after a couple of days the skipper announced they were going to Tahiti. It took ten weeks, through a hurricane that blew every sail to rags, to get there. Reggie had never heard of the place before he arrived, and he has never left.

For a time he was a pool room hustler at Quinn's, then a horse trainer, and in 1932 he bought half shares in a copra plantation in Moorea. They were hard times. It was an eight-mile row along the lagoon to deliver his produce, two tons a trip in exchange for a box of groceries. He sold bundles of firewood. "Life got a bit more cheerful," he told me with a twinkle, "the day I got a wheel for my barrow". Then a French planter chum told him that if he didn't find a girl one would be delivered, and in 1958 he married Céline, a beautiful local girl, now a stout and smiling figure busy in the neat and shiny lino'd kitchen.

Reggie sat in a picnic chair rolling a cigarette. "It was God's own country, this island," he went on. "We had wild pork, wild hens, freshwater shrimps, all the fish in the lagoon, and fruit. There are thirty-two different kinds of breadfruit alone and you can boil it, bake it, steam it or toast and spread it with marmalade. And it's all still here. People forget that when they complain about the old ways dying out."

But that was not quite true, as I found when I scootered along the coast to the Kellums' place.

They were a charming American couple, pushing eighty but looking a score of years younger, who lived in a neat little wood-frame house on a grassy knoll under shady trees above Robinson's Cove in

Opunohu Bay. Medford Kellum had been a Georgia college boy of twenty-two, at a loose end, when he shipped aboard his father's schooner for a South Pacific cruise and took his fiancée Gladys with him. It was some schooner, a 700-ton four-master built for carrying lumber, with a crew of twenty-six. When the ship nosed into the bay it was utterly unspoiled and Gladys said, "Medford, this is the place where I could spend the rest of my life."

He laughed it off at the time but on reaching Papeete made inquiries and discovered that a large block of level and fertile land at the head of the bay, in what had been the crater of the volcano that formed the island, was coming up for auction that very week. They bought it, married in Honolulu, and planned their home. Fully fitted with doors and windows, the entire house was built in pre-fabricated form and loaded aboard the schooner. To get the foreshore track diverted to pass behind their house and garden they called in the local village. Every morning the entire population paddled over in canoes and the few who were not working tended the fires and cooked. At three o'clock work stopped and there was a glorious feast, with singing and dancing, until well after dark when they paddled homeward across the starlit water.

For many years Medford farmed 3,800 acres in the valley, running cattle and growing crops such as vanilla and coffee using Chinese labour. In 1962 he sold the plantation to the administration so it could establish an agricultural school for boys from all over the islands. "But really, the Polynesians don't want to do work and the only people interested in growing things are the Chinese," he said.

Courteous and charming in the best American tradition, the Kellums' love for the island and its people had never dimmed despite the changes that were clearly distressing to them. Medford was mowing his lawn in the cool of the morning, his feet bare on the damp spiky grass, when I arrived. Gladys wore a full length cotton gown of brilliant blue. The polished wooden floor they had brought in thirty-foot sections by schooner was pleasantly cool underfoot when I slipped off my own sandals to enter. The pale green walls were lined with books and homely furniture. The room was breezy and shaded, while down through the palms the lagoon glittered like a level field of mirrors. Didn't they get a little tired of the brilliance and beauty of the place in fifty-five years? Didn't their eyeballs ache just a little from the intensity of sunshine and colour?

"Oh never, never, never!" Mrs Kellum cried, hugging her knees and glancing through the open window as if to reassure herself that the island was still there to be enjoyed. But the signs of the times were troubling.

The Polynesians were buying pineapple in tins and carrots in sacks from California, protested the man who had spent his life growing such things in the valley. Even lettuce was being imported. The natives depended on limes for curing the raw fish they enjoyed so much but they were imported for $6 a kilo from Florida, yet Medford's own garden was full of them. The local people had sold or long-leased their land, permitting ribbon development to encircle the island and cut them off from the lagoon, while coconuts were falling off the trees and nobody bothering to collect them. And most shameful of all, the kindly American explained in a shocked tone, the people down in the village were that week bulldozing out a whole grove of breadfruit trees. Why? To build a football pitch!

Down the road a piece was an American "family" of a different kind. They were the Bali Ha'i boys, Kelley, Muk and Jay. A gang of three young bloods from Newport, California, who – Muk told me – "partied, raised hell and chased tail together", they now lived out a very different kind of dream.

Their particular South Seas dream was a multi-million-dollar paradise resort, but today there was something of a blot on their image. The glass-bottomed raft called the *Liki Tiki*, while loaded with American travel agents on a familiarisation visit to the fabulous Bali Ha'i Hotel, had sunk in the lagoon. A few dozen cameras, travellers' cheques, and corpulent corporate dignities had been wetted. According to one report Jay, who was the financial brains behind the outfit, had locked himself in his office and refused to come out. But Muk, the one-man public relations department and farmer, didn't want to talk about it. "These things happen: you can't expect to enjoy life on a South Sea island without taking a dip in the lagoon."

Donald "Muk" McCallum was a tall, hairy-shouldered, man with long arms and a loping, loose-limbed gait whose open-handed manner suggested that even the faded blue shorts in which he spent his day was over-dressing for the promise of free-and-easy living on Moorea. Muk was working for his family fishing-gear firm, and Jay Carlisle was a broker on the Pacific Coast Stock Exchange, when Hugh Kelley, a lawyer, sailed to Tahiti in a yacht in 1959 and came home to persuade his two red-blooded pals that they should be chasing bronze-skinned Polynesian maidens in the South Seas. They bought land unseen in Moorea, on which they expected to find a vanilla plantation. "What we found was 400 acres of steep jungle with a lot of beautiful pools, like you see in Tarzan movies. We didn't know if vanilla was a tree, a bush, a vine or an animal, but whatever it was we had none of it. In short, we had bought a jungle of lemons."

Undismayed, they lived in a shack on the lagoon beach and when they were broke after twelve months took over the management of a small hotel with four bungalows that was struggling to make a go of it next door. At that time seven airlines came through Tahiti and the crew of each plane would lie over for two or three days. Their success was founded on the $13.50-a-day subsistence allowance paid to crews, who would spurn the hotel rooms provided by their airlines and take the boat over to the Bali Ha'i, a name which the boys had lifted from Michener's book *South Pacific*. Thus their establishment attracted good-looking men who brought their own duty-free booze, and beautiful women, and the tone of the place was set. When they got a few dollars together, Muk explained, they would take a three-day vacation at Quinn's, chasing tail and sleeping aboard whichever schooner happened to be in port.

Some twenty years ago a *Life* photographer had encountered them on the beach and given the fifty-buck establishment a million dollars worth of publicity. The boys were quick to capitalise on it and made shrewd use of their rakish reputations. "They had a vision of an island where liquor flowed instead of rain," proclaimed one of the many magazine articles framed in the hotel foyer. Kelley, whom *Esquire* had photographed in bed with a lovely girl, invented the idea of bungalows built on piles at the edge of the reef. Through a glass panel in the floor you could look down into water a hundred feet deep and switch on underwater floodlights to illuminate the tropical fish grazing around the coral heads. All for $240 a night.

The image of professional bachelorhood continues to be milked though it sits a little uneasily now that the "boys" are fifty-plus. And the three have a less than savoury reputation among other settlers on the island. From them I learned, as if it was the worst thing in the world, that Kelley rode around the island very fast on a big black motorcycle wearing a black leather jacket. That Muk took pot shots at mynah birds from the bar. That Jay, when asked by an angry woman visitor if he thought he was God or something, told her with his hands on his hips: "Sure lady, that's me, I'm God, because I own the place and you'd better watch your step!"

But what really riled the other Westerners on the island, I thought, was that visitors in shabby clothes and floppy hats with no money to spend were made less than welcome to the hotel's style of expensive, sanitised, 55-star luxury.

Muk certainly maintained a bold style as he drove me round in his Land Cruiser. He pointed out a little house near the lagoon – "the compound" – where their children lived. They had fourteen between them, he said, and all were US citizens and properly looked after, the girls sleeping on one side of the bunkhouse and the boys on the other.

Kelley liked to settle with one girl for four or five years, but Muk, he liked to scatter shot, his freedom was too dear. "In any case, a Tahitian girl doesn't want to get married right off the bat. Security is bullshit. They just don't think about it. You don't freeze and you don't starve in Tahiti, so who needs security?"

There was the old plantation house they were restoring, a wooden mansion decorated like a wedding cake with fretwork. It was set in a green lawn where Muk planned croquet parties – "All of us dressed in Panamas, *pareu* blazers, white slacks, and bare feet. It will be a ball!"

At the head of the valley was the farm where Muk experimented with cropping asparagus, grapefruit, oranges, lemons, grapes and everything else in the fruit salad bowl. But the rains kept washing his fertilizer down the hill. They had scored with a chicken farm, which produced a thousand dozen eggs every day, but this climate, he complained, was the Tigris and Euphrates of disease.

And above the farm, high on a rocky bluff, was Muk's own place, a magnificent eyrie furnished as if *Playboy* had designed it as a set for a centrefold. The boys held great parties up here, Muk maintained, as he opened the doors on one hollow and echoing room after another. They put the word around Papeete, a party up top, and the girls flooded in for the weekend and went home with a new *pareu*.

But didn't age intercept all souls? I asked, looking over the savannah of a suede bedspread at the floor-to-ceiling smoked glass. The view was stunning yet static. The green valley dropped dizzily away to the distant carpet of blue stretching to the horizon. The only movement was the remorseless caterpillar crawl of a white wave curling along the reef. Didn't a man of fifty-two want to go to bed that bit earlier, slow down a bit, bask in the glow?

Muk scoffed at my question, as Mrs Kellum had done, but in quite a different way. Okay, so what time did he go to bed? Around nine-thirty. But then he dropped his guard. He liked to read a book in bed, he said, because it helped him off to sleep. And didn't the girls get fed up when he opened a book! Wow, they get real annoyed. The only way to keep them quiet was to give them a couple of thousand (Pacific francs, around $25) to go and have some fun with their friends.

Further along the coast road, out towards the Captain Cook Hotel and Billy's Stop Shop and the Carole Boutique and the Boutique Vahine Kaira, and other touristic fly traps, I found a little ketch moored to a jetty. Opposite, past a tumbledown house surrounded by junk, a track led inland through the palms. Following the directions Reggie Smith had provided, I scootered along it until stopped by a creek, jumped over it, and continued on foot up a steep hillside of high tufted grass. Here, made entirely of thatch and poles, was an unlikely sort of Robinson Crusoe hut on stilts. It had a wide verandah in front, and the shutters all round were propped open with struts. A couple of horses grazed on long halters and horse manure was piled neatly around half a dozen young banana trees. When I stopped at the foot of steep steps, and looked back, the view was as awe-inspiring as that from Muk's bedroom but was all the better for the lack of smoked glass. "Come on up, I don't often see fellow Brits in this part of the world," a voice called.

Jean Shelsher was an English artist who had come to Tahiti five years before and been able to keep on renewing her temporary residential status because she was self-sufficient and it was not tourists but local people, especially Tahitians, who bought the quaint caricatures she painted of ordinary life in Moorea. Her long hair, bleached yellow by the sun, was rigged in plaits and she padded around the bare boards of her picturesque thousand-dollar hut in bare feet. The sink was fixed outside the back window, so it drained directly on to the banana trees. She had everything she needed in her eyrie except cooking Gaz and food which she brought up the hill on horseback. "It can have its problems," she admitted, squeezing limes into a tall glass of rum, "yesterday the horse sat down in the creek on top of my cheese, so it's looking a bit flat."

It was the perfect life, she thought. Especially the sunrises. She woke before dawn and put the coffee on then sat with a Beethoven symphony playing and watched the sun come up. Then she painted until noon, and rode down to the beach for a snorkel and a sun-bathe. There were few difficulties, only the odd centipede in the shower and the boys who want *motoro*.

"Traditionally," she explained, "when a Polynesian lad wanted to pay court he had to sneak into the girl's house through the window. Everyone knew what went on, of course, because the houses were rarely partitioned, but it was a recognised thing that you were safe from discovery once you were inside. The trouble is that nothing gives a Tahitian boy more status than to lie with a *popaa* like me. The other day one of the village boys who had been dared into it by his friends came up in the middle of the night. He was full of beer and hardly knew what he was doing. I was suddenly woken when the string of cans rattled – my burglar alarm. I took a pot-shot over his head with my tear-gas pistol. It made an enormous noise and the boy must have thought a volcano was erupting because he took off like a wild bull and that was the last I saw of him."

I had hunted Jean down partly because I, too, had not seen many fellow Brits on my travels, but mostly because many of her paintings featured life at that establishment of far-distant repute, the One Chicken Inn. It was certainly authentically Polynesian, she promised. Often she had been there, sketching. There were few tourists or Westerners. The people drank a lot and really let their hair down to wild music, and sometimes fell down and stayed down, but there was a great atmosphere, it was unique in Polynesia. Her paintings of the scene captured the spontaneous joie de vivre that I had found so conspicuously lacking elsewhere. Would Jean come with me?

"Love to," she said at once. "Let's go down and see Bill and Donna, they might come too."

Four years ago Bill and Donna Wilder had sailed their ketch *Sea Trek* into Tahiti and discovered that there had been a change of government in Australia, whither they were bound with the aim of starting a lemon and avocado ranch as an extension of their business in California. "We thought we'd better sit it out and see which way the political winds blew, and we're still sitting, a case of comfortable Polynesian paralysis," Bill said. He was a man of fifty-six with a spare wiry frame, tousled grey hair, and thin-rimmed tortoiseshell glasses that gave him an Ivy League look. Donna was a neat and precise body with urchin-cut hair, a merry sense of humour, and a burning intent to complete the writing of a novel that was occupying every waking hour. They lived in the old and cluttered house at the bottom of the track, their ketch was moored over the road. "Welcome to the You-break-it-we-fix-it Ranch," Bill said when I walked through his gate with his two dogs growling and sniffing my legs.

Bill was a natural born Mister Fix-it and in Moorea he had found paradise. In his beaten-up silencerless Beetle he travelled all over the island looking for mechanical trouble and it was never hard to find. Everybody on the island bought machinery but nobody on the island knew how to fix it or even put oil in it. Outboards, fridges, pick-up trucks, scooters, chain saws, radio/tape players, digital watches, generators, lawn mowers ... As soon as anything stopped it was brought to Bill. He had started out with a screwdriver and now he had a large workshop surrounded by heaps of machinery that either he was fixing or could not fix.

"We came out here for the simple life in our little boat and what did we do but bring all our American junk with us," Donna protested. "Micro wave oven, tools galore, walkie-talkie ... Why? So I could talk to him from the cockpit when he was up the mast, of course. Computer ..."

On his South Sea island Bill Wilder even had a computer. It was a do-it-yourself job, just to keep a record of his stock and his avocado farms, he admitted, but sometimes it was harder to get the generator going to power the computer than to do the office work in the old manual way. "You're so dependent on your own two hands in a place like this. Fixing things up is an endless job. Even getting water to run through the tap is a triumph. Psychologically, you have to be as self-sufficient as if you were on a yacht a thousand miles at sea."

Donna, too, had been bothered by young bloods going *motoro*. One night she woke to find a teenager standing by her bed. "It was only when he started to get in with me that I realised it wasn't Bill, because I knew Bill was having one of his all-night computer sessions. But the kid was so drunk he was harmless. Having made it into bed he collapsed in a stupour. We dragged him out on the lawn and flopped him in a deck chair and in the morning he was gone."

But the kids had a rough deal on the island, Bill thought. Just two years ago the people had wanted simple things that made their lives easier, like Gaz, Western food, cassettes. Now television had arrived and their aspirations had made a quantum leap. They wanted Vespas, beefy cross-country Yamahas, outboards, cars. The old generation was still getting by easily, living on the land and the lagoon and paying no rent. But the young people needed money to get what they wanted and there was no work."

Bill saluted the last lingering bud of the setting sun with a tilt of his glass and indicated the group of teenagers silhouetted against the crimson sky. They were sitting under a tree on the shore, next to the road, playing tapes loudly on a radio/player. "That goes on all day, non-stop. Disco music, over and over. Always throwing little stones into the middle of the road until they get bored, then they face the other way and throw stones into the water. Believe me, it's a great day for us when they get a new tape. But what does life in this place hold for them? It's a tragedy."

The American yachtsman in his yard of junk. The English artist up on the hill. The man born in a wool-wagon and cast up on an exotic isle. The Kellums, vintage romantic adventurers. The bachelors, chasing tail and losing heart. And there were others. The Swiss yachtsman who got this far, married a Chinese girl, and now runs a Chinese restaurant. The grumpy Dick Gump, former owner of Gumps, the fashionable San Francisco store ("I'm as open as a book nobody has ever read") who has been coming here for a few weeks every year since 1932 to paint pictures of Florence ("When I'm in Florence I paint pictures of Moorea"). The dark-eyed Israeli girl in a lagoonside house making a business of batik-style painting on cloth. The Dutchman who had closed up his art gallery with a notice thumb-tacked on the door, "Gone Sailing" ... The "beach" European thrived, on Moorea.

It was time to head for the One Chicken. Donna was writing her book. Bill was playing with his computer. Jean led the way on her scooter and I followed at a safe distance because the headlight of my Vespa did not work. The air was cool and sweet in my face and moonlight washed the lagoon but this made the shaded road all the darker.

Jean pulled off the road and propped her bike on its stand. Surely this couldn't be it. There was only one car parked nearby. The darkness was filled only with island whispers. Jean herself looked puzzled as she crossed the road to a crude thatched roof supported on low struts over a dirt floor. One electric light was on at the far end where two people sat at a counter, a fat woman behind and a skinny man on a stool. Both smoked and looked gloomy, and answered Jean's questions only because they knew her. The "Club Med" had for three weeks now been opening its bars to local people and although the prices were higher everybody had left the One Chicken to its fate. "I think One Chicken dead now," the woman said. "We opened three Saturday nights, nobody come."

It was a long ride along the coast to the Club Med and Jean decided not to come. With no comforting tail light to follow I had to go slowly. At the gates I parked at the security hut and asked the guard to keep an eye on the Vespa because they were frequently taken by people who rode them home and left them out on the road to be collected in due course by their owners. The hotel was a big complex of dining areas, bars and discos used by 700 guests, most of whom came from North America on package deals. The bedrooms were little huts staggered through the gardens. A board of photographs showed scenes from the afternoon's programme of organised beach games. The guests revealed a lot of skin and little sense of modesty. One sequence of pictures showed a couple engaged in what seemed to be gross oral indecency, he a handsome young man with hair on his chest and something on a gold chain round his neck, she a scrawny blonde of indeterminate age wearing sun-glasses and a bikini hardly larger than three eye-patches. Only when I looked hard did I detect that somewhere in this elaborately contrived scrum there was a tennis ball (or was it an orange?), which he was rolling with the tip of his nose from one part of her anatomy to another. At the risk of sounding prudish, I thought this conspiracy to cast the afternoon with a flavour of the so-called swinging scene a mortifying horror.

Like the other hotels, the Club Med was not doing too well, mainly because the airlines were steadily reducing their services; even Pan Am had recently pulled out. With the place only half filled it was no surprise that the club management had allowed in the local Poly-nesians in the hope of sparking some island atmosphere. The disco was thunderously loud, the atmosphere redolent of a highway filling station. A crowd of local Polynesians in flowery shirts and dresses were indeed drinking beer and staring gloomily at the flashing coloured lights. I did not waste time buying a drink but went to bed, the One Chicken was not only dead but buried.

Yet romance does still flutter its little wings, even in Moorea. Next day, through Bill and Donna, I met Marty Pease. He was a slim young Yorkshireman sporting a pair of grey shorts, a battered straw hat, and a moustache with a cavalier curl. He lived with his wife Loana and their little girl in a cottage at Paopao, the village in Cook's Bay. And Loana, as Bill promised, was girl worth all the copra and pearls in the South Seas. Tall and slender, with high cheek bones and a perfect complexion, she shook my hand primly. The lovely wide smile and big brown eyes melted my heart. Clad in a simple *pareu* tied beneath her arms to show all her lovely long legs, its red colour faded an exotic ruddy pink that set off the large scarlet hibiscus in her shiny black hair, she moved with the free and easy grace of a seabird soaring on an updraught. Her look was mischievous and knowing and full of fun, but it was not a worldly expression. Loana was twenty-one but had the innocence of a beauty half her age. Marty bounced Gwen on his knee and the little girl, brown-skinned and blonde, giggled loudly. Loana brought me a glass mug of tea with both lemon and condensed milk. "She must think you are somebody pretty important," Marty chuckled, and tilted his hat to the back of his head to grin fondly up at her as she stood by the side of his chair, knowing that he was laughing at her but not understanding why.

Marty had been a water-ski instructor at the Club Med in Greece when he received a telegram telling him to pack his bags and go to Tahiti. He expected to have to speak French but had no idea where the place was, or what colour the people were. Loana was working as a waitress in the restaurant when the tousle-haired Englishman arrived. And one look was enough, though it took him six months. Free love was a thing of the past, girls were more serious about it these days and treated a stranger warily, he said. But she had moved in with him a bit at a time. First it was for an afternoon, then a whole day. Then she stayed the night and did not go to work next morning or ever again. Marty left the Club and they lived with her adopted father, (that is, Marty explained, the man with whom her real grandmother lived in concubinage because Loana, being the youngest of nineteen, had been given away at birth to another member of the family). They were married in a Papeete registry office and celebrated with an ice cream; Marty was twenty-one and Loana nineteen. Their first child had died a few weeks old. Marty worked for the Bali Ha'i boys, first as a cashier, then as an assistant manager, and obtained residential status. But after two years he found he was working eighty hours a week and that, for him, defeated the whole purpose of living in the South Seas. He quit with about $1,300 in hand and looked around for something to do.

Not many of us, with a few hundred bucks and a beautiful Polynesian wife on a beautiful Polynesian island, would write home to Mum in Yorkshire for recipes of the cakes she used to make, and set up in business as a confectioner. But that's what Marty did. He invested his cash in a large gas-fired domestic oven, and sacks of flour and sugar in bulk. First he baked mince pies but the islanders had never seen a mince pie in their lives. What they liked were large squishy sickly colourful cakes, preferably chocolate and smothered in cream.

With his first five iced cakes Marty set off in his beat-up Renault to sell them door to door. But he needed petrol and found his first two customers while he was filling up. In ten minutes all five were gone, at $8 a piece. So he drove home and baked five more.

The only problem was how to carry so many cakes in his little car so he had a word with Bill Wilder, who suggested a cake rack, and Marty knocked one up from bits of plywood. When it rained, so much spray came up through the holes in the floor that his cakes went soggy, though he managed to sell them for a bit less. He glassfibred the car floor and now he was in business, clearing about $20 a day with minimal effort and getting commissions for birthday cakes. Later, maybe, he would go into bees. There was an Arab on Tahiti who would sell him a queen.

So fairy tales do come true in the South Seas, as they do from time to time everywhere else, I thought, as we talked in the shade of Marty's verandah and sipped milky lemon tea. All the while, Loana sat opposite us and because she could speak no English had switched off. After a time, her very stillness attracted my attention. For a long period she sat sideways in a wooden chair, her legs thrown over the arm and her chin resting lightly on the tops of the fingers of one hand. She did not so much as blink, and was not really daydreaming, I suspected, but in neutral. For the moment she was out of gear, just waiting, not even thinking. Marty caught my look and shrugged disarmingly. "Fat, old, skinny, young, there's something about 'em. Loana is beautiful but – my God! – she is difficult sometimes, like a teenager. I have to treat her like a stern father."

As we talked I thought back over my own encounters with the lovely women of the South Seas. Never had I deliberately sought female company, because of the obvious risks to my own contented attachment, and it is likely that this registered in those secret and mysterious vibrations that people unconsciously emit. But neither had I observed nor even heard of much in the way of loose behaviour. On the whole, young women in the South Seas were elegant, shy, and rather prim. There was nothing casual or free about any of them. But it is not until you read more closely the accounts of the early visitors to the islands, and the travellers who were yet in time to enjoy the age of innocence, that you realise with something of a shock how young were the South Seas maidens and Herman Melville's "lovely houris."

Writing of the sexual games of the young boys and girls of Pukapuka where he ran a store there in the 1920s, Robert Dean Frisbie remarked that girls of eighteen were getting dangerously past their prime; "their flowers soon fade". In fact it was their immaturity, he thought, which reduced the chances of conception. Alain Gerbault, writing of the beauties of Bora Bora, noted that at the age of fifteen they were already women. And there are numerous other accounts of the extreme youth of the lovely maidens. It was not uncommon for White men to succumb to the tempting propositions of girls of twelve or thirteen. And that put the entire question in a different light. With our laws concerning the age of consent, we recoil at thoughts of intimacy with one so young, and bury the passing fancy as an evil one. My own daughter was eleven, for goodness sake, and I had no intention of travelling the South Seas making eyes at mere children. Hence I can only report that the young women of the South Seas are no longer recklessly unchaste. And as for the lovely maidens, that was a dream of an erotic nature and I didn't care much to pursue.

But in Marty and his lovely Loana I had found a truth in at least one romantic South Seas legend and I wondered if in fifty years he would be as contented as old Reggie was with his Céline, further along the coast. "Sometimes I do fall to reminiscing," he said in a low and serious tone. "I think it is a shame that Gwen won't tumble around in haystacks like I used to when I was a kid. But what really troubles me is that I can't even talk about haystacks or pubs or cold misty evenings up in the Pennines. Loana has no idea what I'm on about, and doesn't care much. I get lonely sometimes. I look at my pretty wife in this beautiful place and I ask myself how I can – well – make connections."

Then Marty snapped out of it. He tugged his straw hat down over his eyes, got to his feet with a brisk snap of his two palms, and Loana clicked into gear. She looked up at him, half smiling, with her big beautiful eyes.

"Come on, luv," he said, "let's get this birthday cake made. How many candles do we want?"

And while Marty baked his birthday cake and Jean painted pictures and Bill repaired a generator and Donna wrote her book and Muk shot mynah birds then read himself to sleep, I voyaged once more across the Sea of the Moon.

17

DEAR MRS HILL

WHAT NEW NET GOES A-FISHING?

Fittingly, my South Seas Dream concluded with a glorious sunset. I had checked the Post Office for letters from home, taken one last stroll along the line of yachts, and sipped my rum-and-lime punch while sitting on the end of the jetty. The harbour was alive with beetling *piroges*, their teams of paddlers getting into trim for Bastille Day races. At my feet a world of tiny brilliant fish swarmed around antlers of coral. The white sails of a cruising ketch in the reef entrance caught the pink light. When all was black and quiet, I went to my room and packed. I tossed the last of my Kwells into the trash bin, and also my worn-thin "no-walkim-backwards". There was one last lingering scent of frangipani as I crossed the steamy tarmac to the DC-10 at four-thirty in the morning, then I was overwhelmed by the sharp smell of perfumed paper sachets so distinctive of aeroplanes. I took my seat, was catapulted into the air, and after a cup of coffee kicked off the shoes I had donned for the first time in six months and read once more the letter that had been forwarded to me at Papeete Post Office. It was from a complete stranger, Mrs Audrey Hill of Toronto, Canada, and this is what she wrote:

Dear Mr Dyson,

I was very interested in your article on the South Sea Islands. The reason I am writing to you is I would like to re-locate there.

I work every day in the large city of Toronto in jewellery sales and it's crazy: I make a good wage and am getting nowhere fast. I will be 55 this summer and see no improvement in sight. All I want from life at this point is some peace.

The thing is, I can sell some things and that will bring a little cash, but I must work to survive. Could I find work in the South Seas? I would like a small house and perhaps in the future a small business. My husband is a cook and feels the same as I. I love music and play the organ and have done some oil painting as well. We are involved in the Canadian Royal Legion and arrange dances and special event dinners. We would be very interested in community events.

We want a new way of life. We need to be needed. We want to give of ourselves and receive back kindness and consideration. We both feel the South Sea Islands will fill the need. What do you think?

How many barefooted women walking the sandy paths of their islands to little wooden shops selling nothing but half a dozen lines of various tinned foods, I wondered, would exchange their rustic lives for the chance to work among the baubles of a downtown department store, live in an apartment with real carpet and shop every day of the week in supermarkets with five or six thousand lines of goods?

What would happen if all of us simply moved over a bit? If Luama-nuvae Pa'i in Western Samoa motored his *alia* across the sea to Pago Pago and got what he most desired, a comfortable salaried job sitting at a desk for Uncle Sam. If the dissatisfied girl clerk in Pago Pago, educated to high school level in a Western way of life but denied the opportunity to live it, were granted her heart's desire and allowed to work at the jewellery counter of a big store. If Mrs Hill, unhappy and disappointed in life, were able to be spirited to Pa'i's abandoned *fale* with its view of the lagoon, its chickens and its breadfruit trees.

Would Pa'i really be happy imprisoned all day behind a desk with the air conditioner roaring in his ear? Would the girl happily get up early every morning to crush herself into a bus then spend hours on her feet, a creature of the concrete jungle? And how would Mrs Hill get on, rising before dawn to go fishing, and cooking over an open fire; wouldn't she crave the conveniences of the can of food that could be opened with a twist of the hand, the taste of a peppermint after days of insipid coconut, the ability to whisk a Kleenex out of a box when she needed to blow her nose? I didn't think any of them would last three weeks. For it's not until we step outside it that any of us realise how much we are prisoners of our own conditioning.

The letter brought to mind an encounter in Rarotonga, when I met one of the last of the generation of beach Europeans whose ghosts haunt the cane chairs of shady South Seas verandahs. Ronald Syme was forty and working as a company public relations man in London when he gazed out over the Thames and, as so many have done, wondered what life was about, what was in it for him, was he going to have any more fun? But unlike the rest of us he did something about it. He sold up and took ship to the South Seas. He had fetched up in the Cook Islands in 1952 only because it was a sterling area, and he could get his money there.

His little stone cottage was all but buried in blossoming trees when I motorcycled along the coast to see him. A tall bony man with a gaunt complexion and large brown eyes proclaiming quirky, self-mocking humour, he was folded in a canvas chair in the shadows of his verandah, a bottle of moonshine to hand. He thought he was one of the last surviving oddballs who had been able to succumb to a romatic idea, and that he had been just in time "to see the last fading radiance of a flower that has since fallen ..."

Not long before, an American woman had been found sleeping on the beach a little further along the road. She had given up her job in a New York store, left her husband, and spent all she had to come to the South Seas. "She thought you could live under the palms while girls danced, and because of her white skin the natives would be proud to give her two meals a day," Ronald told me in a melancholy tone. "And there she was, down to her last few cents and living rough, lonely and disillusioned and poverty stricken."

Ronald's Maori wife Mari, whom he had married when she was seventeen, had the bearing and beauty of a princess. She came in after closing up her little store and snack bar and sat with us before getting dinner for their daughter, Florence Tia-te-Pa-Tua-a-More, who was now seventeen and equally beautiful and in the next room swotting hard for her university entrance exams.

Only a few days ago, Mari told me, two Americans had been in her shop inquiring about how they could buy land. "They were a bit peeved when I told them to go away, that there was no show of buying land here," she admitted. "I told them God gave you your own land and you can't make a go of it so don't come here sprinkling your cash around expecting to get some native girl to keep your house tidy for a few cents a week. I tell you this place is already owned. It's ours. We don't want you to have it because as soon as you get it you will change things." Mari had stopped speaking abruptly and in the deep silence I saw that she had tears in her eyes. Suddenly she stood up and went to the back of the house.

Ronald had watched her go with a fondness that glowed in his battered face. "These islands are the world's last resort," he said. "We've had the explorers and the missionaries and the exploiters and the do-gooders and they've all left their mark but the islanders have somehow bent in the wind and not been uprooted. But now we're going to see a lot more of what I call the fugitives of the freeways. I have a terrible vision of some great steamer appearing off the port. It will be loaded to the sun-decks with the last evacuees of a burning western civilisation and ashore will stream a horde of over-fed, untidy, helpless, greedy-eyed people clutching their expensive toast racks and all the things they could grab at the last minute from their flamed-out polluted kitchens as they fled ... What in the name of God will we do with them? Mark my words, there will come a time when people in places like these islands will be standing on the shore with machine guns, keeping people off."

Sprawling in the reclined tourist-class seat of a DC-10, jetting towards the freeways and pollution and toasters at nearly the speed of sound, I realised with something of a shock how much I was really looking forward to them, how eager I was to return to the three-ring circus. Life was pleasant in the islands, life was simple, but living was also a mindless activity. The environment is enviable but existence was a sentence of intellectual death. Breadfruit did grow on trees. Fish was easy to spear in the dazzling lagoon. Coconuts did provide a permanently open snack bar atop every palm where the "lemonade" was cool and refreshing and all you had to do was get up there. But life was as limp as washing pegged out in a thunderstorm.

The islanders recognise and fear the mouldy coma into which they are lapsing. It is the root cause of urban drift and of their own dreams of greener, more exciting pastures. In their own culture this gap had been filled by a multitude of elaborate custom, ceremony, and war-making. Denied the stimulus of these events by the austere and unforgiving regimes imposed by missionaries, the people went into a decline which in some of the British-administered islands like Western Samoa was arrested only by the introduction of cricket. Given a communal, competitive activity, the people took a new interest in life. Though it bears little resemblance to the original game, *kilikiti* continues to be an extraordinary spectacle. Village plays against village using a five-sided bat and a latex ball. The stouter batsmen may employ younger ones to do the running. Some games in earlier times turned into open war, with four or five players including the umpire brained to death. When a UN team arrived at Apia to assess relief needs following a devastating cyclone in 1966 the Prime Minister suddenly realised that everybody was out playing cricket among the wreckage so he had to ban the game, except on two days a week, lest the officials get the wrong idea.

The passion for sports and the taste for canned and packaged foods in these isles of plenty are symptoms of the cultural problem—the quest for stimulus. The people are being transfixed, not only by Western consumerism that snows them with temptation, but also by the compulsion to escape terminal boredom. This is why the islander who *needs* nothing works so hard to gain small luxuries that Westerners take for granted. In 1939 the Maori anthropologist Sir Peter Buck wrote in *Vikings of the Sunrise*:

> The old world created by our Polynesian ancestors has passed away, and a new world is in the process of being fashioned ... The members of the divine family of the Sky Father and the Earth Mother have left us. The great voyaging canoes have crumbled to dust and the sea captains and the expert craftsmen have passed away to the spirit land ... The glory of the Stone Age has departed out of Polynesia ... The old net is full of holes, its meshes have rotted, and it has been laid aside. What new net goes a-fishing?

I don't think Sir Peter Buck would have been surprised to discover that the new net which goes a-fishing is the supermarket trolley. The process began long ago, when Captain Cook's men offered Tahitian maidens ships' nails for their favours, often with the connivance of the girls' husbands, but what wouldn't a man give for a steel blade of any sort when his technology centred entirely on the crafting of wood and cord with stone tools? But it does not stop at the problem of how to hew more easily and efficiently. The desire for Western goods is merely a symptom of the longing for a kind of fulfilment that their minds are lacking. That is why, at the top of its brimming cargo of consumer goods, the supermarket trolley bears the radio cassettes, footballs and travel tickets. These are goods which lie most easily to hand and help to fill the voids of aching dullness that the routine of life on sunny islands induces. Besides VD and religion and cash dependence, what Westerners have introduced to these islands is a consciousness of boredom. I wondered if this was a pressure that Mrs Hill would be prepared for. Anybody might support boredom and the crippling psychological suffocation of zero stimulus for a couple of weeks. But for a lifetime?

The letter had to be answered. I folded down my tray and hunted in my bag for some clean paper. What a horribly sweat-stained, salty and damp heap of notebooks I had accumulated! This is what I wrote:

Dear Mrs Hill,

I was interested to receive your letter and pleased that you enjoyed my article in *Reader's Digest*. You are certainly right in thinking that the islands are beautiful, and have a placid tempo of life that I don't suppose has existed in the Western world since the invention of the grandfather clock.

Gone are the days when you could wade ashore from some wandering schooner and build a shack, I'm sad to say. Nowadays, most South Seas countries are independent and you will find a very strict immigration man standing on the high tide mark. The islands tend to be crowded and most native people want to get off them because they want to live in cities and do things like sell jewellery and shop in supermarkets and watch TV and wear shoes, as you do. They don't take kindly to White people who take up jobs that they could do, even if you got permission to stay there, which is virtually impossible.

The main problem is land, which belongs to families or clans. This is not to be regretted for the land is their only cultural base, allowing most traditions of their native society to endure. If they were to lose this base, as they are in danger of doing in Tahiti, the islanders will simply be sucked into a totally Western way of life like the unfortunate Hawaiians.

In general, the only certain way for an outsider to obtain land is to marry into a family. But then, because you are a member of the desirable spend-thrift society, you will also be seen as a means of support and financial comfort for a great number of in-laws.

On the other hand, travellers with onward tickets and visible means of support are welcome everywhere. It is a mistake to look like a hippy because island people are in general a prim and sober-sided lot who take a dim view of dirty and indolent refugees lying around on their beaches. Even the famous painter Paul Gauguin was despised by the natives for his sluttiness.

What I suggest is that, as I did, you experience the joys of the South Seas without committing yourself to a permanent life there. For I am certain that after a few months of it your current life will suddenly begin to glow like a long-forgotten dream! To travel these fragrant and beautiful isles where people always have a courteous smile for the stranger is a dream that I, personally, will always treasure.

It was always a custom in the traditional Polynesian society for groups of people to go travelling. They would take gifts and receive gifts, and have a good party and return to their home islands refreshed in body and spirit. Follow their example and go not as a tourist to lie in the sun, but as a traveller.

In my experience it is a mistake to rely on travel agents for good advice, except with regard to air services on the long-haul routes. Nearly all aircraft which daily cross the Pacific between Australia/ New Zealand and Hawaii/California make a stopover at one island or another. Fiji, American Samoa and Tahiti are the main staging posts and generally there are several daily services in each direction. Other frequent services plug into the Pacific network through Bali and New Guinea in the West, from Tokyo in the north, and from Chile and Easter Island in the east.

From the main international airports, feeder services connect to other countries like Tonga, Western Samoa, and the New Hebrides. Within island groups there are smaller services, many of which tend to be somewhat *ad lib*, in the tradition of romantic sailing schooners, and this sort of travel is part of the fun.

The islands seem a long way from practically everywhere but there are ways of reducing travel costs. One-way advance-purchase tickets between Europe or U.S.A. and Australia greatly reduce the cost of reaching a starting point like Sydney. From there you can take an ordinary economy (to Los Angeles) valid for a year, which allows many stopovers so you can progress more or less in a straight line along the route that I covered largely by little ship.

From Toronto and other points in North America there are many ways of reaching Hawaii cheaply. From there, you fly to Fiji or American Samoa and begin your island-hopping. The Fijian airline Air Pacific ("Your island in the sky") offers a special promotional fare for a circular route through three or four island capitals, and you can join the route without restriction at any point along it.

English is spoken in nearly all islands and French in French Polynesia. The water is usually clean, accommodation is excellent and cheap if you make an effort to avoid the big hotels, there is no disease to worry about, and bugs aren't bad: I came back with most of my original tube of mosquito repellant unused.

If you take my advice and go travelling, be sure to pack a good supply of books for there is nothing much there to nourish the soul except sunshine and beauty, a swimming mask and snorkel, an ankle-length cotton dress (your husband should take a tie and long trousers), a light woolly jumper, and an umbrella. If you are voyaging in local boats, as I did, take an inflatable mattress and seasick pills and lots of patience. But you can leave your shoes behind. Even in church, you don't need shoes in the South Seas.

Yours sincerely,
John Dyson
London
April, 1982

*

I suppose it would have been in keeping to have corked the letter into a bottle and cast it into the sea. Instead, I posted it at Los Angeles Airport and caught the first plane home.

The coral waxes,
The palm grows,
And man departs

(Polynesian proverb)

INDEX

Index